Antique Trader®

CLOCKS

PRICE GUIDE

Including all types of clocks
— 17th through 20th century

Edited by **Kyle Husfloen** | Contributing Editor **Mark Moran**

© 2003 by Krause Publications

Published by

krause publications
An F&W Publications Company

700 East State Street • Iola, WI 54990-0001
715-445-2214 • 888-457-2873
www.krause.com

Please call or write for our free catalog of publications.
Our toll-free number to place an order or obtain a free catalog is 800-258-0929
or please use our regular business telephone 715-445-2214.

Library of Congress Catalog Number: 2002107600
ISBN: 0-87349-450-4

Printed in the United States of America

INTRODUCTION

Time can stand still or time can fly, we can have time on our hands or no time to waste. Time, seems to be a precious commodity that most of us never seem to have enough of, but in order to regulate our time properly we all rely on timepieces, usually clocks and watches. The measurement and recording of time has been a vital part of human civilization for millennia, ever since towns were established and we needed a more dependable way to regulate our daily activities.

The ancient Egyptians used water clocks and the Romans developed sundials, but it wasn't until the Middle Ages that mechanical, weight-driven clocks were first developed and came into use in important cities. These first mechanical clocks were very large and installed in important public places such as churches and town halls so every citizen could at least determine what the hour was. Keep in mind that in those days clocks had only an "hour" hand; no one worried too much about what the exact minute was.

How times have changed. Since the 16th century Western societies have become more and more obsessed with keeping accurate time and developing timekeeping devices that were available to a much wider public. By the mid-1600s, spring-driven clocks were keeping much more accurate time with minute and seconds hands showing up. It wasn't until the early 19th century, however, that the clock became a common object in most households. Much of the credit for developing a clock industry that served a broad public market goes to innovative clockmakers in and around Connecticut. Yankee ingenuity produced cheaper and better clocks in a variety of styles, and by the mid-19th century American-made clocks were being exported around the world. So many thousands of these sturdy timekeepers were made that today it is still possible to acquire an attractive antique example that keeps good time.

Our new price guide will offer you a great overview of all types of collectible clocks, a sampling of rare, museum-quality timekeepers from the 17th and 18th centuries, but many more examples from the latter 19th century and well into the 20th. We have gathered prices and descriptions from a number of sources and are pleased to highlight the listings with abundant large photographs. Included here are more than 800 clocks of every age, shape and size and of these more than 630 are illustrated. In addition to the listings, we are pleased to offer a special feature on "Guidelines for Clock Collecting" written by noted authority R.O. Schmitt, as well as a select "Bibliography" of helpful references. In addition, at the end of the listings we provide a "Glossary of Clock Related Terms."

It took many months and many hands to compile and complete this volume, and my special thanks go to Contributing Editor Mark Moran, who was able to obtain a wonderful selection of photos from a number of helpful clock collectors and dealers. My thanks also to all the other experts and auction firms that generously shared their material with us. I feel we're offering you one of the most detailed and comprehensive guides to the world of collectible clocks and I hope you'll agree. You're welcome to take some time to drop me a line with your comments and suggestions, and I'll do my best to make a timely reply. Meanwhile, *tempus fugit*, so make the most of yours but don't forget to take time to stop and smell the roses, too.

Kyle Husfloen, Editor

SPECIAL CONTRIBUTORS

Special contributors to this volume include:

Mark F. Moran Antiques
5887 Meadow Dr. S.E.
Rochester, MN 55904
(507) 288-8006

The Clocksmith
806 El Camino Real
San Carlos, CA 94070
http://www.theclocksmith.com/

Dale and Lynn Newquist
Rochester, Minnesota

Elden and Jenny Schroeder
Onalaska, Wisconsin

R.O. Schmitt Fine Arts
P.O. Box 1941
Salem, NH 03079
(603) 893-5915

York Town Auction Inc.
1625 Haviland Rd.
York, PA 17404
(717) 751-0211
www.yorktownauction.com

For other photographs, artwork, data or permission to photograph in their shops, we sincerely express appreciation to the following auctioneers, individuals and shops:

Albrecht Auction Service, Vassar, Michigan; Alderfers, Hatfield, Pennsylvania; Charlton Hall Galleries, Columbia, South Carolina; Copake Country Auction, Copake, New York; Craftsman Auctions, Pittsfield, Massachusetts; DeFina Auctions, Austenburg, Ohio; Susan Eberman, Bedford, Indiana; John Fontaine Gallery, Pittsfield, Massachusetts; Garth's Auctions Inc., Delaware, Ohio; Green Valley Auctions, Mt. Crawford, Virginia; Gene Harris Antique Auction Center, Marshalltown, Iowa; Kenneth S. Hays & Associates, Louisville, Kentucky; Jackson's Auctioneers and Appraisers, Cedar Falls, Iowa; Skinner, Inc., Bolton, Massachusetts; Slawinski Auction Company, Felton, California; Sotheby's, New York, New York; Robert and Harriett Swedberg, Moline, Illinois.

Guidelines for Clock Collecting
by R.O. Schmitt

As far back as the glory days of the Egyptian pharaohs and through the height of the Roman Empire, time was measured by draining sand in an hourglass or by dripping water out of a container into smaller containers or scales along the large container that served to measure the hours or minutes. As the world awoke from the Dark Ages, ironworkers learned to fashion the first large public clocks in the 11th century. Progress was slow until the 17th century, when great inventors applied the principle of the pendulum to timekeeping. Skilled workmen and inventors like Christian Huygens, George Harrison, Thomas Tompion and George Graham all helped to define the science of horology that produced more and more accurate timekeeping.

Many clocks from the 17th and 18th centuries are now in museums and private collections. However, hundreds of thousands of affordable antique clocks were produced in factories during the 19th century, and these prove most popular today. There were large clock making centers in southern Germany, Paris and London, while American clock making grew up along the Connecticut River Valley in central Connecticut.

The most influential American clockmaker/inventor in the early 19th century was Eli Terry. His ideas for interchangeable parts and sequential line assembly of components helped produce affordable timepieces for a growing country. Among his apprentices were Seth Thomas and Silas

Top of page: Banjo clock from Massachusetts, 34" long, ca. 1850.

Far left: Grandfather clock, 87" high, by Colonial Mfg. Co. of Zeeland, Michigan, ca. 1919.

Left: Wall Regulator, 39" high, by E.N. Welch Mfg. Co. of Bristol, Connecticut, ca. 1890.

Hoadley, who each made additional contributions. Early clocks were weight-driven, and the arrival of spring-making facilities in the Valley allowed for more portable clocks that were easier to ship. They also began to appear in an endless number of styles and shapes. By the mid 19th century, several firms were busy along the Connecticut River producing clocks, including Seth Thomas Clock Co., E.N. Welch Mfg., Ansonia Clock Company, Wm. L. Gilbert Clock Co., and E. Ingraham & Co. Over in New Haven, Chauncey Jerome was busy, and later the New Haven Clock Company produced a myriad of models. In Boston, E. Howard & Company was setting a high standard for clocks. Even late 20th-century makers such as Elmer Stennes and Foster Campos are sought after today. Space limitations prohibit mentioning every name and company associated with clock making, but several books are available that cover the topic more exhaustively (see bibliography for just a few).

Clocks were made in a multitude of styles and myriad sizes and types of movements, but for ease of discussion, they can be classified into six large groups:

Tall case or "grandfather" clocks grew out of the desire to hide the weights and protect the pendulum.

Wall-hanging clocks eliminated the need for floor or shelf space.

Top of page: German Bracket clock, ca. 1890, 33 1/2" high with bracket.

Left: Pillar & Scroll clock by Elisha Neal of New Hartford, Connecticut, ca. 1830, 31" high.

Right: Swinging Arm clock made in France, ca. 1890, 38 1/2" high.

Below: Mantel clock by Ansonia Clock Co. of Ansonia, Connecticut, with porcelain case by Royal Bonn, ca. 1901, 12 1/4" high.

Mantel or *shelf* clocks are by far the largest category, as nearly every 18th- and 19th-century home had a mantel or wall shelf on which to set a clock.

Novelty and *fantasy* clocks came about as a result of the inventor's desire to mystify observers and make them wonder what they were seeing.

Carriage clocks grew out of the need for portability of accurate time keeping, necessary for keeping schedules; they often included an alarm to assist their owners in rising on time. French officers used the first carriage timepieces.

Marine timepieces are a specific category developed to compensate for the constant motion of a ship as well as the harsh weather conditions and corrosion potential in salt air. Many have naval "ship's bell" striking movements.

Clocks within each of these groups have been made in all industrial countries of the world, and research books on these types and their many subgroups would fill a small library.

Interest in collecting antique clocks continues unabated. At Sotheby's in New York on June 19, 2002, a George Graham (London, England) tall case clock sold for $1.76 million. But fear not. Since millions of collectible clocks were produced, the vast majority of them can be bought today for less than $1,000.

Prominent museums in the United States, including the American Clock and Watch Museum in Bristol, Connecticut, and the National Clock Museum in Columbia, Pennsylvania, offer the public a unique opportunity to see a large variety of clocks and learn their importance in the growth of America.

Top of page: Crystal Regulator shelf clock with cloisonné trim, French, ca. 1900.

Left: Steeple shelf clock by M.W. Atkins & Co. of Bristol, Connecticut, 19 3/4" high, ca. 1848.

Ship's Bell timepiece by Waterbury Clock Co. of Waterbury, Connecticut, ca. 1929, 8" high.

Museums can also help collectors decide the category of clock on which to base a collection.

Which type of clock makes the best investment? No other category has produced such a high rate of return as the attractive and functional American weight-driven wall clock. Price guides abound, both printed and electronic, but the *Antique Trader™ Clocks Price Guide* offers comprehensive information with which to assist collectors in their quest for quality clocks.

Bibliography

Ball, Robert W.D., *American Shelf & Wall Clocks*, revised and expanded 2nd edition. Schiffer Publishing Ltd., Atglen, Pa., 1999.

Distin, William H. and Robert Bishop, *The American Clock*. E.P. Dutton & Company, Inc., New York, N.Y., 1976.

Stein, Mark V., *The Collector's Guide to 20th Century Modern Clocks*. Radiomania Books, Baltimore, Md., 2002.

Swedberg, Robert W. and Harriet, *Encyclopedia of Antique American Clocks*. Krause Publications, Iola, Wis., 2001.

Swedberg, Robert W. and Harriet, *Price Guide to Antique Clocks*. Krause Publications, Iola, Wis., 2001.

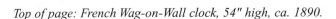

Top of page: French Wag-on-Wall clock, 54" high, ca. 1890.

Above: French-made Carriage clock of brass and beveled glass, ca. 1900.

Right: German "blinking eye" Novelty clock, wood, ca. 1935.

Center right: French automaton Novelty clock with magician figure that moves head and lifts cups, ca. 1835.

Far right: Frying pan-shaped souvenir Novelty clock of the 1901 Pan-American Exhibition in Buffalo, New York.

Small Ansonia Alarm Clock

Alarm clock, Ansonia Clock Co., Ansonia, Connecticut, tin case w/peg feet, round, dial w/Roman numerals & sweep seconds hand, ring handle at top, beveled glass in face, late 19th - early 20th c., 2 1/2" h. (ILLUS.) **$60-70**

Alarm clock, gold-plated brass rectangular case w/border of red, black & white cloisonné Native American-style decoration, quilted pattern metal dial w/radium Arabic numerals & hands, eight-day movement, Switzerland, ca. 1920, 3 1/4" h. (ILLUS. at bottom of page) **224**

Alarm clock, primitive travel-type, upright brass rectangular case w/arched crest partially hiding a 2" bell, hinged glazed bezel over the white porcelain dial w/black Roman numerals, "Davies Chester" engraved on front section below the dial, front wind verge watch movement w/drop off snail for alarm, alarm movement wound & set from rear, alarm dial engraved into rear of case, dial w/hairlines & wear at winding hole, England, ca. 1810, 4 3/4" h. (ILLUS. below) **448**

Primitive Travel Alarm Clock

Colorful Swiss Alarm Clock

Plush-covered Terry Alarm Clock

Alarm clock, Terry Clock Co., Pittsfield, Massachusetts, upright narrow oval case covered w/worn purple plush, angled metal top handle, nickel plated bezel around the dial w/Roman numerals & sweep seconds hand, original glass over dial, alarm rings loudly, 30-hour movement, ca. 1883, 8 1/4" h. (ILLUS.) **134**

Westclox "Baby Ben" Alarm Clock

Alarm clock, Westclox, LaSalle, Illinois, "Baby Ben" model, nickel-plated brass, round case w/Arabic numerals & seconds dial, small peg feet, ca. 1920s, 2 3/4 x 4" (ILLUS.) **40-50**

Alarm clock, Westclox, LaSalle, Illinois, "Ironclad" model, rectangular cast-iron case w/rounded corners on molded base, spandrels around white round dial w/black Arabic numerals & notched brass bezel, one-day time-only movement, alarm-set hand on rear missing, ca. 1935, 5 1/4" h. (ILLUS. below) **88**

Westclox Cast-iron Alarm Clock

German Alarm Music Box Clock

Alarm music box clock, walnut Alt Deutsch-style case w/pressed-brass trim, high peaked top w/knobbed ring-turned finial over a contour splat flanked by two conforming finials on beveled pediment, two three-quarter round baluster-form columns flanking dial frame, original cello dial w/Arabic numerals on white chapter ring, brass bezel & pressed-brass spandrels, on molded rectangular base w/square wafer feet, time-only movement w/alarm, Swiss music box plays tune for alarm, minor veneer cracks, replaced feet, Germany, ca. 1910, 19 1/2" h. (ILLUS. on previous page) **280**

swirled base of urn & up the side, its tongue pointing to time/date, all on stepped white marble square base w/gilt decorated trim & short ringed feet, France, ca. 1895, 9 1/4" h. (ILLUS. bottom left) **4,592**

Japy Clock with Sevres Panels

Annular dial clock, Japy, France, Louis XVI-style, the hour & minute panels w/white number cartouches run around a large ornately decorated gilt-bronze urn w/finial & scrolling handles sitting atop the rectangular gilt-bronze base w/beveled top supporting a serpent that coils around & up the base of the urn, its tongue pointing to the time, each side of the base inset w/an oval Sevres porcelain panel painted w/floral sprays in brilliant colors, short pendulum, time-only movement w/suspension spring, a driveshaft ascends from the movement up the stem of the urn & drives the minute & hour dials, w/Medaille D'Or trademark, ca. 1860, 15" h. (ILLUS.) **7,840**

Lovely French Annular Dial Clock

Annular dial clock, bronze urn-form cobalt blue-enameled case w/gilt bronze embossed finial, handles, feet & trim, Egyptian-style gilt embossed side handles, white bands near top of urn w/Roman numerals give the time & Arabic numerals the date, gilt asp coils around embossed

lever movement, bottom-wound & set, Switzerland, ca. 1955, 3 1/2" h. (ILLUS. below).. **560**

Swiss "Sundial" Style Shelf Clock

Swiss Annular Dial Clock

Annular dial clock, opalescent yellow enamel over damascene patterned silver egg-shaped case, the top w/patterned finial & three h.p. cameos ranged around it & gold border w/scalloped design, number panels directly below, chain decoration swagged under number panels & partially framing h.p. front cameo of woman w/needlework, the top of the swag pointing to the time, on scalloped stem in same pattern as finial, ringed circular base, all on a white marble octagonal base, gold over silver hardware, time-only movement, some oxidation to gold, minor losses to marble base, Switzerland, ca. 1870, 7 1/4" h. (ILLUS.)... **4,200**

Annular dial clock, "Sundial" style, stepped brass circular molded case w/pierced scroll design gnomon on top, incised scrolling designs on either side of gnomon & on one tier of body, gnomon pointing to silvered metal annular dials that are revealed in cut-out section of top, Roman numerals for time & Arabic numerals for date, eight-day jeweled

Louis XVI Annular Dial Shelf Clock

Annular dial clock, "Temple de l'Amour," Louis XVI period, ormolu domical top w/finial, set within four ringed knob-topped columns connected w/ropetwist swags, an arrow suspended between the swags pointing to the black numerals on the white number panels just under the dome, the escapement visible below them, all on a white marble stand w/ormolu gallery, bead border w/chain swags, the top section supported by four green marble columns w/ormolu capitals & bases connecting it to the round white marble w/ormolu bead border & short tapering feet, centered between the columns is an ormolu figure sitting cross-legged on a drum-like pedestal holding a parasol, the movement planted in the case horizontally, the escape wheel driven through a contrate wheel & released by a conventional verge & pendulum, France, ca. 1790, 17" h. (ILLUS. on previous page) **14,000**

w/spread-winged eagle finial above the round dial w/Arabic numerals, brass cut-out side scrolls flanking throat inlaid w/ropetwist & sunburst bordered vine decoration, base w/glass tablet reverse-painted w/scene of Mt. Vernon, within a ropetwist & sunburst border, wooden knobs hanging from bottom of base, ribbed base drop w/drop finial, eight-day time-only movement, ca. 1933, 33" h. (ILLUS. left) **1,120**

Chelsea Clock Co. Banjo Clock

Banjo clock, Chelsea Clock Co., Boston, Massachusetts, serial #207241, mahogany case w/metal surround topped

Chelsea Clock Co. Naval Motif Banjo

Banjo clock, Chelsea Clock Co., Chelsea, Massachusetts, "Willard" model, wooden case w/gilt metal eagle finial, the original dial w/black Roman numerals & engraved w/name of retailer, "Shreve, Crump & Low, Boston," slender pierced brass scrolls along the throat inset w/a glass tablet reverse-painted w/a red, white & blue American eagle & shield & other patriotic motifs, the rectangular base glass tablet w/a reverse-painted scene of the warships Constitution & Guerriere in battle at sea within a floral border, eight-day time & strike lever movement strikes the hours & half hours on deep-toned gong, some dry splits in back of case, ca. 1940, 42" h. (ILLUS. on previous page) **2,912**

Banjo clock, Federal, the mahogany & gilt gesso case w/a molded brass bezel enclosing a white-painted iron dial w/Roman numerals & an A-frame type weight-driven movement above the rectangular églomisé lower tablet showing Helios framed by spiral moldings & the central body flanked by pierced brass side scrolls, possibly Rhode Island, ca. 1820, overall 34" h. (restoration) **4,313**

Howard & Davis "No. 3" Banjo Clock

Banjo clock, Howard & Davis, Boston, Massachusetts, "No. 3" model, molded grained cherry case, round top around the dial w/black Roman numerals, center & bottom panels reverse-painted in black w/gilt highlights, bottom panel w/oval center for viewing pendulum, time-only signed movement, lower baffle board & tie-down missing, weight incorrect, some gold loss to lower tablet, ca. 1855, 38" h. (ILLUS.) **3,360**

Gilbert Banjo Clock

Banjo clock, Gilbert (Wm. L.) Clock Co., Winsted, Connecticut, cast gilt-metal eagle finial, the round metal dial w/brass bezel & Arabic numerals, neck flanked by long brass cut-out scrolls, rectangular lower case w/glass pane reverse-painted w/a scene of a ship under full sail, eight-day time & strike movement w/"bim-bam" strike on two steel rods, ca. 1929, 29 1/2" h. (ILLUS.) **308**

Rosewood Grained Banjo Clock

Banjo clock, Howard (E.) & Co., Boston, Massachusetts, rosewood grained "No. 5" model, the circular molded bezel enclosing a white painted metal dial inscribed "Howard & Co., Boston" & eight-day weight-driven movement above the half-round moldings framing the throat & pendulum box, églomisé black & maroon tablets, mid-19th c., very minor imperfections, 28 1/2" h. (ILLUS. on previous page) **2,415**

Ingraham 1920s Banjo Wall Clock

E. Howard & Co. Banjo Clock

Banjo clock, Howard (E.) & Co., New York, New York, "No. 5" model, dark wooden case w/molded surround, neck & base, tablets w/simple geometric designs in deep red & gold, the original iron dial w/Roman numerals & signature, time-only movement, pattern on pendulum bob mostly buffed away, ca. 1885, 28 3/4" h. (ILLUS.) **4,368**

Banjo clock, Ingraham (E.) Co., Bristol, Connecticut, "Nyanza" model revival-style banjo wall clock, walnut case w/pointed ball finial atop the round dial w/Arabic numerals above the slender tapering neck w/a reverse-painted glass panel over the bottom pendulum box reverse-painted in black w/a narrow gold-bordered window to show the pendulum bob, tapering concave bottom drop, copy of an early 19th c. model, ca. 1920, 4 1/2 x 10 1/8", 39" h. (ILLUS. above right) **450**

Massachusetts Banjo Clock

Banjo clock, knobbed brass finial above original round brass bezel & dial w/black Roman numerals, the case neck w/center glass panel featuring reverse-painted American eagle & shield & scroll design on a cream ground, the sides w/long slender pieced brass scrolls, simple rectangular base w/reverse-painted glass tablet showing a pastoral scene w/building in center, both neck & base bordered in brass ropetwist trim, original time-only movement, neck tablet cracked & glued, recent finial, Massachusetts, ca. 1850, 34" h. (ILLUS. on previous page) **1,148**

Late New Haven Banjo Wall Clock

New Haven Clock Co. Banjo Clock

Banjo clock, New Haven Clock Co., New Haven, Connecticut, solid mahogany case w/gilt metal urn-form finial, the round dial w/raised Arabic numerals, the throat inset w/a glass panel w/gilt stenciled scroll design flanked by pierced brass scrolls, the bottom rectangular glass tablet reverse-painted w/a scene of a ship under sail at sea, graceful tapering rounded base drop, eight-day time & strike pendulum-driven movement, some lifting of throat glass decoration, ca. 1928, 18" h. (ILLUS.) **459**

Banjo clock, New Haven Clock Co., New Haven, Connecticut, "Welton" model revival-style banjo wall clock, ebonized wood case, brass eagle finial above the steel dial w/Arabic numerals, the tall waisted neck w/long edge scrolls & a glass panel above the rectangular pendulum box w/black reverse-painted glass panel w/small gold oval showing the pendulum bob, tapering concave base drop, time only, ca. 1940s, 3 1/2 x 8 1/2", 25" h. (ILLUS.) **150**

Banjo clock, New Haven Clock Co., New Haven, Connecticut, "Whitney" model, mahogany-finished softwood case, a small gilt-metal eagle finial above the round brass bezel enclosing the silvered metal dial w/black Arabic Art Deco-style numerals, the tall slightly tapering throat w/a reverse-painted looping vine panel, the rectangular base frame enclosing a glass pane reverse-painted w/a garden scene, tapering pointed base drop, hour & half-hour rod strike movement, ca. 1930-35, 9 1/2" w., 30 1/2" h. (ILLUS. below) **600-700**

painted glass panel w/gilt scrolls over an eagle & American shield, the rectangular wood base enclosing a reverse-painted glass panel decorated in color w/two sailing ships flanking an American eagle & shield, tapering base drop, late 19th - early 20th c., 6 x 12", 40" h. (ILLUS. below) **2,400**

Older New Haven Banjo Clock

Banjo clock, Noyes (Leonard), New Hampshire attribution, mahogany case w/gilded facade moldings & brass trim, original reverse-painted glass in the waist w/flaking & touch-up, replaced glass in bottom panel, brass works w/weight, pendulum & key, round dial w/Roman numerals & traces of maker's label, early 19th c., 31 1/4" h. (case reinforced w/glue, early finial replaced).. **1,430**

Banjo clock, Sawin (John), Boston, Massachusetts, a gilt-metal eagle finial above the round bezel enclosing the signed metal dial w/Roman numerals, the tall slender slightly tapering waist section fitted w/a reverse-painted pane of glass decorated w/patriotic designs, long pierced brass C-scrolls at the sides, the rectangular bottom section w/a reverse-painted glass pane decorated w/a warship scene, eight-day time-only movement, early 19th c., bottom pane damaged, 31" h. (ILLUS. on next page)............ **2,588**

New Haven 1930s Banjo Clock

Banjo clock, New Haven Clock Company, New Haven, Connecticut, wood & brass, the round dial at the top w/Arabic numerals & surmounted by a spread-winged eagle finial, the narrow tapering tall throat flanked by long brass C-scrolls & inset w/a reverse-

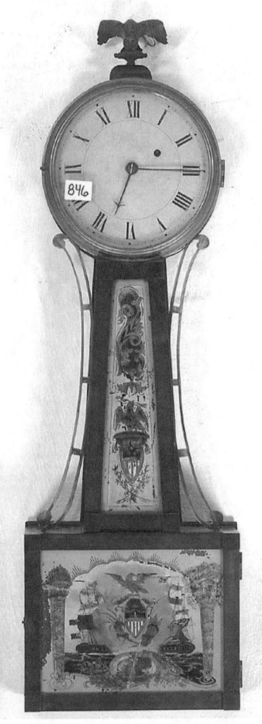

John Sawin Banjo Clock

Newer Elmer Stennes Banjo Clock

Banjo clock, Stennes (E.O.), Weymouth, Massachusetts, flame finial over the white dial w/black Roman numerals, gold-front case w/notched borders on throat & base, delicate cut-out sidearms, both glass tablets w/geometric designs in off-white, pink, blue-grey & gold w/top panel also sporting silhouette of spread-winged eagle over olive branch, beaded base w/ribbed drop incurved to knobbed drop finial, time-only weight movement, stamped "MCIP," "#104" & "'72," ca. 1972, 40" h. (ILLUS.) **5,488**

Banjo clock, Taber (Elnathan), Roxbury, Massachusetts, the round brass bezel w/a tall gilt metal pointed finial at the top & enclosing a painted white dial inscribed "E. Taber" & an eight-day brass weight-driven movement above the trapezoidal églomisé throat glass w/urn & flowering vine flanked by long slender curved & pierced brass mounts, inscribed "Patent" above the pendulum box w/an églomisé sea battle scene, throat & lower case w/half-round narrow moldings, ca. 1820, 33 1/4" h. (replaced tablets)........................ **5,750**

Seth Thomas "Danvers" Clock

Banjo clock, Thomas (Seth) Clock Co., Plymouth, Connecticut, "Danvers" model, inlaid mahogany case, the top round molded frame w/a cast gilt-metal spread-winged eagle finial above the brass bezel enclosing the steel dial w/Arabic numerals, the tapering case & neck flanked by brass scrolls, rectangular base w/contour tapering base drop, eight-day four-jewel lever movement, part of label remains, some crazing, ca. 1930, 18 3/4" h. (ILLUS.) **134**

Seth Thomas "Ramsgate" Clock

Banjo clock, Thomas (Seth) Clock Co., Plymouth, Connecticut, "Ramsgate" model, wooden case w/gilt cast-metal eagle finial, the round top frame enclosing a brass bezel & steel dial w/Roman numerals, the case neck w/an inset narrow tapering glass panel reverse-painted w/gilt leaf decoration on a cream ground, flanked by two slender brass scrolls, the rectangular base inset w/a reverse-painted glass tablet w/a scene of a ship under full sail, curved & tapering drop finial, eight-day seven-jewel lever movement, top capital reglued, ca. 1929, 21" h. (ILLUS.).. **252**

Waltham Miniature Banjo Clock

Banjo clock, Waltham Clock Co., Waltham, Massachusetts, miniature, "No. 1550" model, mahogany case w/gilt spread-winged eagle finial, outcurved cut-out brackets flanking neck, neck & base w/reverse-painted tablets, base w/gilt beaded border & drop finial, white dial w/Arabic numerals & original hands, Hull glasses, eight-day jeweled car clock movement w/stem wind, ca. 1928, 21" h. (ILLUS.) **1,176**

George Washington Banjo Clock

Banjo clock, Waltham Clock Co., Waltham, Massachusetts, serial #31250, large gilt cast-metal spread-winged eagle finial above the brass bezel enclosing the white dial w/black Arabic numerals, the gently tapering case neck inset w/a reverse-painted glass panel decorated w/a gilt arrow spire & wreath enclosing a colored bust portrait of George Washington, flanked by cut-out brass scrolls, the bottom rectangular glass tablet reverse-painted w/a scene of Mt. Vernon within scalloped white border, both neck & base w/ropetwist brass trim, the base w/brass balls hanging from bottom edge & large ribbed base drop w/drop finial, eight-day time-only lever movement, ca. 1930, 42" h. (ILLUS.).. **1,120**

"Willard" Model Waltham Clock

Banjo clock, Waltham Clock Co., Waltham, Massachusetts, "Willard" model, cross-banded wooden case w/brass eagle finial over the original signed white dial w/Roman numerals, throat w/reverse-painted panel of leaves, rectangular base w/tablet of Aurora in chariot, knob border at bottom of base & base drop w/drop finial, weight driven time-only movement, ca. 1930, 42" h. (ILLUS.)................................... **2,128**

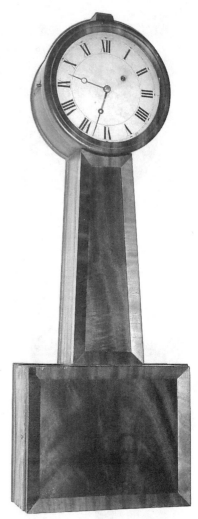

Massachusetts Weight Banjo Clock

Banjo clock, weight-driven style, mahogany case w/clean geometric lines & crotch mahogany panels in neck & large bottom rectangular door, original dial w/Roman numerals, pendulum & weight, time only movement, Massachusetts, ca. 1840, 29 1/2" h. (ILLUS.) **1,400**

Banjo clock, Willard (Simon), Roxbury, Massachusetts, Federal style, inlaid mahogany case w/a top round brass molded bezel enclosing a white painted dial w/Roman numerals & an eight-day brass weight-driven movement w/T-bridge above the long trapezoidal throat, lower case w/white églomisé tablet & pendulum box tablet inscribed "S. Willards Patent," both framed by mahogany cross-banding & stringing w/flanking pierced brass brackets, old finish, ca. 1815, 32 1/4" h. (restoration) **1,955**

Waltham "Willard" Banjo Clock

Banjo clock, Waltham Clock Co., Waltham, Massachusetts, "Willard" model, spread-winged eagle finial, case neck flanked by curved cut-out scrolls, reverse-painted leaf decoration on neck & pastoral scene in tablet on base, both w/white borders, drop finial, original dial w/Arabic numerals & "Waltham" under the 12 & "Smith Patterson Co." above the 6, time only movement, eagle has been glued, tablets repainted, ca. 1925, 40" h. (ILLUS.)............. **1,484**

Early Electric Bank Timer

Bank timer, American Bank Protection Co., Minneapolis, Minnesota, Model #22-3601, square hardwood case w/stenciled model number, round 24-hour dial w/Roman numerals & molded bezel, looks to be eight-day (or longer) lever movement, electric, used to open/lock door or other device, ca. 1910, 8" h. (ILLUS.) **220**

Boudoir clock, Gallet & Co. Swiss eight-day movement in a small rectangular Gorham Mfg. Co. sterling silver case, porcelain dial w/Arabic numerals, early 20th c., lines in the dial, 3 1/4" w **158**

English Georgian Bracket Clock

Bracket clock, Frodsham & Sons, England, ebonized wood case, the pagoda-form flattened rectangular top w/inset beveled glass panel & angled swing loop carrying handle, the upright beveled glass sides showing the works & the ornately engraved brass dial w/Roman numerals, gadrooned base band over the stepped & flaring base over a scrolled apron & bracket feet, signed, England, Georgian period, ca. 1790 (ILLUS.) **3,250**

English Greek-style Bracket Clock

Bracket clock, Greek-style mahogany case w/arched beveled top over molded pediment, molding & inlay decoration all around w/fret side panels, three-quarter round ring-turned columns flanking glassed arch-shaped door, molded-top block base on rectangular wafer feet, the arched silvered metal dial w/engraved brass decoration, Arabic numerals & strike/silent, tune selection & F/S subsidiary dials, eight-day triple fusee movement, clock chimes on eight bells or five gong rods w/choice of Whittington or Westminster tune, made for Theodore B. Starr & Co., small sliver of wood missing from rear, very minor dry splits in veneer, England, ca. 1910, 18 1/2" h. (ILLUS.) **3,584**

Hermlie Music Box Bracket Clock

Bracket clock, Hermlie (Franz), Germany, music box clock, stained fruitwood case w/a domed, stepped top w/bail handle, square front door opening to a brass & enamel dial w/Roman numerals, pairs of knob-turned spindles on each side, platform base w/flat feet, eight-day time & strike movement, 8 1/4 x 11 1/2", 11" h. (ILLUS.).. **300-350**

Junghans Chiming Bracket Clock

Bracket clock, Junghans, Germany, mahogany & poplar case w/stepped beveled cornice w/cove molding, three-quarter round ring-turned columns flank the arched molded door over an arched brass dial panel w/scroll decoration & centering a steel chapter ring w/Arabic numerals below two small subsidiary dials, molded stepped base on square wafer feet, time & strike movement w/Westminster chime, ca. 1915, 17 1/2" h. (ILLUS.) **532**

Late German Bracket Clock

Bracket clock, Linden, Germany, mahogany case w/a domed top & metal loop handle, the square glass front w/molding over a dial w/Roman numerals & applied gilded spandrels, stepped bottom molded on flat tab feet, eight-day time & triple chime movement, ca. 1940s, 7 1/2 x 11", 14 1/2" h. (ILLUS.) **350**

Double Chime English Bracket Clock

Bracket clock, mahogany rectangular case w/molded ogee top w/ormolu swag decoration on front, center urn-form finial & four similar corner finials, the arched ormolu dial panel w/silvered metal chapter ring in round time dial w/Roman numerals & in three subsidiary dials ranged above it, the body accented w/ormolu caryatids at the corners & broad acanthus moldings around waist, heavy cast sound frets & folding handles at the sides, three-fusée double chime time & strike movement, chimes the quarters on a choice of eight bells or four gongs, strikes the hours on a fifth large gong, some dry splits in front of case, England, ca. 1890, 27 1/2" h. (ILLUS.) **5,320**

Bracket clock, miniature mother-of-pearl inlaid rectangular case w/beveled top w/ring handle, sliding front & rear panels, brass dial plate w/floral engraving rotates behind a single vertical hand, calendar indications show in two little openings below the time dial, one showing the 12 Terrestrial branches, the other the 10 Celestial branches, stepped base w/bracket feet, intricate floral displays on all surfaces, original winding key in hidden drawer, fusée time & strike movement w/verge controlled by a balance rotating under the bell, made before Japan adopted Western time keep-

ing about 1873, Japan, mid-1800s, 6" h.
(ILLUS. below) **11,200**

Miniature Japanese Bracket Clock

English Victorian Bracket Clock

Bracket clock, Smith & Sons, Clerkenwell, England, ebonized & bronze-mounted case, an arched top pierced w/square pediment surmounted by a flame finial & small corner finials, over an arched glazed panel door w/pierced bronzed spandrels & open-

ing to an arched silver gilt dial w/Roman numerals, on a platform molded base raised on scroll bronze feet, fitted w/Whittington & Westminster chimes, pendulum needs repair, ca. 1850, 9 x 14", 26" h. (ILLUS. bottom of previous column) **2,800**

Seth Thomas Modern Bracket Clock

Bracket clock, Thomas (Seth) Clock Co., Thomaston, Connecticut, walnut case w/a domed top & brass loop handle, brass & enamel dial w/Roman numerals, based on an 18th c. English design, eight-day time & strike movement w/floating balance, ca. 1950s, 3 3/4 x 7 1/2", 10 1/2" h. (ILLUS.) **180**

German Oak Bracket Clock

Bracket clock, Winterhalder & Hoffmeier, Germany, oak case w/cove molded pediment topped by ringed stemmed orb corner finials & ribbed quatrefoil dome on beveled base, the square brass dial frame w/cast spandrels & center, the steel chapter ring w/black Roman numerals, the case w/reeded side pilasters w/Corinthian capitals, ribbed & beveled decoration at top & bottom, the molded block base w/molded feet, quarter striking time & strike movement, ca. 1900, 15" h. (ILLUS. on previous page)... **616**

Junghans Musical Bracket Clock

German Bracket Clock & Bracket

Bracket clock, Winterhalder & Hoffmeier, Germany, oak case w/molded pediment w/panel of carved decoration topped by flat-topped dome w/carved decoration, the case w/reeded pilasters w/Corinthian capitals flanking the arched brass dial panel w/heavy cast foliate spandrels & three subsidiary dials in the arch above the main dial, each dial w/steel chapter rings, the time dial w/brass Arabic numerals, the subsidiary dials for tune selection (four or eight gongs), the sides of the case w/inset panels w/intricate carving, the bottom w/a band of carved decoration over the molded block base, chime/silent & F/S regulation, quarter-chiming three-train time & strike movement plays Whittington or Westminster tunes, comes w/original molded bracket w/ogee sides & carved apron, ca. 1890, 22" h., w/bracket 33 1/2" h. (ILLUS.) **4,592**

Bracket music box clock, Junghans, Germany, wooden case w/music box in domed top, quatrefoil flattened dome ribbed top w/brass bail handle, molded pediment over border inset w/beads, two half-round Ionic columns w/gilt bases & capitals flanking dial panel w/arch-topped glass-paned door & corner decoration, molded bottom w/border matching pediment, stepped base on gilt square wafer feet, the silvered metal dial w/black Roman numerals & ornate gilt spandrels & arch decoration, eight-day time & strike movement w/Swiss Thorens disc-playing music box activated by clock movement at the hour, w/comb intact & 18 discs & original disc box, ca. 1920, 21 1/2" h. (ILLUS.) **3,360**

Calendar desk clock, DuBois & Fils, Switzerland, tall silver case w/round top dial section w/notched rim & topped by spread-winged eagle finial, a white porcelain time dial w/Arabic numerals framed by a/polychrome scene at top showing a man holding dog & looking toward draped columns, two subsidiary dials for date & days of the week, raised on a flattened waisted support w/a bulbous lower body w/applied flower decoration, all supported by two figural satyrs standing on a rectangular stepped base w/bands of notched decoration & leaf & bead trim, key-wind calendar movement, chain fusée movement w/monometallic balance just visible behind the fancy gilt cock that fits in dial, both dial & movement signed, replaced crystal, ca. 1830, 7" h. (ILLUS. on next page)... **1,960**

tral upright round clock w/bell on top & top ring handle, the white dial w/brass bezel, black Roman numerals for time & red Arabic numerals in outside ring for dates, two subsidiary dials, one black & one red hand, clock flanked by two matching square clear cut-glass inkwells w/brass-hinged integral covers in the form of helmeted Trojans, each on its own stepped square base, ca. 1915, 13" w. x 9 1/2" h. (ILLUS. at bottom of page) **896**

French Calendar Shelf Clock

Early Swiss Calendar Desk Clock

Calendar desk clock, Junghans, Germany, "Inkwell Calendar Clock" set, a rectangular stepped black base supporting a cen-

Calendar shelf or mantel clock, double-dial type, Belgian slate rectangular molded contour case on molded contour block base, both dials in white porcelain w/brass bezels & center rings, the upper time dial

"Inkwell Calendar Clock" Set

w/black Roman numerals, the lower calendar dial w/perpetual indications & moon
phase & a central equation of time hand
that points to the month & to a ring of numerals that gives the minutes each day
that sunlight is increasing or decreasing,
time & strike movement w/open escapement, France, ca. 1875, 16" h. (ILLUS. on
previous page) **2,352**

"No. 10 Farmer's" Calendar Clock

Calendar shelf or mantel clock, Ithaca
Calendar Clock Co., Ithaca, New York,
"No. 10 Farmer's" model, rectangular walnut case w/stepped pediment and base,
molded decoration, white dials, time dial
w/Roman numerals, original pendulum,
time & strike movement, top may have
been added later, some discoloration to
top dial, ca. 1880, 24" h. (ILLUS.) **644**

Calendar shelf or mantel clock, Ithaca Calendar Clock Co., Ithaca, New York, "No. 10
Farmer's" model, tall upright walnut rectangular case w/molded narrow cornice above
the two-pane front, the upper square pane
over a round time dial w/Roman numerals
framed by gilt spandrels, the lower square
pane over the signed calendar dial w/Ara-
bic numerals & rollers, label inside backboard states "Davidson & Co., Watch-mak-
ers and Jewelers, one door west of
Northampton Bank," eight-day time & strike
movement, ca. 1874, 21" h. (ILLUS. top
right) **784**

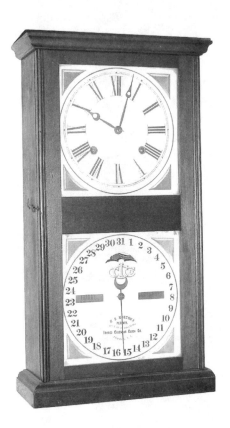

Ithaca Calendar Shelf Clock

Ithaca "No. 4-1/2 Favorite" Clock

Ithaca Calendar Clock Co. "No. 5"

Calendar shelf or mantel clock, Ithaca Calendar Clock Co., Ithaca, New York, "No. 4-1/2 Favorite" model, molded wood case w/arched top & corner finials, broken arch crest w/fancy leaf finial, arch-top door panel w/glass around dials w/delicate line decoration & cartouche separating two dials, the white dials w/brass bezels, the time dial w/brass center ring & black Roman numerals, the calendar dial w/Arabic numerals for dates, rollers for days of week & months, lunette & marked "L.B. & McG, Manufactured for Favorite Calendar Clock Co.," on molded beveled base, eight-day time & strike movement, glued tear on lower dial, ca. 1880, 31" h. (ILLUS.) **3,024**

Calendar shelf or mantel clock, Ithaca Calendar Clock Co., Ithaca, New York, "No. 5" model, arched molded rosewood case on beveled base, the time dial w/Roman numerals & metal bezel, clock dial & calendar dial below it w/original hands, original paper instruction label behind pendulum access door & two old repair stickers from Ithaca, time & strike movement, top dial pan now w/paper dial pasted on it, old pendulum not original, some veneer bubbles, ca. 1879, 22 1/2" h. (ILLUS. top right) **868**

Ithaca Calendar Clock Shelf Model

Calendar shelf or mantel clock, Ithaca Calendar Clock Co., Ithaca, New York, "No. 6-1/2 Shelf Belgrade" model, tall upright walnut case w/ornate carved crown-form crestrail w/a scroll crest & pointed finials over a beveled sawtooth-incised cornice above tall two-pane glazed front, the upper pane over a line-incised wood panel framing the brass bezel & time dial w/black Roman numerals, the lower pane over another incised wood panel centering the calendar dial w/a brass bezel & black Arabic numerals for dates & rollers for days of the week & months, copper-colored pendulum w/fancy scrolled metal bob, on a deep molded base w/an incised band of diamonds above the molded bottom base, overall gilt highlights in the incising, eight-day time & strike movement, some bubbling to calendar dial, ca. 1880, 32" h. (ILLUS. bottom of previous page)................. **2,688**

Rare Ithaca Calendar Shelf Clock

Calendar shelf or mantel clock, Ithaca Calendar Clock Co., Ithaca, New York, upright walnut case w/ebonized trim, the top section w/an arched & pierced leaf-carved crest above columns flanking the round bezel & paper dial w/Roman numerals, the slightly stepped-out deep lower case enclosing a large glass calendar dial exposing the crystal gridiron pendulum & date roles, molded base, eight-day time & strike movement, second half 19th c., 20 1/4" h. (ILLUS.) **3,600**

New Haven Clock "Cabinet No. 7"

Calendar shelf or mantel clock, New Haven Clock Co., New Haven, Connecticut, "Cabinet No. 7" model, ash case w/uncommon dial configuration, the calendar dial forming the top of the case in molded frame w/leaf crest & side garnishes, the calendar dial w/black Arabic numerals & months, the time dial centered in body w/brass bezel & center ring & black Roman numerals, the rectangular body w/contour frame, beading on top & inset w/panels w/various molded or carved decorations, on molded base, time & strike movement, ca. 1885, 21 3/4" h. (ILLUS.)... **2,016**

Calendar shelf or mantel clock, Thomas (Seth) Clock Co., Plymouth, Connecticut, "Parlor Calendar" model, rosewood rectangular case w/beveled cornice & base, multi-sided half-round columns w/the capitals forming sides of cornice & flanking the three-paned door over two octagonal dials & rectangular tablet in between w/black ground & gilt scene of a globe w/locomotive & sailing ship in ornate leafy border, the upper time dial w/Roman numerals, the lower calendar dial w/Arabic numerals for dates, rollers for month & day of the week, column bases form sides of block base, eight-day two-weight time-only movement, some chips, upper dial papered over, lower dial w/some paint loss, ca. 1865, 30 1/2" h. (ILLUS. below) **1,344**

S. Thomas "Parlor Calendar" Clock

S. Thomas "Parlor Calendar No. 3"

Calendar shelf or mantel clock, Thomas (Seth) Clock Co., Plymouth, Connecticut, "Parlor Calendar No. 3" double-dial model, upright rectangular rosewood case w/ogee molded cornice & beveled block base, round molding around each dial, the top time dial w/Roman numerals, the bottom calendar dial w/Arabic numerals for dates & rollers w/days & months, eight-day time & strike movement, good label on back of front door, lower dial repainted, case refinished, minor repairs, ca. 1880, 27" h. (ILLUS. bottom left) **672**

"Parlor Calendar No. 6" Clock

Calendar shelf or mantel clock, Thomas (Seth) Clock Co., Plymouth, Connecticut, "Parlor Calendar No. 6" model, walnut case w/flattened knob finial in center of scroll crest on molded pediment, glass door w/knob & flanked by square ribbed columns, white painted dials w/brass bezels, the upper time dial w/black Roman numerals, the calendar dial w/Arabic numerals for dates & rollers for days of week & months, original hands & pendulum bob, the molded base w/carved apron & bracket feet, eight-day time & strike w/R.T. Andrews 1876 patent calendar movement, date code for 1896 stenciled on back, label w/directions for setting up calendar on back of door, 1896, 27" h. (ILLUS.) **2,912**

Southern Clock Co. Calendar Clock

Calendar shelf or mantel clock, Thomas (Seth) for the Southern Clock Co., "Fashion" model, tall upright walnut case w/an arched, molded cornice w/three urn-form turned finials above the case w/slender turned columns flanking the tall arched door over two large dials, the upper time dial w/Roman numerals & subsidiary seconds dial, the lower calendar dial w/days printed in Arabic numerals & w/two openings for rotating day & month, the word "Fashion" printed between the dials on the glass door, stepped & blocked base, eight-day time & strike movement, late 19th c., 32" h. (ILLUS.) **2,363**

Calendar shelf or mantel clock, Thomas (Seth), Plymouth, Connecticut, "Parlor Calendar No. 8" model, wooden case w/beveled pediment topped w/ornately scrolled crest & four finials, the glass front w/decorative borders at top & bottom & between dials & two three-quarter round baluster-form columns at sides, the top dial w/black Roman numerals & marked "W. & C.A., 184 Oxford St., London," the lower dial w/Arabic numerals for dates & rollers for days of week & months, both dials white w/metal bezels, on stepped multi-sided block base, ca. 1886, 27 1/2" h. (ILLUS. below) **5,040**

"Parlor Calendar No. 8" Clock

Waterbury No. 43 Calendar Clock

Thomas Double-dial Calendar Clock

Calendar shelf or mantel clock, Thomas (Seth) Clock Co., Plymouth, double-dial, walnut case w/arched coved crest fitted w/three urn finials above an arched glazed door flanked by slender turned colonettes, on a deep flaring molded base, the upper black dial w/Roman numerals, the lower black perpetual calendar dial w/Arabic numerals, time & strike movement, late 19th c. (ILLUS.) **2,400**

Calendar shelf or mantel clock, Waterbury
Clock Co., Waterbury, Connecticut, No.
43 model, ornate pressed oak case, the
high paneled & scroll-carved & impressed
pediment w/long central block above a flat
cornice w/matching long blocks above
corner fan design over the tall round-
topped glazed door w/a reverse-painted
black ground & gilt band trim opening to
an upper clock dial w/Roman numerals &
a lower calendar dial, reeded side columns w/scroll capitals & blocked bases,
stepped flaring wide base, original finish,
eight-day movement, time & strike, ca.
1910, 5 1/2 x 16 1/4", 29 1/8" h. (ILLUS.
bottom of page 32) **800-900**

E.N. Welch Calendar Shelf Clock

Calendar shelf or mantel clock, Welch
(E.N.), Bristol, Connecticut, "Arditi" double-dial model, tall upright walnut case
w/molded pediment topped by cut-out
scrolling border at front & sides, the cut-
out decoration continues at top & bottom
sides of case, a tall arch-topped glass
door over a time dial w/black Roman numerals at top above the large calendar
dial w/black Arabic numerals for dates &
subsidiary dials for months & days of the
week, both dials w/brass bezels, eight-
day time & strike movement, Gale patent
calendar mechanism fully perpetual, cor-
recting for short months, stepped molded
base w/short bracket feet & shallow rectangular apron matching feet, good Arditi
label on calendar label inside, some wear
to time dial, front glass replaced, ca.
1885, 27" h. (ILLUS.) **1,064**

Rosewood Veneer Calendar Clock

Calendar wall clock, Carter (W.W. & L.F.),
Bristol, Connecticut, double-dial calendar,
molded rosewood veneer case w/cove
molded base drop, the large round top
molding around the white painted time dial
w/black Roman numerals & subsidiary
hand pointing to days of the week, the long
drop case enclosing the smaller calendar
dial w/Arabic numerals for dates & subsidiary hand pointing to months, both dials
w/wooden bezels & original hands, eight-
day weight time & strike movement of
Welch manufacture, clean label inside
case & B.B. Lewis label on back of calendar dial, some flaking to time dial, minor lifting of veneer, small dings in bezels, two
iron weights not original, ca. 1865, 31" h.
(ILLUS.) **1,688**

Calendar wall clock, Carter (W.W. & L.F.),
Bristol, Connecticut, wooden case w/mold-
ed round upper section & long drop base
w/molded beveled base drop, the upper
white time dial w/black Roman numerals &
subsidiary hand pointing to days of the
week, lower dial w/molded bezel & black
Arabic numerals for dates & smaller hand
pointing to months, glass panel below dials

covers pendulum bob & weights, Welch upside-down eight-day seconds pendulum, two-weight time & strike movement, Lewis patent calendar label intact, ca. 1865, 57" h. (ILLUS. below) **3,360**

"Ionic Calendar" Double Dial Clock

Carter Drop Wall Calendar Clock

Calendar wall clock, Ingraham (E.) & Co., Bristol, Connecticut, "Ionic Calendar" model, double dial perpetual calendar model w/a rosewood figure-eight case, wide round upper molding enclosing the time dial w/Roman numerals & subsidiary dial pointing to days of the week, slightly smaller round lower molding enclosing the B.B. Lewis calendar dial w/Arabic numerals for the days of the month & subsidiary dial pointing to the months, a small roundel on each side of the case center, eight-day time & calendar movement, original label in case back, top bezel w/small dry split, upper dial darkened w/age, cover on back of calendar dial missing, ca. 1888, 29 1/2" h. (ILLUS. top right) **1,680**

Ithaca "Iron Case" Calendar Clock

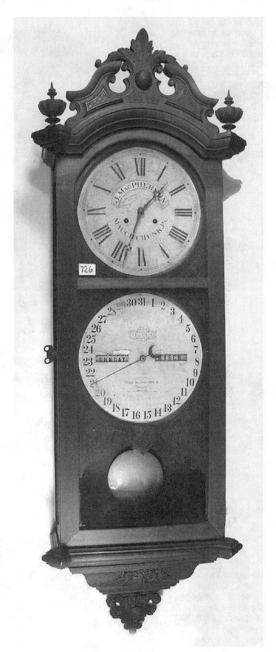

Fine Ithaca Calendar Wall Clock

Calendar wall clock, Ithaca Calendar Clock Co., Ithaca, New York, Bank Model No. O, long walnut case w/a high broken-scroll pediment centered by a cartouche on an arched, molded cornice w/urn-form turned corner finials, a long two-pane front w/the upper arched pane over the large time dial w/Roman numerals, the lower pane over the large calendar dial w/Arabic numerals & small slots for rotating day & month rolls, the large brass pendulum bob visible below, a molded base over a stepped, tapering base drop w/a scroll-carved drop finial, paper dials, time dial marked "J. MacPherson, Mauch Chunk, PA," loss & discoloration on lower paper dial, door restoration, late 19th - early 20th c., 60" h. (ILLUS.)... **7,650**

Calendar wall clock, Ithaca Calendar Clock Co., Ithaca, New York, "Horton's Patent Iron Case" double-dial calendar model, pear-shaped case w/smaller upper time dial & larger lower calendar dial, dials w/brass bezels, the time dial w/black Roman numerals, the calendar dial w/black Arabic numerals for dates & rollers for months & days of the week, panel between dials h.p. w/daisy-like flowers, ornate cast-iron floral & shell trim at top, bottom & sides, Hubbell's Patent 30-day time-only pendulum movement, original backboard w/good labels, case missing about one third of its decoration to wear & rust, dials w/wear & water stains, center panel a replacement, ca. 1866 (ILLUS. on page 35) **3,109**

Ithaca Hanging Calendar Clock

Calendar wall clock, Ithaca Calendar Clock Co., Ithaca, New York, "No. 4 Hanging Office Calendar" model, walnut contoured case w/time on top dial, smaller calendar on bottom, both dials w/original paper over zinc, the time dial w/Roman numerals, original rollers, 30-day time & strike movement, Welch double spring time movement, some wear, part of label missing, ca. 1880, 28" h. (ILLUS.) **1,120**

Jerome & Co. Wall Calendar Clock

Calendar wall clock, Jerome & Co., New Haven, Connecticut, "REGISTER, Hanging" model, wooden case w/molded cornice w/arched crest & corner knob finials, beveled frame around glass pane over the upper time dial w/Roman numerals & subsidiary dial pointing to days of the week, the lower calendar dial w/Arabic numerals for dates & subsidiary dial pointing to months, both dials w/brass bezels, on molded base w/ogee drop & short finial, time & strike movement, some discoloration to time dial, ca. 1880, 31" h. (ILLUS.) **1,792**

Calendar wall clock, Lewis (B.B.), Bristol, Connecticut, "Lewis Calendar No. 6" model, figure eight mahogany case, round molding & carved scroll & leaf decoration around the smaller upper time dial w/brass bezel & Roman numerals & days of the week, a larger round molding enclosing the lower calendar dial w/dates in Arabic numerals & months, further leaf & scroll carving at the bottom & at the sides between top & bottom sections, Hubbell eight-day lever double-spring time-only movement, calendar label notes this clock made "By the inventor," replacement bottom carving, both dials re-papered, brass tension washer has come off, ca. 1867, 30" h. (ILLUS. below) **2,800**

Thomas Office Calendar No. 2 Clock

"Lewis Calendar No. 6" Wall Clock

Calendar wall clock, Thomas (Seth), Plymouth, Connecticut, "Office Calendar No. 2" model, walnut veneer rectangular case w/low pediment & molded cornice, stepped block base, round molding enclosing glass over the upper time dial w/Roman numerals & the word "Regulator" under the 12, matching lower calendar dial w/"Seth Thomas Clock Co. - Plymouth Hollow," time only movement, original label, weight, pendulum & rollers, ca. 1875, 42 1/2" h. (ILLUS. top right) **1,344**

Waterbury Calendar No. 25 Clock

Calendar wall clock, Waterbury Clock Co., Waterbury, Connecticut, "Calendar No. 25" model, quarter-sawn oak case w/beaded cove-molded cornice w/molded arched scroll top w/scalloped crest, the body w/ribbed frame & scroll side garnishes at top & bottom flanking the arched glass door panel w/knob decoration in top corners, the upper time dial w/black Roman numerals & subsidiary dial, the calendar dial w/Arabic numerals for dates & rollers for days of week & months, both dials w/brass bezels, on molded base w/drop gallery flanked by drop chimneys w/drop finials, original pendulum, hands & weights, weight hooks replaced, some flaking to upper dial & some discoloration to lower dial, ca. 1908, 49 1/2" h. (ILLUS. bottom right previous page) **4,480**

time dial w/brass bezel, center ring & black Roman numerals, the calendar dial w/brass bezel & Arabic numerals for dates & rollers for days of week & months, base w/beading, shell-like base drop & corner drop knob finials, eight-day time & strike movement w/hour & half hour strike on cathedral gong, original signed Waterbury key, instruction label on rear only partially legible, ca. 1900, 39 1/4" h. (ILLUS. left) **2,352**

Waterbury Calendar No. 36 Clock

Calendar wall clock, Waterbury Clock Co., Waterbury, Connecticut, "Calendar No. 36," oak case w/scrolling crest flanked by round ringed corner blocks w/finials & molded pediment, body w/contour design side splats & half-round ropetwist columns w/urn-form capitals & bases, glass-paned front panel over the white dials w/brass bezels, the upper time dial w/brass center ring & black Roman numerals, the calendar dial w/Arabic numerals & rollers, the molded base w/long ornately carved back splat & shallower apron in front w/molded scroll design, time-only movement, original glass & pendulum, old key, some paint flakes, date wheels darkened from age, ca. 1891, 28" h. (ILLUS.) **2,352**

Waterbury Calendar No. 33 Clock

Calendar wall clock, Waterbury Clock Co., Waterbury, Connecticut, "Calendar No. 33" model, oak case w/beaded broken arch crest & urn finial on molded pediment, molded case w/glass door w/corner contour garnishes over the upper

Calendar wall clock, Waterbury Clock Company, Waterbury, Connecticut, oak, double-dials, a large molded round upper frame enclosing the clock dial w/Roman numerals above a mid-band w/small carved roundels above the smaller molded lower frame enclosing the calendar movement, brass works w/pendulum & double, paper label also reads "Patented July 30th, 1889 - Calendar No. 34," w/instructions, 29" h. (repairs) **908**

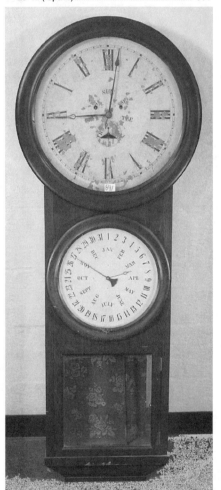

Welch, Spring & Co. Calendar Clock

Calendar wall clock, Welch, Spring & Co., Forestville, Connecticut, rosewood grained case, the large round molded top enclosing the brass bezel & large time dial w/Roman numerals, the long rectangular drop case w/a round molding enclosing the repainted calendar dial w/Arabic numerals, a square glass pane at the base, eight-day time-only movement, late 19th c., time dial flaking, 56 1/2" h. (ILLUS.) **1,913**

Regulator-Calendar Clock

Calendar wall clock, Welch, Spring & Co., Forestville, Connecticut, variant of "Round Head Regulator No. 2," wood veneer case w/molded round top over the time dial & simple molded drop w/calendar dial, time dial w/Roman numerals & subsidiary hand pointing to days of the week, the calendar dial w/Arabic numerals for dates & subsidiary hand pointing to months, molded base drop, two-weight time & strike movement, excellent Lewis calendar label, minor flaking & chips, age crack, ca. 1872, 34" h. (ILLUS.) **1,120**

Carriage clock, Ansonia Clock Co., Ansonia, Connecticut, brass & glass, upright rectangular glass-sided case w/large round dial w/Roman numerals above a mercury-filled glass pendulum, rectangular platform base, time & strike movement, w/key, late 19th c., 9 3/4" h. **275**

Carriage clock, Ansonia Clock Co., Ansonia, Connecticut, "Extra" model, nickel-finished case w/glass front & sides, fancy pierced swivel handle, one-day movement, half-hour strike & alarm, 6 1/2" h. **169**

Bechot, French Brass Carriage Clock

Carriage clock, Bechot, France, cast brass upright rectangular case w/overall foliate design & bail handle at top, beveled glass front & sides, white porcelain dial w/black Roman numerals & subsidiary dial, time, strike, alarm & repeat lever platform movement w/butterfly extension on lever, backplate of movement signed "Bechot & Fils, à Paris" & numbered 133, bottom cover & one case screw missing, ca. 1850, 6 3/4" h. (ILLUS.) **1,344**

Carriage clock, brass Anglaise-style case w/embossed gilded bands around top & bottom, case held together by threaded finials on top & screws through ring-turned feet, beveled glass front & sides, gilt-metal dial mask w/white porcelain time dial w/ornate embossed floral decoration in center & subsidiary alarm dial below w/plain gilt center, both w/molded bezels, eight-day time & alarm silvered lever platform movement, front glass w/minor chip, France, ca. 1900, 6 1/4" h. (ILLUS. bottom left) **392**

French Brass Carriage Alarm Clock

Carriage clock, brass case w/rounded corners & beveled glass front & sides, top handle, low bracket feet, white porcelain rectangular dial w/black Arabic numerals & subsidiary alarm dial, cylinder platform time-only movement w/alarm, minor chips on glass, French, ca. 1910, 5 3/4" h. (ILLUS.) **420**

French Carriage Clock with Alarm

French Brass Carriage Clock

Carriage clock, brass case w/simple block corners & beveled glass front & sides, top & bottom held in place by eight balls w/integral screws also serving as feet, top handle, white porcelain rectangular dial w/black Arabic numerals, cylinder platform time-only movement, French, ca. 1920, 5 1/4" h. (ILLUS.) **218**

J.E. Caldwell Carriage Clock

Carriage clock, brass case w/top handle, embossed bands around top & base molding, turned bun feet, beveled glass front & sides, the dial w/Roman numerals & subsidiary seconds dial marked "J.E. Caldwell Co. - Philadelphia," original lever platform, time only movement w/alarm, replaced minute hand, made in France, retailed by Caldwell, ca. 1900, 5 3/4" h. (ILLUS. bottom left) **336**

Carriage Clock with Corniche Case

Carriage clock, brass Corniche case w/rounded corners, cornice & molded bracket base, bail handle at top, beveled glass front & sides, white porcelain dial w/black Roman numerals & subsidiary seconds dial, grand sonnerie w/alarm, selector lever on base engraved with "Gde Sonnerie, Silence, or Hours & Quart's," France, ca. 1909, 7" h. (ILLUS.) **1,344**

Carriage clock, brass Doucine case w/serpentine-sided top & bottom bands decorated w/bands of embossed & gilded rococo scrolls, flat scroll-shaped bail handle on top, beveled glass front & sides, gilt-metal dial mask w/white porcelain chapter ring w/black Arabic numerals & original hands, short ringed round wafer feet, eight-day time-only cylinder platform movement, France, ca. 1900, 6 1/4" h. (ILLUS. top of next page) **336**

French Doucine Carriage Clock

Drocourt French Carriage Clock

Carriage clock, Drocourt, France, gilded brass case w/molded pediment & base, bail handle, beveled glass front & sides, the square white dial w/black Roman numerals, subsidiary seconds dial & original hands, backplate signed with "D-C" trademark w/tiny carriage clock between & serial number 13661, selector lever for "Striking" & "Silent" on base, petit sonnerie w/alarm, ca. 1890, 6 1/4" h. (ILLUS. bottom of previous column) **1,064**

Carriage Clock with Porcelain Panels

Carriage clock, gilded brass case w/molded top & cove molding over plain base w/block feet, square corners, angled bail handle at top, glass front & two sides each w/porcelain panels of birds, butterflies & flowers, the white chapter ring w/black Arabic numerals, time & strike movement w/original silvered lever platform intact, "Harris and Shafer, Washington" on dial mask, France, ca. 1905, 7 1/2" h. (ILLUS.) **2,576**

French Brass Carriage Clock

Carriage clock, H&H, rectangular brass case w/stepped cornice w/straight ring handle, beveled base & bracket feet, beveled glass front & sides, white dial w/Arabic numerals, original lever platform, time, strike & repeat movement, replaced minute hand, France, ca. 1900, 5 3/4" h. (ILLUS.) **420**

French Carriage Clock for Tiffany

Carriage clock, Hour (Ch.), France, Grand Sonnerie-type, gilt-brass upright rectangular gorge case w/floral engraving on sides & top, twisted bail top handle, beveled glass panels on front & sides, grey porcelain dial w/black Arabic numerals, original hands & subsidiary dial directly underneath, thin bracket feet, 13-jewel time, strike & alarm movement w/lever platform signed "Ch. Hour, France - 13 - Thirteen Jewels," made for Tiffany & Co., ca. 1900, 7 1/4" h. (ILLUS. bottom left) **4,200**

Carriage clock, Jennings Brothers, Model 699, ornately scroll-cast upright brass-plated spelter case w/scroll swing handle on top, round glass over the dial w/Arabic numerals & subsidiary seconds dial **124**

Miniature Enameled Carriage Clock

Carriage clock, miniature, upright brass case w/enameled porcelain panels under the beveled glass on front framing the dial & on the sides & top, the inset top panel depicts a pair of doves, the sides show pastoral scenes w/lovers dressed in lavender, pink, blue, red & white, the front shows Cupid w/bow lying under the dial near a tree that branches around dial, simple bail top handle & block base, the white porcelain dial w/brass bezel & star-like center ring & black Roman numerals, time-only movement w/tiny lever platform spanning the top of the plates, tiny chip in glass, hairline in porcelain, France, ca. 1900, 3 1/2" h. w/handle (ILLUS.) **1,680**

French "Pendule D'Officier" Clock

Carriage clock, "Pendule D'Officier" style, gold-plated domed case w/ornate over-all decoration, the top w/a flat rectangular platform for the scrolled bail handle, white porcelain glass-paned dial w/black Roman numerals & hands & signed w/dealer's name, "Lescurieux & Cie.," flattened knob feet, time & strike movement, France, ca. 1880, 8 1/4" h. (ILLUS.) **2,016**

Elaborate Decorated Carriage Clock

Carriage clock, Oudin (Chs.), Paris, France, gilt-brass upright rectangular case ornately cast w/Rococo style blossoms, swags, scrolls & leaves, gargoyles at each top corner, elaborate cutout scroll bail top handle, glass front & side panels, the gilt-metal dial surround w/intricate engraving, the white porcelain dial w/black Arabic numerals & signed "Chs. Oudin - Paris," subsidiary dial directly underneath, time, strike, scroll & leaf feet, a face in relief w/frame forming apron at base, repeat & alarm movement numbered 13859 w/single coiled gong struck from above for the hours & from the underside for the alarm, most of the gilding rubbed off, ca. 1880, 7 3/4" h. (ILLUS.) **2,800**

French Carriage Clock

Carriage clock, petite sonnerie-type, upright brass Corniche case w/rounded corners, molded top w/scroll bail top handle, beveled glass on front & sides, dial w/Roman numerals, on a block base w/bracket feet, time & strike movement w/lever platform strikes ding dong quarters & full hours & quarters on demand, comes w/original leather traveling case minus strap, France, ca. 1900, 7" h. (ILLUS. on previous page) **1,568**

English Gilt-Brass Carriage Clock

Carriage clock, Rossiter (Wm.), London, England, "#3528" model, gilt-brass upright rectangular case w/molded pediment & base, bail handle on top, round columns at each corner below acorn finials, the sides & front all w/finely engraved decoration, round white porcelain dial w/black Roman numerals & gilt-brass bezel, the rear w/door for winding & setting the hands & engraved silvered plaque w/Rossiter's name & clock's number, circular wafer feet, time-only movement, small hairline in dial, ca. 1825, 4 3/4" h. (ILLUS.) **1,904**

French Carriage Clock

Carriage clock, round ormolu & brass case w/pierced design around sides, scrolling leaf-design handle & short feet, round glass front over white porcelain dial w/Arabic numerals, platform cylinder escapement mounted on the back plate, movement marked "France," ca. 1900, 5 1/4" h. (ILLUS. bottom left) **252**

1950s German Carriage Clock

Carriage clock, Schmitt, Germany, brass case w/tall beveled glass front & sides framed by colonettes enclosing a steel dial w/Roman numerals suspending a brass lyre-form pendulum, ca. 1950s, 3 1/2 x 6 3/4", 10 1/2" h. (ILLUS.) **180-200**

French Carriage Clock with Columns

Carriage clock, upright brass "Anglais Riche" case w/fluted Corinthian columns & fluted top bail handle, dentil borders at top & bottom, beveled glass panels on front, sides & top, striped & spotted dial mask, white porcelain dial w/black Roman numerals, gilt minutes & original hands, signed "G. Edward & Sons, London & Glasgow" for the retailer, block base w/molding at top & square wafer feet, time, strike, repeat & alarm lever platform movement numbered 6172, France, ca. 1900, 7 3/4" h. (ILLUS. on previous page) **1,960**

Carriage clock, upright brass frame enclosing glass sides & front, angled swing top handle, dial w/Roman numerals, made in Paris, France for Sir John Bennett Ltd., England, eight-day movement, 4 1/4" h. (corner crack in side glass) **169**

Carriage clock, Waterbury Clock Co., Waterbury, Connecticut, "Conductor" model, brass upright case w/glass sides & front, porcelain dial w/Arabic numerals, in original velvet-covered case, 4" h. **84**

French Gilt Bronze Cartel Wall Clock

Cartel wall clock, Louis XVI-Style, gilt bronze, ornate openwork works, ribbon & vine top suspending the round enameled dial w/Roman & Arabic numerals surrounded by large scrolling leaf & flower cornucopia borders, a twisted ribbon pendent base drop, two train chiming movement, France, early 20th c.,14" w., 35" h. (ILLUS.) **3,105**

French Ormolu Cartel Wall Clock

Cartel wall clock, Hour (Charles), France, Louis XVI-Style, ormolu case w/round dial topped w/ribbon decoration & small ring handle, the white porcelain dial w/polychrome floral decoration & ormolu pierced hands, Arabic numerals for hours & in increments of five for minutes, the case bottom flanked by an applied leaf wreath centered by an ornate drop, round time-only movement w/Swiss jeweled platform escapement, leaf decoration loose in one spot, ca. 1900, 11 1/2" h. (ILLUS.) **392**

French Carved Oak Cartel Clock

Cartel wall clock, ornately carved oak case composed of a large pierced leafy wreath enclosing a round molding around the dial w/enamel cartouches w/black Roman numerals, eight-day time & strike movement, France, ca. 1880-90, 18" w., 25" h. (ILLUS. on previous page)...................... **1,500-1,750**

Walnut & Ebony Cartel Clock

French Ovoid Cartel Wall Clock

Cartel wall clock, ovoid oak case w/heavily carved rococo design of scrolls w/crest & drop finial of carved grapes & grape leaves, molded circular wooden dial w/black Roman numerals on white porcelain cartouches, original pierced-brass hands, time & strike movement strikes the hours & half hours on coiled wire gong, France, ca. 1890, 28" h. (ILLUS.) **532**

Cartel wall clock, Victorian carved Baroque-style walnut case w/leaf, fruit & scroll designs w/ebony accents, dark round dial w/molded bezel & white number cartouches w/black Roman numerals, replacement movement resulting in three filled holes in backboard, France, ca. 1890, 27" h. (ILLUS. top right)... **896**

Crystal regulator, 400-day model, French-style rectangular upright case w/a cherry wood top & base & four slender brass columns flanking the glass front, back & sides, brass bezel enclosing the dial w/Arabic numerals, Germany, late 19th - early 20th c., 11 1/4" h. **731**

Fine Ansonia Crystal Regulator

Crystal regulator, Ansonia Clock Co., Ansonia, Connecticut, & New York, New York, gold-painted cast-spelter case w/a large urn finial, pierced cast scrolls at the top & base corners, beveled glass front, back & sides, large brass bezel enclosing the enameled dial w/Roman numerals, open escapement, faux mercury pendulum, late 19th - early 20th c., 6 1/2 x 7 1/2", 15 1/4" h. (ILLUS. on previous page) **700-800**

"Delphus" Crystal Regulator

Boston Clock Co. Crystal Regulator

Ansonia "Peer" Crystal Regulator

Crystal regulator, Ansonia Clock Co., New York, New York, "Peer" model, brass case w/beveled glass front & sides, ornate scroll design on cornice, base, trim & doorknob, trifid feet, round porcelain dial w/brass bezel & black Roman numerals, original fancy pendulum, eight-day time & strike movement, glass chips on door & back panel, ca. 1917, 12" h. (ILLUS.) **599**

Crystal regulator, Boston Clock Co., Boston, Massachusetts, "Delphus" model, upright rectangular brass case w/reeded columnar corners & beveled top w/notched & beaded panels below, beveled glass sides & front, round porcelain dial w/applied gilt numbers, bezel & center decoration, original hands, molded base w/beaded rim on top, bracket feet, nickel-plated rear plates w/"damaskeen" finish, eight-day time & strike 11-jewel lever movement, ca. 1890, 10 1/2" h. (ILLUS. top right) **952**

Crystal regulator, Boston Clock Co., Boston, Massachusetts, upright brass case w/glass sides & front enclosing the large dial w/Arabic numerals in the porcelain outer ring around a relief-cast cast-brass dial center, tandem wind eight-day time & strike movement, 10 1/4" h. (crack in side glass) **563**

Crystal regulator, Boston Clock Co., Chelsea, Massachusetts, "Crystal" model, upright brass frame w/some molding at top & rounded front corners, beveled glass front & sides, cream-colored porcelain dial w/black Arabic numerals in raised round white shields, brass bezel, brass pendulum w/spool-type bob, beveled base w/bracket feet, eight-day seven-jewel tandem-wind time-only movement w/lever escapement w/patent date of 1880, most gilding worn off, scratch in left glass pane, ca. 1890, 9 3/4" h. (ILLUS.) **560**

Cloisonné Crystal Regulator

Crystal regulator, bow-front brass case w/cloisonné corner panels enclosing beveled glass front & sides, top w/brass molding & quatrefoil cloisonné decoration, more cloisonné in top & bottom borders, molded bracket base, gilt dial w/Arabic numerals, original hands & center sunburst pattern, eight-day time & strike movement, made in France for J.E. Caldwell & Co., Philadelphia, ca. 1900, 11 1/4" h. (ILLUS.)... **1,568**

Crystal regulator, Chelsea Clock Co., Chelsea, Massachusetts, upright brass frame w/four beveled glass sides, signed porcelain dial, eight-day time & strike balance movement w/a cathedral gong, made for Tiffany & Co., New York, ca. 1920, 10 1/2" h.. **500-600**

Decorative Crystal Regulator Clock

Crystal regulator, gold-painted cast-spelter upright case w/an arched top w/five flower basket finials, an egg-and-dart cornice over a scroll-cast panel above the long beveled glass door & sides, porcelain dial w/Arabic numerals & decorated w/flower swags, glass tube pendulum, rectangular platform base cast w/a scroll & floret band on flat tab feet, eight-day time & strike movement, early 20th c., 5 3/4 x 8 3/8", 15" h. (ILLUS. bottom left)........................ **600-650**

Marti Crystal Regulator Clock

Crystal regulator, Marti, France, domed brass case w/molded arched top & molded base each w/rounded corners & bracket feet, beveled glass in front & sides, white porcelain dial w/brass bezel & center ring, black Roman numerals & open brocot escapement, grid pendulum w/large bob, time & strike movement, minute hand too short, some hairlines in chapter ring, ca. 1900, 18 1/2" h. (ILLUS.) **1,960**

Crystal regulator, simple upright brass molded frame on bracket feet w/beveled glass panels in front & sides, white porcelain dial w/brass bezel & center ring, open escapement & black Roman numerals, ship's wheel under dial rotates back & forth as long as the clock is wound, eight-day time & strike movement, some hairlines to dial, France, ca. 1900, 11 1/2" h. (ILLUS. top of next page)............................. **2,968**

Crystal Regulator with Ship's Wheel

Crystal regulator, Thomas (Seth) Clock Co., Plymouth, Connecticut, upright brass frame w/beveled glass sides, signed porcelain dial w/original hands, mercury-style pendulum, eight-day movement w/cathedral gong, late 19th - early 20th c., 10" h............................... **250-350**

"Empire No. 65" Shelf Clock

Crystal regulator, Thomas (Seth) Clock Co., Thomaston, Connecticut, "Empire No. 65" model, brass bow-front case w/slightly arched stepped cornice, four fluted columns at sides & aproned base w/block

feet, white dial w/Arabic numerals & bezel, columns missing some gold finish, ca. 1909, 11" h. (ILLUS. bottom left) **504**

French Crystal Regulator Clock

Crystal regulator, upright case w/quatre-foil flattened arch mahogany top w/large ormolu & cut crystal urn at center, gilt-metal pine cone finial at each corner, four cut & polished crystal columns w/ormolu capitals at corners flanking the glass sides & the porcelain dial ring w/Roman numerals around an engine-turned center w/original gilding, mahogany platform base w/ormolu front ribbon decoration on flattened urn feet, brass mounts, mercury pendulum, rack time & strike movement, signed "Made in France," early 20th c., 15 1/2" h. (ILLUS.) **3,024**

Crystal regulator, upright rectangular all-glass clear crystal cut case w/fluted frame & starburst designs on front, block base w/bands of circular decoration, enclosing an ormolu dial & bezel w/ornate scroll, floral & leaf design around chapter ring & in center, black Roman numerals & original moon hands, time & bell strike movement w/silk thread suspension & Mougin trademark, replacement pendulum, France, ca. 1840, 10" h. (ILLUS. top of next page) **1,036**

French Crystal Regulator Shelf Clock

Vermont Clock Co. Crystal Regulator

Crystal regulator, Vermont Clock Co., Fair Haven, Vermont, upright rectangular brass case w/rounded corners & beveled top, beveled glass panels in front & sides, round white porcelain dial w/brass bezel, black Roman numerals & original hands, two-jar mercury pendulum, molded base w/bracket feet, damascened nickel-plated round eight-day time & strike movement w/time train located outside main plates, ca. 1915, 9 1/2" h. (ILLUS.)................... **672**

Crystal regulator, Waterbury Clock Co., Waterbury, Connecticut, "Chalons" model, cast-brass frame w/ornate scrolls & pierced finial & rings enclosing beveled glass sides, porcelain dial w/open escapement & original hands, mercury-style pendulum, original key, eight-day time & strike movement w/cathedral gong, late 19th - early 20th c., 14" h... **700-850**

German Carved Cuckoo Clock

Cuckoo shelf or mantel clock, linden wood case w/walnut peaked roof carved w/oak leaves cascading along the top & down the sides centered by a carved pheasant perched on peak, the round dial w/darker wood chapter ring, carved hands & white Roman numerals, the arched base covered w/carved ferns & forest plants, a steer standing below the dial, heavy brass 56-hour time & strike movement, old bird, nice tone on old flutes, bellows recovered, Germany, ca. 1925, 24" h. (ILLUS.) **1,680**

Cuckoo shelf or mantel clock, wooden house-shaped case w/pairs of leaves on vines twining up from base to peaked "roof," spread-winged bird finial, beveled base w/valanced skirt & bracket feet, original dial w/bone hands & grommets around winding holes, Roman numerals, cuckoo w/articulated beak & wings, original flutes, time & strike movement, cast lyre-shaped plates geared for 56 hours, Germany, ca. 1920, 15" h. (ILLUS. top of next page)... **980**

German Cuckoo Shelf Clock

American Cuckoo Co. Wall Clock

Cuckoo wall clock, American Cuckoo Clock Co., Philadelphia, Pennsylvania, fumed oak Neo-Gothic Arts & Crafts case, stepped flat top above Gothic arched & flat pilasters flanking the cuckoo door & brass dial w/Arabic numerals, eight-day weight-driven movement, time & strike, oak pendulum bob in a wheel design, tall obelisk-shaped iron weights, early 20th c., 5 1/4 x 9 1/4", 12 3/4" h. plus chain & weights (ILLUS. disassembled) **200-250**

German Black Forest Cuckoo Clock

Cuckoo wall clock, Black Forest-style, carved hardwood, a large figural stag head w/antlers at the top of the oak leaf-carved crest w/crossed rifles above carved dead game flanking the cuckoo door & round dial w/white Roman numerals, a pair of carved small birds, game bag & leaves at the base, chain & weight mechanism, dial marked "Germany," probably post-World War II, 13 1/2 x 15", 23" h. plus chains (ILLUS.) **200-250**

Cuckoo wall clock, carved hardwood Black Forest-style, typical house form, topped by a carved bird & flanked by clusters of fruit, the face w/ivory hands, two-train weight-driven movement, Germany, late 19th c., 23 1/2" h. (restoration) **348**

German Cuckoo Wall Clock

Cuckoo wall clock, carved wood chalet-style case, 30-hour movement, Germany, ca. 1950, 9" w. (ILLUS. on previous page) **225**

Cuckoo wall clock, Keebler pendulette, molded wood, red & green foliage, 30-hour movement, time only, spring-driven, 5 x 6 1/2" **45**

Waltham Deck Watch Clock

Deck watch clock, Waltham Clock Co., Waltham, Massachusetts, square mahogany display-top gimbaled case stamped "1203," suspended round white dial w/black Arabic numerals & subsidiary seconds dial marked "Waltham USA," brass bezel & gimbals, 15-jewel time & strike movement adjusted for changes in temperature & Isochronism, some dings & scratches to case, ca. 1930, 5" h. (ILLUS.) **896**

"Vanderbilt" Desk Clock

Desk clock, Chelsea Clock Co., Boston, Massachusetts, "Vanderbilt" model, chrome case in shape of ship's wheel mounted on circular base w/wood & felt insert, 4" d. brushed dial w/black Arabic numerals & marked "London Harness Company," time & strike movement, ca. 1960, 6 3/4" h. (ILLUS. bottom left) **773**

Desk clock, Chelsea Clock Co., Chelsea, Massachusetts, mahogany case w/yoke top & molded edge, cast-brass bezel enclosing a convex glass over the signed dial, eight-day balance movement w/cathedral gong, ca. 1915, 11 1/2"h............ **500-600**

Desk clock, clock-inkstand combination, cast-brass, Rococo style, the small clock w/a round dial w/Roman numerals framed by ornate pierced scrolls in an upright case above a rectangular inkstand w/ornate scroll trim & fitted w/two inkwells w/domed covers, on small peg feet, 30-hour movement, probably French, late 19th - early 20th c., 6 x 10 1/2", 8 1/8" h. (ILLUS. at top of next page) **180-200**

Desk clock, Elgin Company, World Time battery-operated electric model, a long horizontal rectangular upright case enclosing a long world map w/a small time dial at one end, w/original box, mid-20th c., 7" h. **146**

Desk clock, General Electric Company, electric Art Deco model, an oval wood base supporting a three-sided chrome frame w/narrow stepped side supports flanking the upright rectangular blue glass front printed in white w/Arabic numerals around a rectangular white center panel, 6" h................. **56**

Swiss Desk Clock

Desk clock, horizontal rectangular brass case w/raised Arabic numerals on rectangular white border band of dial, enameled hands, eight-day jeweled lever movement, Switzerland, ca. 1950, 6" h. (ILLUS.) **196**

Cast-brass French Inkstand-Clock

Dwarf Grandfather Clock   *W.L. Gilbert Floor "Regulator No. 8"*

Dwarf grandfather, attributed to Noah Ran-
let, Gilmanton, New Hampshire, Federal
style, pine case, broken-scroll pediment
w/three brass urn finials above a molded
cornice above the round molded circle
around the painted dial w/Roman numerals above another molded crestrail above
the waist w/a narrow short door w/an oval
opening flanked by small pilasters,
stepped-out lower case on simple French
feet, eight-day weight-driven movement,
old refinish, replaced dial, early 19th c.,
48" h. (ILLUS. bottom left on previous
page).. **6,325**

Floor regulator, Gilbert (William L.), Winsted, Connecticut, "Regulator No. 8" model, walnut case w/stepped pediment
w/beveled & ribbed band & scroll-topped
molded panels slanting up to meet center
rectangular panel w/ornate crest w/relief
bust of Pharaoh figure under band of
molded bull's-eye decorations topped by
arch w/sunburst design & spiked knob
finial, w/matching spiked knob decorations on either side of arch, the body
w/glass front & side panels within wood
frame w/ribbed corners, scroll, loop, scallop & cut-out designs applied to top &
bottoms of side panels, the front arched
glass pane w/decorations in upper corners & engraved in wood around arch,
the white porcelain dial w/brass bezel,
black Roman numerals & sweep seconds
hand, the grid iron lyre-form pendulum
signed by retailer "M.L. Sheehan, 785 8th
Ave., N.Y.," the stepped molded bottom
section w/inset panels, the front w/mold-
ed design, on base w/bracket feet & contour apron, pinwheel time-only movement, most of walnut dial surround
missing, small chip in dial, ca. 1885,
106" h. (ILLUS. bottom right on previous
page) **19,600**

Gallery clock, Cochran (Samuel), London,
England, round mahogany wall-mounted
case enclosing a large signed silvered
metal dial w/Roman numerals, fusee
w/eight-day crown wheel movement,
15" d. (ILLUS. bottom left) **2,925**

Gallery clock, Hubbell (Laporte), Marion,
Connecticut, octagonal walnut wall-
mounted case framing a brass bezel &
paper dial, signed movement w/1865
patent date, eight-day time-only move-
ment, 12 1/2" w.. **150-200**

Iron Octagonal Gallery Clock

Gallery clock, iron octagonal case painted
black w/mother-of-pearl inlaid accents
around the sides framing the round white
dial w/black Roman numerals, open escapement & brass bezel, hangers at top
& bottom cast into iron backboard, 30-
hour lever/balance time-only movement
signed "N. Pomeroy," loss of paint on
case, ca. 1850, 9" h. (ILLUS.) **392**

Self Winding Clock Co. Gallery Clock

Gallery clock, Self Winding Clock Company,
battery-operated electric model, a wide
round walnut frame enclosing a large white
dial w/bronzed metal Roman numerals &

Early English Gallery Clock

subsidiary seconds dial, 20th c., case 24" d. (ILLUS. on previous page) **1,406**

Gallery clock, Thomas (Seth) Clock Co., Plymouth, Connecticut, wall-mounted octagonal mahogany case enclosing a brass bezel & signed paper dial, 1878 patent date on label, 11" w **125-150**

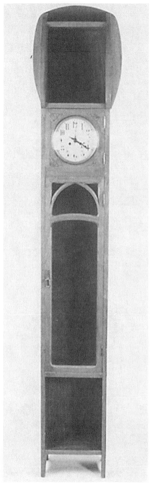

Arts & Crafts Grandfather Clock

Grandfather clock, Arts & Crafts style, tall slender oak case w/an oblong top backboard behind an open compartment over a square door w/scroll-carved corners flanking the round bezel opening to a round dial w/Arabic numerals above a tall slender amber glass door w/arched loop at the top, an open compartment at the bottom, low arched bootjack feet, applied brasses, Europe, early 20th c., 86 1/4" h. (ILLUS.) **1,265**

French Gothic Style Grandfather Clock

Grandfather clock, Bentejec, France, oak Gothic Revival style tall case, the ornate Gothic arch-carved top enclosing the signed round steel dial w/Arabic numerals above the tall narrow case w/a two-panel Gothic arch & linenfold-carved narrow door flanked by quarter-round ropetwist edge bands, the stepped out base section w/a carved linenfold panel above the flared rectangular foot, late 19th c., 12 x 22", 95" h. (ILLUS.) **8,050**

American Gothic Grandfather Clock

B.D. Bingham Grandfather Clock

Grandfather clock, Bingham (Belden D.), Nashua, New Hampshire, jeweler's master regulator, mahogany arched-top case w/peaked molded crest, molding & inset beveled panels in base & sides, mirrored back, the arched glass door panel showing round 17" silvered brass dial signed "B.C. Bingham, Maker, Nashua, N.H." w/typical "astro" layout w/center minutes in Arabic numerals & subsidiary dials for hours (Roman numerals) & seconds (Arabic numerals), two-jar mercurial compensating pendulum, the pulley, weight & hardware all original, time-only movement, ca. 1845, 89" h. (ILLUS.) **47,040**

Grandfather clock, Blunt & Co., New York, New York, Gothic Revival style, mahogany & mahogany veneer, the hood w/molded Gothic arched cornice w/central plinth & spire flanked by smaller spires above a round molded brass bezel enclosing a round engraved silver regulator dial w/Arabic numerals & signed by the maker, the waist w/a tall glazed Gothic arch door framed by crossbanding above a crossbanded rectangular panel flanked by lambrequin corners over the tall base section w/slender cut-out feet, eight-day weight-driven movement, old finish, ca. 1840, minor imperfections, 94 1/2" h. (ILLUS.)..................................... **12,650**

Grandfather clock, Caldwell (J.E.) & Co., Philadelphia, Pennsylvania, Colonial Revival mahogany case, the top hold w/full pillars in the front & quarter pillars in the rear, fretwork side windows, brass dial w/cast spandrels & separate chapter rings chased in the center & w/an engraved eagle boss at the top, crossbanded waist & base on the case, heavy brass movement w/hour bell strike, ca. 1900, 7'6" h.................. **3,500-4,200**

Grandfather clock, Claggett (William), Newport, Rhode Island, Queen Anne-Chippendale transitional style, cherry, the case w/a flat top w/small corner blocks & pointed ball finials above an arched cornice molding & glazed tombstone door w/engaged columns enclosing the eight-day weight-driven movement & brass dial engraved w/Roman numerals w/strike-silent indicator in the arch flanked by cast dolphin spandrels, an engraved chapter ring seconds hand, calendar aperture below & engraved panel signed "Wm. Claggett Newport" w/cast spandrels, the arch-molded tall rectangular waist door w/a glazed bull's-eye panel on the stepped-out molded base w/ball feet, old refinish, 18th c., 100" h. (restored)............................ **9,200**

Colonial Clock Grandfather Clock

Grandfather clock, Colonial Clock Company, New York, New York, Neoclassical-style mahogany case, the rectangular top w/a flaring cornice over a carved dentil band above roundels & reeded panels over carved bellflower drops flanking the tall glazed door w/an upper small panel over the white & brass dial w/Arabic numerals & the lower panel w/Gothic arch lattice, a bottom panel w/a carved swag above small block feet, original finish, ca. 1920s, 10 x 14", 64" h. (ILLUS.).................. **1,000**

Colonial Mfg. Co. Grandfather

Grandfather clock, Colonial Mfg. Co., Zeeland, Michigan, "Model 1216," Queen Anne Revival mahogany case w/molded broken-scroll pediment w/urn finial above an arched molding & glass door opening to a brass-framed steel dial chapter ring & black Arabic numerals, moon phase movement in arch above it, the dial flanked by small colonettes & glass-inset side panels, the case front w/a narrow rectangular glass panel showing the weights & pendulum, the stepped-out tall lower case w/cove molding above the sides, on short ogee legs w/square feet, five-tube time & strike movement made by Herschede, case slightly crazed, click on strike side repaired but needs additional attention, finial's dowel broken, ca. 1919, 87" h. (ILLUS.) **1,512**

Colonial Revival Grandfather Clock

Grandfather clock, Colonial Revival carved mahogany case, broken-scroll pediment centered by a lotus-form finial & carved w/rosettes & scrolling decoration above the arched glazed door bordered by carved beading, beveled glass door opening to an arched gilt-brass & silvered metal dial w/two small upper dials over the main dial w/Roman numerals & ornate spandrels, the upper case flaring out & bead-carved above the long case fitted w/a long door w/nine small square beveled panes above & below the large beveled central pane showing the large brass pendulum, the stepped-out lower case w/an ornately scroll-carved central panel over a scalloped apron & boldly carved hairy paw feet, Westminster & Whittington chimes, retailed by Bigelow, Kennard & Co., Boston, late 19th - early 20th c., overall 95" h. (ILLUS.) **4,888**

Exceptional Carved Oak Grandfather

Grandfather clock, Colonial Revival, carved oak, the very high broken-scroll pediment over a wide frieze boldly carved w/scrolls centering a lion mask above scrolled sides flanking the arched glazed door opening to a steel & brass dial w/moon phase & Arabic numerals, the tall body topped by a carved flaring cornice above an oblong door w/beveled glass flanked by serpentine sides w/front scroll carving, the stepped-out lower case w/a wide carved flaring band over a bombé section boldly carved on the front w/leafy scrolls, serpentine apron & bold front paw feet, original finish, Europe, ca. 1890, 16 x 22", 108" h. (ILLUS.) **20,000**

Grandfather clock, Colonial Revival, mahogany, the high broken-scroll pediment w/a raised central flame-turned finial w/matching corner finials above the ornate scroll-carved frieze above reeded columns flanking the set-back arched glazed door opening to a steel & brass dial w/moon phase & Arabic numerals, pierced brass sides, the tall body topped by a carved egg-and-dart band above the arched door w/beveled glass flanked by reeded columns, beveled glass side panels, the stepped-out lower case w/a gadrooned band above pilasters flanking an ornate scroll-carved panel, molded base on heavy paw front feet, nine-tube chiming movement, signed "Elite Germany," original finish, ca. 1885, 16 x 20", 100" h. (ILLUS. top of next page) **12,000**

Beautiful Colonial Revival Grandfather

Fine Tiffany "Elite" Grandfather Clock

Grandfather clock, Colonial Revival, Tiffany & Co. "Elite" model, dark carved oak case, a high broken-scroll front pediment w/a large central carved urn finial & smaller corner urn finials w/smaller broken-scroll pediments & finials at the sides of the top, an arched glazed top door over the arched dial w/moon phase movement over the brass filigree-trimmed dial w/brass Arabic numerals, the tall waist w/rows of small raised square panels at each side & a glazed tall front door opening to the large weights & flanked by quarter-round columns at the sides, the stepped-out bombé base section w/a lappet-carved band above wide bands of scroll carving, on carved paw feet, nine-tube three-weight movement, late 19th - early 20th c. (ILLUS. below left) **14,850**

Grandfather clock, Cummens (William), Boston or Roxbury, Massachusetts, Federal mahogany & mahogany veneer case, the arched top w/a pierced fretwork & three plinths each w/a brass ball finial, over a molded arched crest & glazed tombstone door opening to a gilt & polychrome floral-decorated white enamel dial w/Roman numerals & Arabic numeral chapter ring & centering a calendar aperture & inscription "Warrented by Wm. Cummens," all flanked by free-standing columns w/brass capitals & bases over the tall waist section w/a molded tall door flanked by quarter-engaged fluted columns on the box-form base w/a molded panel, on French feet, old refinish, ca. 1800, 9 x 17 1/4", 86" h. (repair to dial) **10,350**

Grandfather clock, Cummens (William), Roxbury, Massachusetts, Federal inlaid mahogany case, the hood w/a pierced fretwork joining three inlaid plinths above the arched cornice molding & glazed tombstone inlaid door enclosing a white-painted gilt-decorated dial w/Roman numerals & a rocking ship flying an American flag in the concave arch, seconds hand & calendar aperture inscribed "Warranted by Wm. Cummens," housing an eight-day brass weight-driven movement, all flanked by brass stop-fluted free-standing columns, the waist w/molded rectangular door inlaid w/crossbanding & stringing flanked by brass stop-fluted quarter columns on conformingly inlaid base on flaring French feet, ca. 1790, 97" h. (refinished, minor restoration, imperfections) **27,600**

Grandfather clock, Durfee (Walter), Providence, Rhode Island, Colonial Revival-style walnut case, a high broken-scroll pediment centering a large carved pineapple finial above the swag- and ribbon-carved frieze band above the arched glazed door opening to a steel dial w/brass Arabic numerals below the moon phase dial all flanked by free-standing colonettes & cloth-lined latticework sides on a projecting cornice over the waist section topped by a band of leafy swag carving above an arched, geometrically-glazed front door flanked by columns & w/glazed sides, the projecting base section w/shaped panels centering swagged leaf & blossom carving, carved base band above scroll-carved feet, tube striking movement, retailed by Tiffany & Co., New York, late 19th - early 20th c., 102" h. (ILLUS. below)................................ **20,000**

Fine Durfee Grandfather Clock

Grandfather clock, Elliott, London, England, Gothic Revival mahogany case, the Gothic arch crest topped by a large flame-style finial & flanked by spiked spire corner finials over the arched glass door opening to a moon phase dial over the clock dial w/Arabic numerals, the lower glass panel of the door w/Gothic arch muntin opening to the weights & chimes, the door flanked by blocked pilasters above the paneled base platform w/Gothic trefoil carving, molded base band on beveled bun feet, dial labeled "Elliott, London," brass works w/tubular Westminster & Whittington chimes, w/key & pendulum w/its mercury vials removed, England, late 19th - early 20th c., 97" h. (ILLUS. top of next column)............. **7,700**

Fine Gothic-Style Grandfather Clock

Renaissance-Style Grandfather Clock

Grandfather clock, Elliott of London, England, Renaissance-Style carved oak case, the arched pediment mounted w/a pair of winged griffins flanking a central shield above a panel of acanthus leaf carving over another arched panel of leaf carving above the ornate filigree dial w/Arabic numerals & a moon phase action flanked by columns over a scroll-carved band above the tall waist w/a paneled door finely carved w/delicate fruit & flower vines flanked by reeded columns, the stepped-out base w/a gadrooned band around the top above leafy scroll & shield-carved panels above the flared stepped base on paw feet, two-train quarter striking movement on gongs, ca. 1890, 104" h. (ILLUS. on previous page) **13,800**

Cherry Federal Grandfather Clock

Grandfather clock, Federal style, cherry case, arched scroll-carved crest on conforming molded cornice above the matching glazed door flanked by freestanding colonettes, opening to a white-painted dial w/Roman numerals & a painted moon phase, the narrow body of the case w/quarter-round columns at the sides flanking the narrow line-inlaid door, stepped-out lower case w/band inlay & a shaped apron & short French feet, old refinish, ca. 1810, 12 x 15", 86" h. (ILLUS.) **3,500**

American Mahogany Grandfather

Grandfather clock, Federal style mahogany case w/molded pediment & cut-out crest w/center & corner four-piece cast brass ball finials, the dial panel w/arched glass door & oval side panels over the white dial painted w/pink roses & green leaves in the arch & spandrel areas, black Roman numerals for hours surrounded by Arabic numerals in increments of 5 for minutes, subsidiary seconds dial, top flanked by two colonettes w/metal capitals & bases, simple tall case w/quarter-round colonettes flanking the long door w/cove-molding at top & bottom, the rectangular base section on short bracket feet, eight-day time & strike movement, brass works, original pendulum & tin can weights, false plate between movement & dial stamped "Wilson, Birmingham," a nailer board screwed to the back for attaching the clock to a wall, American, probably New Hampshire, ca. 1820, 90" h. (ILLUS.) **8,400**

Oak English Grandfather Clock

Grandfather clock, Georgian, oak, broken-scroll pediment above a square glazed door opening to the white dial w/Roman numerals & painted spandrels, flanked by free-standing colonettes, the tall body w/a long solid door, tall stepped out lower section missing the footed base, old refinish, England, ca. 1820, 12 x 15", 80" h. (ILLUS.).. **900**

English Inlaid Oak Grandfather Clock

Grandfather clock, Georgian, oak case w/banded inlay, the broken-scroll pediment centering a brass ball & eagle finial w/matching corner finials, a wide frieze above the arched glazed door opening to a painted dial w/moon phase, Roman numerals & painted figurals in corner, the door flanked by slender squared columns, the waisted body w/reeded pilasters flanking the crossbanded door, the stepped-out lower case w/banded inlay & raised on small bracket feet, wooden works, England, ca. 1800, refinished, 12 x 18", 84" h. (ILLUS. bottom left)........................... **2,600**

Boldly Carved Oak Grandfather Clock

Grandfather clock, Georgian, oak, the broken-scroll pediment centered by a brass ball & eagle finial above a frieze band carved w/bold stylized leaves over the arched glazed door opening to the brass & filigree dial w/moon phase & Roman numerals all surrounded by a narrow carved gadrooned band flanked by slender colonettes & serpentined back side rails, the tall body w/quarter-round columns flanking the tall door w/carved gadroon bands enclosing a large stylized carving of a pot issuing a long flowering leafy vine, the stepped-out lower case carved at the front w/bold stylized leaves & flowers, short serpentine apron & tiny ogee feet, probably English, ca. 1830s, refinished, 12 x 16", 88" h. (ILLUS.) **3,300**

Herschede Gothic Grandfather Clock

Grandfather clock, Herschede (Frank)
Clock Co., Cincinnati, Ohio, Gothic Revival style mahogany & mahogany veneer case, pointed arch crest w/wide
molding above a tall arch-topped door
w/the upper section covering the steel
dial w/Arabic numerals below a moon
phase movement, the lower door
w/Gothic arch glazing opening to the
large weights & large pendulum, long
pilasters down the sides of the case,
octagonal block front feet, early 20th c.
(ILLUS.) **3,650**

Grandfather clock, Herschede (Frank)
Clock Co., Cincinnati, Ohio, "Model
215," mahogany molded case w/arched
top & stepped base, beveled glass panels in front & sides, the ornate brass
dial plate & steel chapter ring w/black
Arabic numerals below the arched rolling moon phase section, slender reeded columns down the front above the
deep, slightly stepped-out base section
on flat block feet, nine-tube two-tune
(Whittington & Westminster) time &
strike movement, door lock intact &
w/original Herschede-signed winding
crank, minor repair to top dust
cover, ca. 1950, 80" h. (ILLUS. top of
next page).. **2,464**

French Grand Sonnerie Grandfather

Grandfather clock, grand sonnerie-type,
French Provincial oak case w/rectangu-
lar top w/molded pediment, a narrow floral-carved frieze band on front, a narrow
carved molding around the tall front
glass pane over the round white dial
w/brass bezel & black Roman numerals
& the bar pendulum w/large brass bob,
tall lower case section w/a rectangular
carved molding enclosing carved fruit
cluster, molded base w/carved edges
raised on circular wafer feet, three-train
Morbier time & strike movement strikes
two bell quarters followed by full hours
on a third large bell, brass-sheathed
weights, spider web crack in dial, black
dial mask not original, minor dings in
bob, replacement weights, France, ca.
1860, 97" h. (ILLUS.) **3,920**

Rare Southern Grandfather Clock

Grandfather clock, Krause (John J.), Northampton, Pennsylvania, Federal cherry case, the broken swan's-neck pediment terminating in carved rosettes & centering a reeded plinth over a glazed tombstone door opening to a white enamel dial w/Arabic numerals centering a calendar aperture & signed "John Krause - Northampton," & decorated w/fruit & flowers in the spandrels & arch, all flanked by ring-turned freestanding columns over the tall case fitted w/a double-arch tall door flanked by slender quarter-round reeded columns above the square base w/similar columns, on short French feet, old surface, 30-day weight-driven movement, early 19th c., 10 1/2 x 19 1/2", 83 1/2" h. (imperfections)........................... **4,888**

Herschede "Model 215" Grandfather

Grandfather clock, Herwick (William), North Carolina, Federal style inlaid mahogany case, the molded broken-scroll pediment above an arched frieze band w/line inlay over the set-back arched door opening to a painted dial w/Roman numerals & a moon phase dial & flanked by slender colonettes, the tall waist w/decorative band inlay flanking the tall door w/corner fan inlay & a central oval inlaid band, the stepped-out lower case w/further decorative inlay banding & an inlaid central circle, on small French feet, signed indistinctly, untouched & unrestored, early 19th c. (ILLUS. top of next column)... **8,750**

English Mahogany Grandfather

Grandfather clock, Queen Anne Revival mahogany case w/arched top & brass corner ball & spike finials, molded cornice above ogee side splats & simple colonettes w/brass capitals & bases flanking the arched glazed door opening to the 12" brass dial w/black Roman numerals framed by cast shell spandrels & a sunburst in arch, tall center case w/a long wood door, deep molding atop the stepped-out base w/a molded panel on the front, serpentine apron & bracket feet, eight-day signed Salisbury movement striking on a giant cathedral gong mounted to the back of the case, door key in bag taped to movement, small dry splits & scrapes, knob to top door has been pulled out & screwed into nearby location, England, ca. 1900, 86" h. (ILLUS.) **1,736**

French Grandfather Clock

Grandfather clock, mahogany case w/rectangular flat top w/ogee molded cornice above the round white porcelain dial w/brass bezel & black Roman numerals & sweep seconds hand, bracket-topped glass-fronted compartment for long multi-strand pendulum w/large brass bob, base w/beveled molding, Morbier pinwheel movement, weight from another clock, movement lacks dust cover, France, ca. 1890, 78" h. (ILLUS.) **3,080**

Renaissance Revival Grandfather

Grandfather clock, Renaissance Revival-style, carved walnut, a male & a female caryatid flanking either side of hood, the face w/painted lunar phases in arch, brass mounts & subsidiary dials, the case w/glass door flanked by carved terms, square base w/winged beast terms to sides, carved paw feet, late 19th c., 97 1/2" (ILLUS.)... **9,775**

Grandfather clock, Renaissance Revival-style, walnut case, the hood w/fruit & scroll carving, the round face w/painted stylized sun w/brass hands as stylized rays, weight-driven movement, the case open w/bobbin-turned columns on acanthus bases topped by carved female faces, the columns flanking a carved grotesque, the base w/fruit & scroll carving, ca. 1900, Germany, 79" h. (ILLUS. top of next column)........... **1,955**

Renaissance Revival German Grandfather

Grandfather clock, Rittenhouse (Benjamin), Philadelphia, Pennsylvania, Chippendale carved cherrywood, the broken swan's neck pediment w/pinwheel terminals & urn & flame finials above an arched glazed door opening to an engraved brass dial inscribed "BENJAMIN RITTENHOUSE - FECIT 1790," w/second hand, date hand & moon phase dial flanked by colonettes, the arched door below flanked by fluted quarter-columns above a "turtle-mounted" base w/similar columns on ogee bracket feet, ca. 1780, 11 x 19 1/4", 8' 3" h. (ILLUS. top of next page) **17,250**

merals, an upper moon dial w/engraved sun & globe & applied castings in the spandrels painted grey, door flanked by small reeded quarter-round columns w/brass caps & bottom applied w/brass wire decoration a quarter of the way up from bottom, the tall narrow body w/a tall arched-top door flanked by similar columns, stepped-out base w/base molding & serpentine apron, 18th c., pieced restorations on hood & base ended out, pendulum needs repair & weights, missing winding key, 90" h. (ILLUS.bottom left) **3,850**

Chippendale Cherrywood Grandfather Clock

Rare Joseph Taylor Grandfather Clock

Grandfather clock, Taylor (Joseph), York, Pennsylvania, Chippendale style tiger stripe maple case, broken-scroll pediment w/an urn-form central urn & matching corner finials above an arched recess & glazed door flanked by slender colonettes, opening to a painted dial w/upper moon phase in color, floral-painted spandrels & Arabic numerals, tall narrow body w/narrow paneled door, stepped-out base w/paneled front on small French feet, early 19th c. (ILLUS.) **30,250**

Mahogany English Grandfather Clock

Grandfather clock, Storr (Marmaduke), London, England, Georgian, figured mahogany case w/an arched & molded crest & frieze band over the conforming door opening to a painted dial w/Roman nu-

Victorian English Grandfather Clock

Grandfather clock, Victorian Baroque-style, carved oak case w/a scrolled pediment centered by a turned knob finial above a leaf-carved frieze over an arched molding & conforming glass door flanked by colonettes, opening to the brass & silver dial w/scrolls & round plaque above dial w/Roman numerals & ornate scrolled spandrels, the tall body topped by a carved band of acanthus leaves over a tall narrow paneled door carved w/a lion mask at the top & bottom & swags & scrolls down the middle, leafy scroll vines down the sides, the stepped-out base w/a raised square panel carved w/leafy scrolls framing a small classical head, leafy scrolls around the edges, the molded base over a scalloped apron centered by a carved shell, England, ca. 1890, 14 1/2 x 23 1/2", 91" h. (ILLUS.) **1,792**

Grandfather clock, Watson (Luman), Cincinnati, Ohio, Federal style cherry case w/mahogany accents, broken-scroll pediment w/urn finial & matching corner finials, slender baluster-form colonettes flanking the arch-top glass door over the signed dial w/delicate floral spandrels & black Arabic numerals, the simple tall case w/narrow wooden door flanked by beveled front corners, base section w/top molding & inset panels on front & sides, cove molding at bottom above short baluster-turned feet, 30-hour Hoadley-type wooden time & strike movement, dial w/small chip & minor loss of black, door glass w/small crack, winding barrel w/small chip on rim, ca. 1820, 94" h. (ILLUS. below) **4,704**

Luman Watson Grandfather Clock

Lantern Clock of Mixed Origin

Lantern clock, brass w/parts of mixed origin, 17th c. dial & frame by William Holloway of Strowd, England, ca. 1679, the rectangular frame on knob feet w/circular dial w/Roman numerals applied to front, top border w/curlicue design that forms the initials "RSM," the domed top in ring frame w/finial, two-fusee Victorian movement, chain fusee strikes the hours on top bell, England, ca. 1890, 15 1/2" h. (ILLUS.)... **1,624**

Lantern clock, Colver (John), Woodbridge, England, upright brass case w/a domed bell at the top above an arched & pierced brass gallery over the signed & engraved round brass dial w/Roman numerals, on small brass ball feet, 1739-47, 30-hour movement, missing brass cross arms over bell, no pendulum, 11" h..................... **1,800**

Lantern clock, Cotsworth (John), London, England, brass, the brass dial w/engraved chapter ring & alarm mechanism engraved w/the maker's name "John Cotsworth Londini," the brass weight-driven movement housed in an iron & brass four-column case w/cross arched bell at the top w/an urn-form finial, the clock set in an oak wall shelf, ca. 1670, 15" h. (restorations)..................................... **5,175**

English Renaissance Style Clock

Grandfather clock, Whitehurst, Derby, England, Renaissance-Style oak case, a broken-scroll crest w/three brass ball finials over the scroll-carved frieze & arched glazed door flanked by elongated scroll carvings & opening to the metal dial w/Roman numerals & a moon phase & date crest above the narrow case w/narrow front panel carved w/scrolls above a full-length carved figure of a standing medieval king over a grotesque mask panel, all flanked by slender carved Gothic-style side caryatids, the lower case w/a scroll-carved panel flanked by carved mask & scroll corner bands over the deep scroll-carved apron, two-train chiming movement, late 19th c., 9 5/8 x 18 1/4", 92 1/2" h. (ILLUS.) **2,645**

English Lantern-style Mantel Clock

Lantern clock, upright brass case w/a bell forming the domed top w/ring-turned finial, four straps attach finial to matching corner finials, the front w/a circular dial w/Roman numerals overhangs the case, the center w/engraved leafy scroll decoration, reticulated floral panels between the straps over the domed top & on four sides between corner finials, sides of case w/engraved decoration, corner ring-turned columns ending in knob feet, eight-day chain fusee time & strike movement strikes the hour on the top bell, chapter ring has lost its silver, movement a bit gummy, England, ca. 1890, 15 1/4" h. (ILLUS.) **1,232**

Early English Lantern Clock

Lantern clock, Wheeler (Thomas), London, England, brass, the sides w/hinged plates, the top bell w/straps applied to finials centering pierced plates, the silvered chapter ring w/Roman numerals centering an alarm indicator, w/one hand, on bun feet, signed "Thomas Wheeler near ye French Church, London," Charles II period, late 17th c. (ILLUS. bottom left) **4,889**

Ornate French Lyre Clock

Lyre shelf or mantel clock, Berthoud (F.), Paris, France, blue cobalt enameled case festooned w/swags of gilt metal leaves, berries & flowers, trimmed w/tiny gilt-metal beading, gilt finial in the form of the head of a person w/flowing hair against sunburst background, the white porcelain dial w/brass bezel & center open pinwheel escapement, Arabic numerals, & painted w/1-31 concentric calendar, all connected to base on molded stepped shaft also adorned w/brass trim, oval base consisting of blue cobalt, white porcelain & gilt-metal layers, pendulum bob circled w/brilliants, time & strike movement w/original signature, restoration to blue porcelain & escapement, hands replaced, ca. 1785, 22" h. (ILLUS.) **12,880**

Lyre wall clock, Chandler (Abiel), Concord, New Hampshire, carved mahogany, a pointed brass ball finial above a narrow round molded frame enclosing the dial w/Roman numerals above a tall carved lyre-form throat w/pairs of large leafy scrolls up the front above a gadroon-carved band over a lower paneled box over a reverse-stepped & tapering base w/a half-round pointed drop finial, 1825, 43" h. (imperfections) **17,250**

Modern Foster Campos Lyre Clock

Lyre wall clock, Foster Campos, Pembroke, Massachusetts, wooden case w/large maple leaf crest above the round dial w/brass bezel & black Roman numerals, the lyre-shaped body w/ornate scroll carving w/center panel reverse-painted w/figure of woman in classical garb w/lyre, all within floral border, the molded base w/drop tapering to rounded drop finial, signed on dial, movement, back of case & weight, time-only movement, original Campos box, glued crack in leaf crest, ca. 1979, 42" h. (ILLUS.) **3,192**

Lyre wall clock, Sawin and Dyer, Boston, giltwood, a gilt figural eagle finial above a round leaf-carved frame enclosing a dial w/Roman numerals above a large lyre-form throat w/bold carved leafy scrolls flanking an églomisé panel painted w/a tall leafy scroll design in red, green & gold on a white ground, the lower case w/a molded small rectangular box section w/an églomisé panel painted w/classical scrolls & trophies in green, red & gold on white, a scrolled cartouche base drop, ca. 1820s, 40" h. (imperfections)................................. **13,800**

Mantel garniture set: clock & a pair of porcelain urns; the large round porcelain dial w/Arabic numerals & the works framed by delicate ornate openwork ormolu scrolls, wreath & flower basket finial & suspending a flower basket pendulum between four marble-topped columns w/ormolu pineapple & urn & flower finials, the columns in dark blue-glazed porcelain w/gilt wreath decoration & all set on an oblong white marble base w/small brass feet, the matching porcelain tall urns w/domed covers & ormolu finials, handles & a pedestal

Fine French Bronze & Porcelain Set

Fine French Mantel Garniture Set

foot on a white marble platform w/small brass feet, France, ca. 1880, eight-day movement, time & strike, clock 5 1/2 x 9", 15 1/2" h., the set (ILLUS. above) **1,400-1,500**

Mantel garniture set: clock & candelabra; Louis XV Revival, gilt-bronze & porcelain, the tall upright gilt-bronze clock case cast w/ornate scrolls & swags & topped by a porcelain & bronze urn finial, the round porcelain dial w/Roman numerals cen-

tered by painted cupids above a lower porcelain plaque also painted w/cupids, on a pierced swag-footed base, w/a pair of five-light candelabra w/four upturned arms & a taller central shaft each ending in a candle socket above an urn-shaped porcelain & bronze shaft raised on an ornate scroll-cast footed base w/insert porcelain plaque, France, late 19th c., the set (ILLUS. bottom of previous page) **1,500**

Crystal Regulator Garniture Set

French Art Deco Garniture Set

Mantel garniture set: clock & pair of candelabra; Marti, France, ormolu & bronze crystal regulator clock w/stepped pediment topped by a figural spread-winged eagle, the case w/glass sides & ormolu columns on either side of arched glass dial panel below ormolu winged horse mounts on a dark green bronze panel, the white dial w/ormolu bezel & center & black Roman numerals, the pendulum decorated w/concentric rings of tiny leaves, a narrow dark green bronze panel w/further ormolu mounts below the dial door, on a molded rectangular ormolu base w/stepped feet, time & strike movement w/Marti Medaille D'Or trademark; the candelabra each w/four candleholders, the center one inset w/a flame finial, each w/curlicue embellishments raised on green bronze shafts w/ormolu ringed capitals & bases, on square bases similar to clock's w/ormolu decorations on front bronze panel, ca. 1900, 22" h., the set (ILLUS. bottom of previous page) **2,464**

"Amour et Psyché" Garniture Set

Mantel garniture set: clock & pair of urns; Art Deco style, all pieces of gilded metal w/fine engraving filled w/multicolor enamel floral decoration, the crystal regulator clock case of rounded rectangular form w/radiused sides, top & bottom, on short legs w/ball feet & molded scroll & shell decoration, glass front & sides, topped by scroll-handled covered urn similar to the two matching covered six-sided urns w/straight slender side handles sharply angled at top & square bases w/beveled corners & ring-turned feet (urns convert to candlesticks by inverting covers), the gilt dial w/Roman numerals & open escapement, the dial center & surround & pendulum bob also w/colorful enamel decoration, time & strike movement, made in France for Wm. Batty & Son, Manchester, ca. 1910, 19 1/2" h., the set (ILLUS. top of previous page) **2,800**

Mantel garniture set: clock & two urns; "Amour et Psyché" model, spelter w/pantinated bronze finish, large cast figures of Cupid & Psyche embracing on a domed mound enclosing the small white dial w/brass bezel & black Arabic numerals, all resting on an ovoid base w/rim of cream & light pink marble w/grey veining & tiny brass ringed feet, eight-day pendulum time & strike movement; the matching urns w/scrolling outcurved side handles & long necks topped w/domed covers & flame finials, on stepped ring-turned outcurved shafts on marble bases similar to clock's, France, ca. 1900, 22" h., the set (ILLUS. bottom of previous page) **1,960**

Mantel garniture set: figural clock set w/matching urns; Japy, France, "Le Raisin" ("The Grape") model, bronze patinated white metal figures & clock case & urns, each on a green & white veined rectangular beveled marble base w/gilt flower-form feet, the center piece w/figure of barefoot woman in clinging garment sitting w/ewer in one hand & the other arm reaching up to a cherub that stands above the clock case holding a/basket of grapes, a brass bezel around the round white porcelain dial w/black Arabic numerals, the short clock pedestal base w/a brass plaque inscribed "LE RAISIN," gilt-metal scroll decoration on front of marble base, the urns w/tapering lids w/upturned rims & trifid finials, ornate C-scroll side handles, molded decoration w/grape motif throughout, round French time & bell strike movement signed, ca. 1900, 14 1/2" h. (ILLUS. bottom of page) **728**

Mantel garniture set: swing clock & two facing statues; Junghans, Germany, gilt cast metal clock case w/ornate decoration on top & bottom of round white dial w/black Arabic numerals, decorated swing arm w/spiked ringed orb bob, the top of the arm connected to green onyx column w/stepped circular base & gilt-metal accents, side statues of bronze patinated metal, titled "L'Epav" & "Le Sauveteur" after originals by Moreau, one features a woman in diaphanous gown & flowing hair shielding her eyes w/one hand, the other features a scantily clad male holding a rope, both figures on molded domed stepped base on green onyx socles w/title plaques on front, time-only movement, ca. 1900, 11 1/2" h., the set (ILLUS. top of next page) **1,568**

French "Le Raisin" Garniture Set

German Swing Clock Garniture Set

Mantel Regulator with Sevres Panels

Mantel regulator, upright rectangular brass-framed case w/rounded corners & molded top & bracket base, Sevres porcelain front & side panels w/pink grounds, the signed dial w/black Roman numerals on white signet panels & delicate gilt spandrels, center of dial w/a scene of two cupids, lower front panel painted w/a garden scene w/18th c. figures, a standing musician playing stringed instrument for a seated woman, side panels w/delicate paintings of birds, flower garlands & ribbons, all accented w/gilt border w/tiny aquamarine dots & additional tiny white pearl-like decorations, the rear panel w/beveled glass for viewing movement, the movement, pendulum & panels all numbered "#40355," time & strike movement, made in France for J.W. Benson, London, ca. 1900, 11 3/4" h. (ILLUS. left) **3,696**

Scarce Early Mirror Wall Clock

Mirror wall clock, attributed to Benjamin Morrill, Boscawen, New Hampshire, Classical style, the rectangular frame case w/a hinged split-baluster border in gilt & black w/the stenciled dial tablet framing the white-painted dial w/Roman numerals, a rectangular mirror in the lower door, w/a brass "wheelbarrow" weight-driven movement, minor imperfections, ca. 1830, 4 x 14", 30" h. (ILLUS. on previous page)..... **5,175**

French Annular Night Alarm Clock

French Mystery Clock

Mystery shelf or mantel clock, Gebard & Cie, France, "#136" model, gilded gesso case w/arch-top square dial panel w/ribbed & decorated frame & beveled glass on ring-turned shaft connecting to the stepped rectangular base, the dial w/black Arabic numerals & gilt hands, lever movement, movement & cover both signed w/Gebard's trade stamp & the number 136, the base of the clock w/a plaque from the retailer marked "Lebolt & Co, New York - Chicago," base brushed w/gold paint, ca. 1890, 14 1/4"h. (ILLUS.)........................ **15,120**

Night clock, annular alarm-type, a flat-topped milk glass globe w/Roman numerals around center indicating the time, smaller Arabic numerals low on the globe for alarm, a short ringed neck holds the globe above a cylindrical brass base w/embossed scroll band around the middle, flaring base w/short feet, 30-hour pendulum-driven movement, bell present inside case, alarm set hand stuck to main drive w/dried grease, alarm winder missing, France, ca. 1890, 6" h. (ILLUS. top next column) **616**

Glass & Spelter Annular Clock

Night clock, annular type, Louis XVI-Style case topped by a pierced gilt-spelter crown-like finial over an/ovoid milk glass chimney w/pink band at top & pink scalloped design at base, white middle panel w/black Arabic numerals, waisted ring-turned neck connects globe to ornae gilt spelter base w/applied swags, notching, ribbing & high scroll feet, large cut-out hand indicating time, 30-hour time-only pendulette movement, France, ca. 1890, 13" h. (ILLUS. on previous page) **2,016**

French Match Strike Alarm Clock

Novelty shelf or mantel clock, alarm, match strike type, figural spelter case in form of a standing bearded man wearing a wide-brimmed hat & long top coat, the dial mounted in the man's chest, notched brass bezel around the dial, white number plaques w/black Arabic numerals against a pale blue ground, on a molded base w/bracket feet & decorated throughout w/scalloped & floral decoration, friction strike pad missing, small chip in dial, some cracks in base, France, ca. 1890, 10" h. (ILLUS.) **784**

Lighthouse-form Night Clock

Night clock, patinated metal case in the form of a lighthouse w/a spired domed top over slender baluster-form colonettes flanking the annular-style cylindrical white dial w/black Arabic numerals, the cylindrical body w/incised "bricks" & applied doors & windows on molded base, time movement in base, a driveshaft up the tower turning a ventilated base plate that holds the lens, ca. 1880, 21 1/2" h. (ILLUS.) **2,800**

Alarm-Type Novelty Clock

Novelty shelf or mantel clock, alarm-type, Toulouse-Lautrec, France, hand moves down when alarm goes off to light a match on clock base & returns to the candle on top, 5 1/2 x 10" (ILLUS.) **800**

Japanese Novelty Annular Clock

Novelty shelf or mantel clock, annular clock set in a clear glass globe enclosing the orbital dial on shaft w/two animated fish keeping time, a smaller fish forms pendulum & wiggles back & forth w/each tick, the bigger fish does a full revolution around dial one tick at a time, globe set on beveled chrome base w/Art Deco geometric decoration, six molded saucer feet, time-only movement, Japan, ca. 1950, 5" h. (ILLUS.) **1,176**

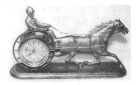

Jockey & Trotter Novelty Clock

Novelty shelf or mantel clock, Ansonia Clock Co., Ansonia, Connecticut, brass, jockey w/trotter, 30-hour movement, time only, 6 1/2 x 10 1/2" (ILLUS.) **600**

Novelty shelf or mantel clock, Ansonia Clock Co., Ansonia, Connecticut, cast iron w/black enamel, ship's brass wheel rotates as escapement moves, 15 x 18 3/4" **2,000**

Novelty shelf or mantel clock, Ansonia Clock Co., Ansonia, Connecticut, enameled pot metal, squirrel in tree, 30-hour movement, time only, 6 x 7" **400**

Brass Baby Novelty Clock

Novelty shelf or mantel clock, Ansonia Clock Co., Ansonia, Connecticut, model of a brass baby holding fan, 30-hour movement, time only, 5" h. (ILLUS.) **375**

Novelty shelf or mantel clock, Ansonia Clock Co., Ansonia, Connecticut, "Novelty 34 or The Advertiser" model, 30-hour movement, time only, 7" h. **500**

Ansonia "Echo" Automaton

Novelty shelf or mantel clock, Ansonia Clock Co., New York, New York, "Echo" model automaton, nickel-plated case w/cast figure of boy holding hammer & sitting next to bell set at an angle on cylindrical dial case, boy strikes bell w/hammer on the hour, dial w/Roman numerals on tiny ring-turned feet, 30-hour time & strike movement, some roughness on case, nickel plating on back worn, ca. 1880, 7 3/4" h. (ILLUS.) **1,960**

Ansonia "Jumper No. 1" Clock

Novelty shelf or mantel clock, Ansonia Clock Co., New York, New York, "Jumper No. 1" model, cast metal lamp post design w/a round clock mounted at the top side of a slender ringed shaft, the clock case w/a leaf & scroll crest & a support scroll bracket suspending a tiny doll figure on a swing, the white patent-dated dial w/black Roman numerals & subsidiary seconds dial, time-only movement, incorrect replacement doll is too light to activate the works, but movement is complete, set knob is probable replacement, ca. 1889, 15 1/4" h. (ILLUS. on previous page) **1,120**

Sheet Brass Parade Lantern Clock

"Topsy" Blinking Eye Clock

Novelty shelf or mantel clock, Bradley & Hubbard, Meriden, Connecticut, "Topsy" blinking eye model, cast-iron figure of a black girl in white blouse & stockings, green skirt w/red polka dots & bandanna on head, on black stepped circular base, original paper dial located on front of skirt w/a brass bezel, Roman numerals, lunette & original hands, 30-hour time-only lever movement, w/eyes that blink to movement of escapement, some paint loss, ca. 1870, 17" h. (ILLUS.) **2,352**

Novelty shelf or mantel clock, Bradley & Hubbard Mfg. Co., Meriden, Connecticut, lantern-form "parade" type (carried in torchlight parades & hung outside for evening parties), the upright rectangular stamped sheet brass case w/a four-sided peaked top w/two side peaked dormers inset w/a colored jewel, the sides of the case also inset w/assorted sizes of colored jewels & pierced cutouts, round translucent dial w/white numbers that glows when a candle is lit inside the case, signed w/B&H trademark, 30-hour time-only movement, chain at top added, hands not original, ca. 1885, 13" h. (ILLUS.) **784**

Novelty shelf or mantel clock, "Bras en L'Air" model, the figure of a gowned woman standing w/arms outstretched within an ormolu arch w/swirl columns & shell & spike decorations around top, the woman points to two flanking enamel chapter sectors, one w/hours & one w/minutes, her arms falling when they reach the top, the blue enamel background w/ormolu scroll design throughout, stepped rectangular dark variegated green marble base w/ormolu trim & low square stepped feet, rectangular plated movement w/platform escapement, base w/front-to-back glue repair, feet glued on, crack through numeral 10, France, ca. 1890, 17" h. (ILLUS. top of next page) **15,120**

"Bras en L'Air" Novelty Clock

George W. Brown Novelty Clock

1856 stamped on top plate, early spider cast-metal winding key on bottom, original Roman numeral dial, bezel & pendulum bob, hands are old replacements, time & strike movement, ca. 1860, 7 3/4" h. (ILLUS. below left)............................ **672**

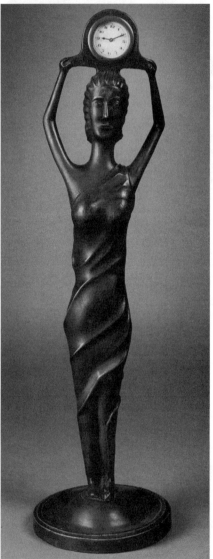

Unusual Figural Folk Art Clock

Novelty shelf or mantel clock, Brown (George W.), Forestville, Connecticut, "Briggs Rotary" model, wooden footed round base & glass dome enclosing the metal-framed dial w/Roman numerals w/the metal ball pendulum suspended at the front, early production model w/John C. Briggs, patents of Aug. 1855 & July

Novelty shelf or mantel clock, carved & stained maple, a hand-carved folk art figure of a standing woman w/wavy hair & a long draped gown, her arms over her head holding the round frame for the clock w/a brass bezel & Arabic numerals, on a dished round base, original surface, American, early 20th c., 8" d. base, overall 29" h. (ILLUS.) **3,450**

Unique French Novelty Bell Clock

Novelty shelf or mantel clock, cast brass frame, a large bell w/ornate cast designs centered by an enameled dial w/Roman numerals & enclosing the clock works suspended from a Gothic arch-form framework w/four open arches joined at the top by a temple & urn-form finial & each resting on an ornate columnar leg on a wooden platform base, French, late 19th - early 20th c. (ILLUS.) **1,350**

Elephant Mantel Clock

Novelty shelf or mantel clock, cast iron, model of elephant, France, time only, 4 x 7" (ILLUS.).. **75**

"The Jester" Novelty Clock

Novelty shelf or mantel clock, figural "The Jester" model, patinated spelter figure of a standing jester in knee pants & jacket w/gilt trim, he holds the 2" ball-shaped clock on a shaft in his right hand, white dial w/black Roman numerals, on a molded stepped circular base, the tiny seven-day key-wind time-only movement contained within the ball, some touch-ups to dial, France, ca. 1880, 17" h. (ILLUS.) **2,240**

Novelty shelf or mantel clock, figural, upright china model of a windmill w/moveable blades, a small round dial in the base, blue Delft-style decoration, Kienzle, Germany movement, 8 1/4" h. **146**

Novelty shelf or mantel clock, Gilbert Mfg. Co., Winsted, Connecticut, figural gilt cast spelter case in the form of two horses leaning over a water trough w/cast leaf decoration, a small round dial w/Arabic numerals inset at the left end of the trough, 6" h. (slight wear) **135**

German Whistler Novelty Clock

Novelty shelf or mantel clock, Griesbaum (Karl) Co., Germany, "Clock Peddler & Whistler" model, carved & painted wood figure of a standing man dressed in white shirt & stockings, red vest, black knee pants, tie, bowler-type hat, shoes & red-lined coat, carries six clocks in a pack on his back & holds a working clock in his right arm, the working clock dial w/black Arabic numerals in white number circles on black surround, all on a rectangular black base, arch above dial shows scene of chalet & trees against blue sky, weight & pendulum dangle from bottom, whistles two repeated notes, ca. 1925, 13 1/2" h. (ILLUS. left) **1,400**

Novelty shelf or mantel clock, Haddon Clock Co., electric motion clock, "Home Sweet Home," model of a house in plastic & composition, a square large window over the dial on the left, a window on the right w/a scene of an old woman in a rocker, when plugged in woman rocks & fire shimmers, 20th c., 3 1/2 x 12 1/4", 7 3/8" h. (ILLUS. top of next page) **185**

Novelty shelf or mantel clock, Hamburg American Clock Co., brass, a disk foot & slender turned shaft supporting the model of a ship's wheel enclosing the dial, early 20th c., 7 1/2" h. **79**

Novelty shelf or mantel clock, Imhof, Switzerland, inclined plane model, the long narrow wooden top board raised on a slim brass baluster form spindle & mounted at the front w/a brass plate engraved w/days of the week along the side, the round brass clock case w/white dial & Roman numerals rolls down the incline indicating the days of the week as it descends, the long narrow base board raised on four tiny knob feet, 15-jewel time-only movement powered by gravity, w/original Franklin Mint booklet & certificate of authenticity from the Musée International d'Horologerie, ca. 1984, 24" w. x 9" h. (ILLUS. bottom of page) **1,080**

Novelty shelf or mantel clock, Lux Clock Mfg. Co., Waterbury, Connecticut, rotary metal, tape measure type w/copper fish, time only, ca. 1920, 5" d. **45**

Novelty shelf or mantel clock, Lux Clock Mfg. Co., Waterbury, Connecticut, wooden, girl & soldier on blue base, 30-hour movement, time only, spring driven, 7 x 9" **800**

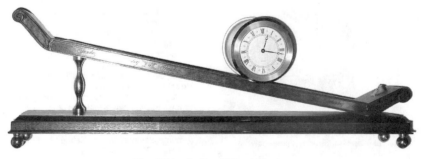

New Swiss Inclined Plane Clock

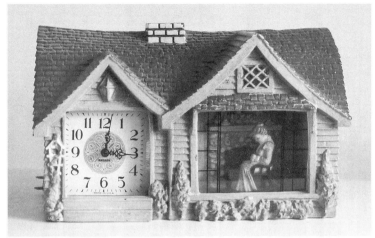

Haddon Electric Motion Clock

French "Magician" Automaton Clock

Novelty shelf or mantel clock, "Magician" automaton, ormolu & bronze, top w/automated Blackamoor figure in formal dress & turban standing at table draped w/star-decorated fringed cloth & lifting inverted gold cups alternately w/his left & right arms & turning his head to right & left, ormolu case w/porcelain dial w/Roman numerals & ormolu hands & signed "Grout, R'de la Feronnerie S.," case front ornately decorated w/floral swags, scrolls & shells scrolling up around dial & extending beyond the case to form cut-out designs at sides & forming apron & heavy outcurved feet, time & strike silk thread movement, France, ca. 1835, 14 1/2" h. (ILLUS.) **28,000**

Novelty shelf or mantel clock, Mastercrafter electric motion clock, a brown plastic model of a fireplace w/fender, fireplace shimmers when plugged in, large round frame & dial at the top, white dial w/Arabic numerals, ca. 1950s, 4 3/4 x 7 1/4", 10 1/2" (ILLUS. right, bottom next page) **85**

Novelty shelf or mantel clock, Mastercrafter electric motion clock, the brown plastic case designed to resemble an open stage w/railing showing a boy & girl who sit on moving swings, the large round top centering a steel dial w/Arabic numerals & a sweep seconds hand, ca. 1950s, 5 x 7 1/4", 10 3/4" h. (ILLUS. left, top of next page)... **180**

Novelty shelf or mantel clock, Mastercrafter electric motion clock, the brown plastic case w/an opening showing a girl sitting on a moving swing, large rounded top enclosing a steel dial w/Arabic numerals, ca. 1950s, 3 x 7 1/4", 10 3/4" h. (ILLUS. center, top of next page).. **165**

Novelty shelf or mantel clock, Mastercrafter electric motion clock, the tall copper-colored plastic case w/molded green & brown fir trees flanking an opening w/a painted waterfall scene that shimmers when plugged in, ca. 1950s, 5 x 7 1/4", 10 3/4" h. (ILLUS. right, top of next page)... **125**

Novelty shelf or mantel clock, Mastercrafter electric motion clock, white plastic case in the form of a stylized church, a bell ringer standing in the door pulls a string to ring the bell in the steeple, large steel dial w/Roman numeral & sweep seconds hand, ca. 1950s, 2 3/4 x 7 1/4", 12" h. (ILLUS. left, bottom next page)............................ **125**

Novelty shelf or mantel clock, New Haven Clock Co., New Haven, Connecticut, a fancy cast metal gilt & bronzed figural case w/a cherub atop the round dial frame enclosed w/leaf branches all on a

Three Mastercrafter Motion Clocks

wheeled base pulled by two oxen, dial w/Roman numerals, 6 3/4" h. (missing chain to oxen).. **371**

Novelty shelf or mantel clock, New Haven Clock Co., New Haven, Connecticut, figural lighthouse model, the cast-metal case in the form of a lighthouse w/an oxidized silver & gilt finish, the spired top above a revolving glass lantern, a small round clock dial inset below the lantern at the top of the building, late 19th - early 20th c., 12 1/2" h.. **703**

Novelty shelf or mantel clock, New Haven Clock Co., New Haven, Connecticut, "Fort" model, a cast-spelter figural case in the form of a castle w/a series of towers on a hillside across from another hill topped w/a figural cannon above an inset dial, late 19th - early 20th c., 8" h. **203**

Novelty shelf or mantel clock, "Oarsman" model from the Industrial Series, figure of oarsman & clock dial in wrought brass sailboat w/mast & rigging, rudder & tie down, the boat on separate casting of

Two Mastercrafter Motion Clocks

waves mounted to a stepped rectangular red marble base on four gilded skids, the original dial w/Arabic numerals & signed by the London retailer "Dibdin & Co., Ltd, 189 Sloane St, SW-1," eight-day movement, oarsman suspended from a three-point mystery suspension as used in a swinging arm clock & w/a heavy counterbalance that swings down into the base, his paddling motion continuing for full duration of the clock (eight days), France, ca. 1880, 16 1/2" h. (ILLUS. below) **12,320**

"Oarsman" Novelty Clock

"Panting Dog" Novelty Clock

Novelty shelf or mantel clock, "Panting Dog" model, wooden case carved in the form of a log structure w/a dog looking out an upper window, a man below peering through a side window to see a kissing couple on the other side of the building, all on an oval stepped base, the dog & figures in gold-painted gesso over wood, the white round dial in the center of

the front w/a brass bezel & black Roman numerals, dog's tongue goes in & out, peering man shakes his head, time-only movement, Germany, ca. 1885, 6 1/2" h. (ILLUS. bottom left) **1,680**

Sambo Blinking Eye Clock

Novelty shelf or mantel clock, "Sambo" blinking eye model, painted cast-iron figure of a standing black man playing banjo, which encloses the white paper dial w/Roman numerals & lunette, on a thin rectangular beveled base w/short feet, black hat & tie, cream-colored shirt & trousers, red vest, gold buttons & banjo, strong time-only movement in running & blinking order, replacement paper dial, unmarked, ca. 1875, 16" h. (ILLUS.) **1,960**

Novelty shelf or mantel clock, "Ship's Quarter Deck" automata from the Industrial Series, bronze & silvered metal case in the form of a ship's quarter deck, a sailor at the helm on the upper deck gallery w/the clock dial directly below him & flanked by another sailor on one side & the ladder leading to the upper deck on the other, all on a stepped black marble base on gilt brass feet, the gilt dial w/Roman numerals, two-train signed French time & strike movement w/platform escapement & striking the hours & halves on a coiled gong, the helmsman at top forms the top of the compound pendulum & rocks back & forth w/each tick,

"Ship's Quarter Deck" Automata

France, ca. 1890, 12 1/2" h. (ILLUS.
above)... **7,952**
Novelty shelf or mantel clock, souvenir,
LeCoultre, Switzerland, "Rue de la Paix"
model, brass case in the form of a street
lamp, the white "lamp" within a brass
frame w/ringed finial above the round
signed dial w/Roman numerals & pierced
hands, all on a ringed shaft tapering out
to a circular base, rectangular sign on
shaft reads "Rue de la Paix," seven-jewel
eight-day movement, ca. 1955, 11" h.
(ILLUS. at right).. **364**

Welch "Briggs Rotary" Clock

"Rue de la Paix" Souvenir Clock

Novelty shelf or mantel clock, Welch (E.N.) Manufacturing Co., Bristol, Connecticut, "Briggs Rotary" model, visible brass mechanism w/an upright white dial w/Roman numerals behind a wire pendulum w/ball bob, all on round black-painted wood base w/carved scroll feet, time & strike movement, w/original glass dome cover, ca. 1878, 8 3/4" h. (ILLUS. bottom, left column, previous page) **912**

"Little Lord Fauntleroy" Clock

Novelty shelf or mantel clock, Welch (E.N.) Manufacturing Co., Bristol, Connecticut, "Little Lord Fauntleroy" model, nickel-plated horizontal oblong case on button feet & a top loop handle, a brass bezel around the white dial w/Roman numerals, some tarnish, scratches, loose foot, ca. 1891, 2 3/4" h. (ILLUS.) **252**

Novelty shelf or mantel clock, Welch (E.N.) Mfg. Co., Bristol, Connecticut, "Little Grip" model, bronzed metal model of a small suitcase w/clock dial w/Roman numerals inset on the side, original handle, 3" w. **394**

Novelty wall clock, American Clock Co., a celluloid front & Lucite case modeled as a banjo w/a thermometer in the lower panel below the dial, 20th c., 13" l. **169**

Novelty wall clock, carved walnut frame in the form of the Masonic emblem w/compass & square enclosing the round clock dial, round dial w/Roman numerals, time & strike movement, paint loss on dial, case repair, late 19th - early 20th c., 12" h. **169**

Novelty wall clock, figural Oswald Scottie carved wood case w/revolving eyes telling the time, label under base, Germany, early 20th c., 5 3/4" h. **366**

Souvenir Novelty Clock

Novelty wall clock, hanging clock in the form of a frying pan, souvenir of the 1901 Pan-American Exhibition in Buffalo, black metal w/dial featuring panel in center w/color transfer of angels & brass Arabic numerals & hands, one-day balance wheel movement, back of upper handle embossed "C.P. Chouffer, Jeweler," who claims to have manufactured the clock, original "Official" stencil, some rust, New York, 1901, 11" h. (ILLUS.) **364**

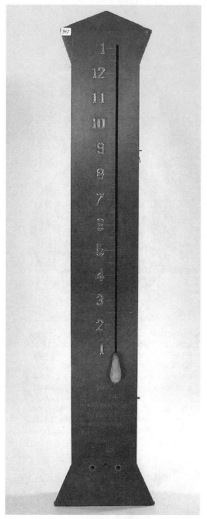

Hickory Dickory Dock Novelty Clock

Novelty wall clock, Hickory Dickory Dock model, a tall slender upright wooden case w/a vertical line of Arabic numerals w/a "1" at the top followed by numbers from 12 to 1 down the front beside a narrow slit fitted w/a model of a small mouse which ascends to tell the time, all original, made for Dongan & Klump Co., late 19th - early 20th c., 43" h. (ILLUS.) **2,194**

Hickory Dickory Dock Novelty Clock

Novelty wall clock, New Haven Clock Co., New Haven, Connecticut, "Hickory Dickory Dock" model, tall narrow black rectangular wood case w/peaked top, base slants out at bottom, brass Arabic numerals inset in middle panel, starting w/1 on the bottom & going through 12, another 1 at the top after the 12, a white mouse runs up the side of the panel to indicate the time, the Hickory Dickory Dock nursery rhyme imprinted below the dial, eight-day time & strike lever movement mounted in the bottom of the case also raises the mouse via a ladder chain running over two sprockets, part of label remains, made for Dungan & Klump, Philadelphia, ca. 1910, 43" h. (ILLUS.) **2,240**

Novelty wall clock, Oswald Uhrenfabrik, Germany, "Owl" model, carved wood model of an owl perched on a wooden base in the form of a book, large eyes rotate when wound, time-only movement, minor nicks & scrapes, ca. 1935, 7 1/2" h. (ILLUS. below left) **644**

German "Scottie" Novelty Clock

Novelty wall clock, Oswald Uhrenfabrik, Germany, "Scottie" model, carved wood model of a Scottie dog w/outsize head, large eyes rotate when wound, comes w/original "Osuhr" dust cover w/1926 patent information, time-only movement, wear to original finish, holes for dust cover filled, ca. 1926, 7 1/2" h. (ILLUS.) **560**

Novelty wall clock, Parker & Whipple Co., a flat round wooden case h.p. on the front w/a snowy winter landscape scene w/a clock tower in the background fitted w/a small working clock dial, Hotchkiss patent works, late 19th - early 20th c., 11 1/2" d. **51**

German "Genie" Rotating Eye Clock

Novelty wall clock, Oswald Uhrenfabrik, Germany, "Genie" model, carved wood figural head of a turbaned genie holding a tray, large round eyes rotate when wound, comes w/original "Osuhr" dust cover carved from wood, time-only movement, some paint flaking on eyeballs, doesn't run consistently, ca. 1927, 9 1/2" h. (ILLUS.) **1,120**

German "Owl" Rotating Eye Clock

Austrian Animated Novelty Clock

Novelty wall clock, picture-frame style, rectangular gilt plaster frame case w/ornate molded scrolling border, inset cartouche panel w/blue ground surrounded by gilt floral & scroll-decorated mat, gilt bezel, spandrels & flourishes beneath dial w/white chapter ring w/black Arabic numerals, center of dial w/animated figure of Tirolean wood cutter, silk thread time & strike movement strikes the hours & halves on a coiled wire gong & the wood cutter swings his axe at the same time, once for each strike, Austria, ca. 1820, 20" h. (ILLUS. on previous page) **2,240**

Novelty wall clock, United Clock Corp., figural cast-spelter case in the form of a guitar, the body w/a small round dial above the larger time dial w/Arabic numerals & a printed musical scene, early 20th c., 18" l. **236**

German Monk Novelty Clock

Novelty wall clock, walnut case w/arched & stepped pediment over a panel forming the backdrop to an inset nook w/carved figure of monk standing by bell flanked by large corner blocks & tall turned corner finials, the case w/ring-turned columns on each side of arched glass front enclosing

a brass bezel around the dial w/Arabic numerals & an embossed brass center, a multi-rod pendulum w/a brass bob embossed in matching style, base w/corner drop finials, ribbed base drop incurved to shallow rectangular shaft ending in drop finial, time & strike movement, movement strikes on large external bell, wire running up to the monk makes it appear that he is striking the bell, Germany, ca. 1900, 34" h. (ILLUS. bottom left)............................ **1,120**

Paperweight clock, Ansonia Clock Co., Ansonia, Connecticut, square clear diamond-cut case enclosing the round dial w/Arabic numerals, made for H.D. Phelps, 3" w. **135**

Ansonia Plato "Flick" Clock

Plato calendar clock, Ansonia Clock Co., New York, New York, upright round brass & glass lantern-style case w/molded top w/bail handle, case encloses three ring-turned columns around a stack of two dark blue flip cards w/gold numerals showing time & date, stepped circular base on short feet, ca. 1907, 6" h. (ILLUS.) **543**

Plato calendar clock, Ever Ready Fitch Clock Co., upright gilt-brass French-style case w/ornate loop top handle, reeded columns down the sides & a wide floral-cast band along the base, two stacks of white turning pages w/numbers indicating the date, 4 7/8" h....................................... **214**

Plato calendar clock, Junghans, Germany, upright brass & glass cylindrical case showing two stacks of digital white turning pages w/numbers to indicate the date, swivel handle... **101**

Plato calendar clock, upright brass French-style case w/glass front showing two stacked digital numbered white turning pages to indicate the date, swivel handle **84**

Plato calendar clock, upright brass & glass French-style case w/swing handle on top, two stacks of digital white pages w/numbers to indicate the date, 4 3/4" h. **180**

Chauncey Jerome Schoolhouse Clock

Schoolhouse wall clock, Jerome (Chauncey), New Haven, Connecticut, mahogany & mahogany veneer, the octagonal top case w/wide veneer border around a round glazed door over the large dial w/Roman numerals, a short rectangular drop compartment w/angled lower edge & centered by a small decorated glass panel over the short pendulum, ca. 1850, 5 x 17", 22" h. (ILLUS.) **2,520**

Seikosha Schoolhouse Clock

Schoolhouse wall clock, Seikosha Co., Tokyo, Japan, celluloid veneer case w/octagonal top w/round molded frame enclosing a brass bezel & white dial w/black Roman numerals, molded rectangular drop case w/pointed bottom features conforming glass panel over original pendulum & ringed brass bob, time & strike movement, original label, some tears & losses to veneer, ca. 1910, 22" h. (ILLUS. bottom left) **112**

Shelf or mantel clock, a tall upright ornate French porcelain case w/elaborate scrolls across the top & down the sides ending in high arched scroll front legs, a wide brass bezel around the upper round dial w/Roman numerals, a lower front scroll reserve painted w/a scene of florals & cherubs w/a harp, floral decoration down the sides, eight-day time & strike movement, late 19th c., 16" h. (lines in dial) **563**

Shelf or mantel clock, alarm-type, Ansonia Clock Co., Ansonia, Connecticut, "Amazon" model, 5" dial... **150**

American Clock Co. Gothic Clock

Shelf or mantel clock, American Clock Co., New York, New York, Gothic-style iron-front case w/bronze finish, the Gothic arch facade cast w/flowering vines, round brass bezel around the white dial w/Roman numerals above a center panel of repainted red, white & green flowers over a small round pendulum window, block-molded base, 30-hour movement, time only, ca. 1855, 12" h. (ILLUS.) **280**

Ansonia Bank-Clock with Scene

Shelf or mantel clock, Ansonia Clock Co., Ansonia, Connecticut, bank-clock, pointed arch gilt cast-spelter case, the front cast in relief w/a wild boar hunt in a forest, dial w/Arabic numerals, flat molded base, two slots for coins in the back, ca. 1920s, 2 3/4 x 4 3/4", 5 3/4" h. (ILLUS.) **100**

Shelf or mantel clock, Ansonia Clock Co., Ansonia, Connecticut, black cast-iron "Irving" model case, two full fluted green columns on the front w/applied gilt ornaments, enameled dial w/Roman numerals, eight-day movement, time & strike, ca. 1910, 5 x 11 3/8", 12" h. **595**

Shelf or mantel clock, Ansonia Clock Co., Ansonia, Connecticut, black marble temple-style case, thin flat rectangular top above the blocked front w/a central brass bezel around the dial w/Roman numerals, the side panels w/incised scrolls & small inset blocks of tan marble, deep rectangular flat base w/inset

tan marble trim, eight-day movement, time & strike, open escapement, ca. 1890, 7 x 17 1/2", 10 1/4" h. (ILLUS. bottom of page) **400-450**

Ansonia Iron Clock with Large Dial

Shelf or mantel clock, Ansonia Clock Co., Ansonia, Connecticut, black-finished iron temple-style case, the flat rectangular top above a wide ornate brass bezel w/beveled glass around the dial w/Arabic numerals & a raised central gilt-brass center ring, gilt-trimmed incised sprigs flank the dial, the thick platform base w/further gilt sprigs, eight-day movement, time & strike, ca. 1900, 6 x 9", 10 1/2" h. (ILLUS.) **300-350**

Shelf or mantel clock, Ansonia Clock Co., Ansonia, Connecticut, black-painted iron temple-style case, a flat rectangular top above a large brass bezel enclosing the dial w/Roman numerals, incised gilt

Ansonia Marble Temple Clock

scrolls at corners, deep stepped base w/further incised gilt scrolls, gilt-metal scroll & paw feet & lion head masks at the ends, eight-day movement, time & strike, ca. 1900, 5 3/4 x 10 1/4", 12 1/4" h. (ILLUS. at bottom of page)...................... **300-350**

Shelf or mantel clock, Ansonia Clock Co., Ansonia, Connecticut, cast-iron temple-form case w/black enameled finish & molded sides w/line-incised decoration, brass bezel around the paper dial, eight-day time & strike movement, late 19th - early 20th c., 10 1/2" h............................ **125-150**

Ansonia "Chemung" Shelf Clock

Shelf or mantel clock, Ansonia Clock Co., Ansonia, Connecticut, "Chemung" model, upright porcelain case w/arching top & serpentine sides, a wide decorative stamped brass bezel enclosing the round white dial featuring elaborate reticulated brass enclosing the black Arabic numerals, the case in white w/pink & gilt floral & scroll designs around the border & delicate pastel flowers in the area below the dial, on the top & sides, time & strike movement, heavy wear to gold trim, ca. 1910, 10 1/2" h. (ILLUS. left).......................... **336**

Ansonia-Royal Bonn China Clock

Shelf or mantel clock, Ansonia Clock Co., Ansonia, Connecticut, china case w/arched pierced scroll crest w/large scrolled leaf finial & scroll-molded sides & ornate scroll-molded apron on small block feet, decorated around the dial w/stylized water lilies in pink & yellow on a turquoise shaded ground w/gilt trim, stamped brass bezel around the dial w/Arabic numerals, Royal Bonn china case marked "La Bretagne," ca. 1900, minor imperfections, 15" h. (ILLUS.).......... **1,320**

Ansonia Iron Case Temple Clock

"Crystal Palace No. 1 Extra" Clock

Shelf or mantel clock, Ansonia Clock Co., Ansonia, Connecticut, "Crystal Palace No. 1 Extra" model, two gilt cast-metal figures lean against a central walnut case topped by a large round white glazed dial w/decorative brass bezel & center ring, floral decoration at top & bottom & black Roman numerals above a scroll-stick pendulum, on a walnut oval base w/button feet, eight-day time & strike Ansonia-signed movement, comes w/good reproduction glass dome, original gears for the Geneva stops that mount on winding arbors have been lost, ca. 1880, 14 1/2" h. (ILLUS.) **672**

Ansonia "Crystal Palace No. 1" Clock

Shelf or mantel clock, Ansonia Clock Co., Ansonia, Connecticut, "Crystal Palace No. 1" model, walnut oval platform base

supporting a walnut-framed upright center mirror below a large scrolled brass bezel enclosing the dial w/a center brass ring & outer chapter ring printed w/Roman numerals & suspending a pendulum w/cylindrical small bob, the mirror flanked by gilt cast-metal figures in 18th c. garb, one a woman, the other a man, bezel marked w/patent date of 1876, eight-day time & strike movement signed "Ansonia," dial darkened w/age, mirror shows some tarnish, restored, ca. 1878, 18" h. (ILLUS. bottom left) **896**

Ansonia Mantel Clock

Shelf or mantel clock, Ansonia Clock Co., Ansonia, Connecticut, "Crystal Palace No. 1" model, dial w/ornate brass bezel, Roman numerals and brass center ring, mercury pendulum is flanked by two cast-metal figures, all on molded oval wooden base w/button feet under glass dome, time & strike movement, 15 x 19" (ILLUS.) **1,500**

Shelf or mantel clock, Ansonia Clock Co., Ansonia, Connecticut, "Denis Papin" model, the top w/a cast-metal figure of a man in 18th c. dress seated next to a column supporting the cast-brass bezel & beveled glass over the signed porcelain dial w/original hands & open escapement, a cast-metal finial & drop pendants at the sides, on a platform base, eight-day time & strike movement, late 19th c., 17" h. **700-800**

Ansonia "La Cannes" China Clock

Shelf or mantel clock, Ansonia Clock Co., Ansonia, Connecticut, "La Cannes" model, Royal Bonn china rectangular case w/decorative scrolling & floral crest above the porcelain dial within ornate notched brass bezel & center ring, white chapter ring w/Roman numerals & open escapement, on square feet, decorated in lime green at top shading to yellow in center to dark green at base, trimmed w/yellow & purple flowers painted in area under dial, Royal Bonn trademark, time & strike movement, ca. 1905, 11 3/4" h. (ILLUS.)... **1,064**

"Elysian" Footed Shelf Clock

Shelf or mantel clock, Ansonia Clock Co., Ansonia, Connecticut, "Elysian" model, gold-painted case w/ornate scroll decoration on top & base, urn-form finial, sides of beveled glass, base on scrolled upturned feet, white dial w/brass bezel & Arabic numerals, eight-day time & strike crystal regulator movement, one side replaced w/plain glass, hour hand replaced, gold paint brushed over original finish, ca. 1914, 16 1/2" h. (ILLUS.).............. **672**

Shelf or mantel clock, Ansonia Clock Co., Ansonia, Connecticut, gilt-metal, seated figure of a 17th c. writer or poet beside the upright ornately scroll-cast case surrounding the porcelain dial w/Arabic numerals, long ornate scrolling base on scroll feet, eight-day movement, time & strike, case repainted, ca. 1890, 7 x 14 1/4"., 11 1/4" h.............................. **600-700**

Shelf or mantel clock, Ansonia Clock Co., Ansonia, Connecticut, "Hermes" model, the top w/a cast-metal figure of the god Hermes resting next to a column supporting the signed porcelain dial w/open escapement framed by a heavy cast-brass bezel, the platform base decorated w/cast-metal scrolls & cartouche, late 19th c., eight-day time & strike movement, late 19th c., 15" h.......................... **500-700**

Ansonia Royal Bonn Mantel Clock

Shelf or mantel clock, Ansonia Clock Co., Ansonia, Connecticut, "La Claire" model, Royal Bonn china case w/scroll-molded sides, apron & feet, urn-form finial, lime green & cream color overall w/gold accents, flowers painted in shades of pink & blue under dial, porcelain dial w/Arabic numerals & fancy gold bezel, time & strike movement, ca.1905, 15" h. (ILLUS. on previous page) **1,540**

Ansonia "La Palma" China Clock

Shelf or mantel clock, Ansonia Clock Co., Ansonia, Connecticut, "La Palma" model, Royal Bonn china rectangular case w/a molded arched top w/blossom crest, the porcelain glazed dial w/brass decorative bezel, white chapter ring w/black Arabic numerals & open escapement, the case w/a dark green border decorated w/bright yellow & gold flowers, the sides in the form of tree trunks entwined w/yellow blossoms, short leaf feet on square bases & fleur-de-lis in apron, the dial surround in shades of lime green, yellow & cream w/purple, pink & yellow & gold flowers, time & strike movement, dark hairlines on dial, wrong hands, mismarked "LaRita," ca. 1905, about 11 3/4" h. (ILLUS.)................................ **1,288**

Ansonia "La Vendee" China Clock

Shelf or mantel clock, Ansonia Clock Co., Ansonia, Connecticut, "La Vendee" model, Royal Bonn china case, a tall waisted upright case scrolling out widely at bottom to form feet, the porcelain dial w/a notched brass bezel & center ring, white chapter

ring w/black Arabic numerals & open escapement, case sides w/cut-out loops at the top flanking an upright scrolled crest, teal blue top, the center & lower sides in shades of yellow & tan, a cluster of large pink & red poppies below the dial, all accented w/gilt, time & strike movement, ca. 1915, 14 1/2" h. (ILLUS. bottom left)............. **1,456**

Ansonia-Royal Bonn "La Vera" Clock

Shelf or mantel clock, Ansonia Clock Co., Ansonia, Connecticut, "La Vera" model, upright Royal Bonn china case w/an arched scroll-molded crest tapering down to open S-scrolls flanking the waisted center case & continuing to form wide front panels, the white porcelain dial within a beaded brass bezel, black Arabic numerals & open escapement in center, the case w/deep reddish purple scrolls & sides, the area around the dial decorated w/yellow daisies & purple violets, the top & sides w/further scroll & floral decoration, time & strike movement, Bonn trademark on rear, ca. 1901, 12 1/4" h. (ILLUS.)................ **3,016**

Shelf or mantel clock, Ansonia Clock Co., Ansonia, Connecticut, miniature Royal Bonn china case "Granite" model, arched & scrolled top & waisted sides on scroll feet, small brass bezel enclosing the dial w/Roman numerals, overall floral decoration, late 19th c., 6 1/2" h. **214**

Ansonia "No. 411" China Clock

Shelf or mantel clock, Ansonia Clock Co., Ansonia, Connecticut, "No. 411" model, domed china case w/ogee sides & slightly peaked crest, original round paper dial w/a decorative brass bezel & center, black Arabic numerals, case in forest green shading to cream under dial w/floral decorations of large white & pink blossoms, gold highlights, time & strike movement, replaced hands, dial darkened w/age, ca. 1910, 11" h. (ILLUS. on previous page) **672**

Shelf or mantel clock, Ansonia Clock Co., Ansonia, Connecticut, "Opera" model cast-metal case, the tapering rectangular base w/sawtooth apron & cast-metal scroll feet supporting a large cast-metal figure of a seated classical woman on an elaborate stool & holding a wreath w/a lyre at the side, the ornate upright cast-metal clock case to one side enclosing a brass bezel around the porcelain face w/Roman numerals, eight-day movement, time & strike, open escapement, minor surface wear, ca. 1885-95, 8 x 21", 16 1/4" h. (ILLUS. at bottom of page) **800-1,000**

Shelf or mantel clock, Ansonia Clock Co., Ansonia, Connecticut, ornate porcelain case w/a high scalloped & arched top & wide serpentine sides flaring to scroll feet & a serpentine apron, brass bezel around the large round dial w/Arabic numerals & a visible escapement, front decorated w/transfer-printed color scenes of cherubs & children, time & strike movement, late 19th - early 20th c. **534**

Shelf or mantel clock, Ansonia Clock Co., Ansonia, Connecticut, ornate porcelain "Wyoming" model case, high upright scroll-bordered waisted case decorated w/blue florals around the large brass bezel & dial w/Arabic numerals, time & strike movement, 11 3/4" h. **534**

Shelf or mantel clock, Ansonia Clock Co., Ansonia, Connecticut, ornate Royal Bonn china "La Lomme" model case, wide serpentine top & wide scroll-case serpentine sides on a low footed case, overall floral decoration around the large brass bezel & dial w/Roman numerals, time & strike movement, 11" h. **647**

Fine China Clock & Ansonia Works

Shelf or mantel clock, Ansonia Clock Co., Ansonia, Connecticut, ornate Royal Bonn "La Mine" model china case, the tall upright arched case w/waisted sides molded at the top w/a central shell flanked by long open scrolls w/further scrolls down the sides & across the base w/incurved scroll feet,

Ornate Figural Ansonia Clock

painted a deep magenta at the top w/pale yellow in the center shading to dark green at the base, decorated on the front w/large h.p. white & magenta blossoms & green leaves, the large brass bezel around the porcelain dial, Arabic numerals, open escapement, eight-day movement, time & strike, ca. 1900, 6 1/4 x 11", 13 1/2" h. (ILLUS. on previous page)...................... **1,000-1,200**

Simple Ansonia Cottage Clock

Shelf or mantel clock, Ansonia Clock Co., Ansonia, Connecticut, simple dark hardwood case w/veneering removed, upright rectangular case w/a two-pane door, the large upper pane over the large faded dial w/Roman numerals & gilt trim above a narrow rectangular glass panel reverse-painted black w/geometric gilt loops, deep molded base, time & strike, second half 19th c., 4 x 8 1/2", 11 3/4" h. (ILLUS. left) **90**

Shelf or mantel clock, Ansonia Clock Co., Ansonia, Connecticut, temple-style cast-iron case, the sides w/applied half-columns w/leaf capitals flanking the brass bezel & dial w/sunburst center, original hands & pendulum, eight-day time & strike movement, late 19th - early 20th c., 10" h. **80-100**

Shelf or mantel clock, Ansonia Clock Co., Ansonia, Connecticut, "Tunis" model oak case, an arched notch-cut crest centered by a crown-form cut-out block above a conforming incised frieze band over the round stamped brass bezel enclosing the brass dial w/Arabic numerals, flat pilasters flank the dial, on a rectangular base w/angled sides, eight-day movement, time & strike, original varnished finish, paper label on back, ca. 1880-1900, 5 1/4 x 11 1/2", 14" h. (ILLUS. below) **250-300**

Ansonia Oak "Tunis" Model Clock

Quality Ansonia Victorian Clock

Shelf or mantel clock, Ansonia Clock Co., Ansonia, Connecticut, Victorian walnut Renaissance Revival style case w/a high scroll-carved crest centered by a classical head over the arched, molded cornice w/urn-form finials above an arched glass door w/gilt stencil decoration of cupids & ferns, white dial w/Roman numerals, the door flanked by tall narrow angled mirrors backing gilt-metal standing cupid figures, base w/curved, molded sides flanking a front panel w/gilt-metal scroll boss, eight-day movement, time & strike, third-quarter 19th c., 5 1/2 x 16 1/2", 24 1/4" h. (ILLUS.) **750-800**

blue w/relief images of cherubs & floral garlands in white & relief scrolls in white forming the border, white porcelain dial w/black Roman numerals & beveled glass w/decorative brass bezel, 30-hour time-only movement, ca. 1901, 5" h. (ILLUS. below left)..................... **336**

Ansonia "Goblin" Shelf Clock

Shelf or mantel clock, Ansonia Clock Co., New York, New York, "Goblin" model, Royal Bonn china case, high rounded case w/scrolls at top & down the sides continuing to form outcurved scroll feet, lime green shading to lighter green ground w/aster-like flowers in yellow, magenta, orange, gold & aqua, a decorative brass bezel enclosing the white dial w/Roman numerals, the decoration w/gilt highlighting, good Royal Bonn trademark, 30-hour time-only movement, dial pan loose in bezel, set stem missing, some loss of gold highlights, ca. 1904, 6 1/4" h. (ILLUS.) **336**

Ansonia "Cameo No. 1" Shelf Clock

Shelf or mantel clock, Ansonia Clock Co., New York, New York, "Cameo No. 1" model, arched serpentine-sided German jasper ware ceramic case in pale

Ansonia "La Chapelle" Shelf Clock

Shelf or mantel clock, Ansonia Clock Co., New York, New York, "La Chapelle" model,

Royal Bonn china case in green & aqua w/h.p. deep pink roses underneath dial & on sides, crest formed by head of a woman in the Art Nouveau style w/flowing hair & floral wreath on her head, flanked by open scroll handles on upper sides, the bottom sides scrolling to form feet, all highlighted w/molded floral & leaf decorations accented in gilt, Bonn trademark on rear of case, dial w/brass notched bezel, black Arabic numerals & open escapement, time & strike movement, ca. 1901, 12" h. (ILLUS. on previous page) **1,960**

Ansonia-Royal Bonn China Clock

Shelf or mantel clock, Ansonia Clock Co., New York, New York, "La Charny" model, Royal Bonn china case, the upright arched case molded at the top w/a grotesque mask & scrolls continuing down the sides flanked at each corner by a stylized figure of a seated griffin, the borders in gold & brown shaded to golden yellow & green & decorated w/large red & yellow iris-like flowers, brass door & bezel around the porcelain dial w/Roman numerals, eight-day movement, time & strike, ca. 1900, 5 1/2 x 11 1/4", 11 3/4" h. (ILLUS.) **700-800**

Ansonia "La Charny" Shelf Clock

Shelf or mantel clock, Ansonia Clock Co., New York, New York, "La Charny" model, Royal Bonn china case, aqua at top, dark green at bottom shading to yellow around dial, yellow & pink water lilies on pond h.p. beneath dial, griffins scrolling at 45-degree angles at either side, griffin head crest, gilt accents, Royal Bonn trademark on rear of case, dial w/gold-tone beaded bezel, open escapement & black Roman numerals, time & strike movement, ca. 1905, 11 1/2" h. (ILLUS. below left) **1,848**

Ansonia "La Layon" Shelf Clock

Shelf or mantel clock, Ansonia Clock Co., New York, New York, "La Layon" model, Royal Bonn china waisted case w/pink & yellow ground & pink & yellow roses & green leaves around dial, gilt scroll crest, S-scroll brackets on either side, four ribbed scroll feet, white dial w/brass notched bezel, black Roman numerals & original hands, time & strike movement, chip by right winding hole, ca. 1910, 14 1/2" h. (ILLUS.)..................................... **1,792**

Shelf or mantel clock, Ansonia Clock Co., New York, New York, "Model 502," upright Royal Bonn china case w/a scrolled crest on the domed top above a panel w/criss-cross design, slanted side columns flank the dial w/ornately decorated brass bezel, Arabic numerals & open escapement, the base scrolled out & resting on leaf & scroll feet, the case trimmed in pale green & cream highlighted w/flowers in pinks, light blues, yellows & lavenders, all with gilt line accents, Royal Bonn trademark on rear of case, time & strike movement, some discoloration to case, ca. 1900, 10 1/2" h. (ILLUS. top of next page).. **1,960**

Ansonia-Royal Bonn "Model 502"

Shelf or mantel clock, Ansonia Clock Co.,
New York, New York, "Music and Poetry"
cast metal case w/two standing classical
female figures flanking the upright dial
case topped by an ornate figural urn &
raised on a square plinth, the white porcelain dial under beveled glass w/decora-
tive brass bezel, center ring & original
hands, open escapement & black Arabic
numerals, all on a rectangular base w/gilt
metal center & reticulated corner embellishments, one figure stands beside a
small three-legged table, the other plays
a harp, signed time & strike movement,
dirty condition, black paint needs to be
removed from metal, ca. 1894, 20 1/2" h.
(ILLUS. bottom of page)............................... **1,456**

Ansonia "Parisian" Shelf Clock

Ansonia Double-statue Shelf Clock

Shelf or mantel clock, Ansonia Clock Co., New York, New York, "Parisian" model, upright walnut molded case w/arched top featuring knobbed finials on crest & turned drop finials at the corners, an arched molded frame enclosing a long glass panel over the brass bezel around the dial w/Roman numerals surrounded by small Arabic calendar numbers, the lower pane decorated w/ornate silver stenciled flower & scrolling vine decoration, the lower sides flanked by S-form brackets, on a deep rectangular stepped base, fancy Ansonia Indicator pendulum, eight-day time & strike movement w/calendar, ca. 1880, 23 1/2" h. (ILLUS. on previous page)............. **448**

Shelf or mantel clock, Ansonia Clock Company, New York, New York, "Regal" model, gilded metal Louis XV-Style upright case, the footed base, corner posts & top cast overall w/ornate leafy scrolls, rounded top corners centered by a pointed scrolling finial, beveled glass sides & a round enameled dial w/Arabic numerals, late 19th c., 18 1/2" h. **1,870**

Art Nouveau Mantel Clock

Shelf or mantel clock, Art Nouveau, gilt-metal, the circular clock face w/black Arabic numerals surrounded by three fully sculpted female busts, each w/long hair & smiling, angular tapering base terminating in a quatrefoil foot, works impressed "Medaille d'Argent," ca. 1900, France, 10 1/2" h. (ILLUS.)............................. **977**

Ansonia "Watteau" Mantel Clock

Shelf or mantel clock, Ansonia Clock Co., New York, New York, "Watteau" model, rococo gilt spelter footed case w/painted porcelain panel of two cherubs, cast-brass French-style sash w/beveled glass, porcelain dial w/Roman numerals & Ansonia trademark, eight-day time & strike movement, hairline on dial, hands not original, over-painted gold has darkened, ca. 1900, 18 1/2" h. (ILLUS.) **616**

Small Atkins Rosewood Cottage Clock

Shelf or mantel clock, Atkins Clock Co., Bristol, Connecticut, cottage-style w/rosewood case, paneled arched top over a conforming door w/two glass panes, the top pane over the white dial w/Roman numerals & some paint loss, lower pane reverse-painted w/a colorful floral bouquet against a black ground, ogee molded base, small piece of veneer missing on right base, 30-hour movement, time only, ca. 1865, 10 1/4" h. (ILLUS. on previous page) **179**

Atkins "London" Shelf Clock

Shelf or mantel clock, Atkins Clock Co., Bristol, Connecticut, "London" model, upright rosewood case w/molded pediment over gilt three-quarter round ring-turned columns flanking glazed two-panel door, the upper pane over the white dial w/gilt spandrels, brass bezel & black Roman numerals, the lower pane w/gilt leaf decoration, on a high base w/molding & bracket feet, eight-day time & strike movement, some dial restoration, ca. 1865, 16 3/4" h. (ILLUS.) **476**

Atkins Rounded Double-Ring Clock

Shelf or mantel clock, Atkins Clock Co., Bristol, Connecticut, walnut round-topped model, a half-round molding around the top & continuing to slender columns flanking the face w/double large wooden rings, the upper ring enclosing the dial w/Roman numerals, the lower ring decorated w/a reverse-painted scene of a robin on a branch of cherries w/paint loss, molded base, eight-day movement, strike & alarm, missing minute hand, ca. 1880, 4 1/4 x 9", 15 1/4" h. (ILLUS.) **400**

Shelf or mantel clock, Atkins & Downs, Bristol, Connecticut, carved & painted Classical style case, carved eagle crestrail flanked by small turned finials over a long two-pane door opening to a painted dial w/Arabic numerals, door flanked by half-round carved columns, overall black paint w/gilt accents, small carved paw front feet, mirrored lower door, ca. 1830-40, 39 1/4" h. (loss & restoration to case) **578**

M.W. Atkins Steeple Clock

Shelf or mantel clock, Atkins (M.W.) & Co.,
Bristol, Connecticut, steeple style, case
w/rosewood veneered front & mahogany
veneered sides, flat base, original Fenn
faux acid etch-style glass on front, white
dial w/raised Roman numerals & chapter
ring, original label, OG-style movement
w/curved riveted extensions to extend
plates & convert to an eight-day spring-
driven movement, some veneer loss, replaced hour hand, ca. 1848, 19 3/4" h.
(ILLUS.).. **515**

Atkins & Downs Double Deck Clock

Shelf or mantel clock, Atkins & Downs for
George Mitchell, Bristol, Connecticut, tall
double deck upright mahogany case
w/carved eagle crest & corner blocks
w/ringed knob finials, long two-pane
door, the upper pane over a white dial
w/gold painted spandrels & center ring &
black Arabic numerals, the lower pane
w/replacement mirror, door flanked by
black columns w/gilt stenciled floral decoration & gold carved paw feet, eight-day
time & strike wood movement, label quite
bright, chip to eagle wing, eagle head repaired, replacement hands, stenciling
enhanced w/brush, ca. 1832, 39 1/2" h.
(ILLUS.) **1,344**

Fine Steeple-on-Steeple Mantel Clock

Art Deco Atmos Clock

Shelf or mantel clock, Atkins & Porter, Bristol, Connecticut, steeple model, mahogany case w/a sharply peaked top above a pair of slender columns w/tapering spires flanking the two-pane glazed door, the tall pointed upper pane over the painted metal dial w/Roman numerals & the narrow rectangular lower pane reverse-stenciled w/a leafy cartouche enclosing an American eagle, the slightly stepped-out lower case w/small columns flanking a lower door w/a larger rectangular pane reverse-painted w/a wreath enclosing a color scene of the navel battle between the Constitution & the Guerriere against a black ground, small button feet, wagon spring candlestick eight-day time & strike movement, good label inside, two cracks in upper pane, ca. 1840-50, 28" h. (ILLUS.) **2,925**

Shelf or mantel clock, Atmos, France, Art Deco style w/an upright square flat black enameled frame centered w/a square chrome bezel surrounding the square dial w/Roman numerals, a small rectangular opening below the dial, raised on a narrow rectangular chrome base, retailed by Abercrombie & Fitch, ca. 1930s, 9 1/2" h. (ILLUS. top of right column) **2,419**

Attleboro Clock Company Clock

Shelf or mantel clock, Attleboro Clock Co., Attleboro, Massachusetts, late Victorian Neo-Gothic oak case, the wide pointed & scallop-notched crest w/incised line decor above a tall paneled arch door w/beaded molding, gilt stencil decoration of geometrics & birds & cattails, large brass bezel & dial w/Roman numerals, angular side cutouts flank the door, deep arched & stepped base, ca. 1890 (note that no clocks were actually made in Attleboro but were supplied by other makers), 4 1/2 x 15", 22" h. (ILLUS. on previous page) **300-350**

Barr Mfg. Co. Domed Shelf Clock

Shelf or mantel clock, Barr Mfg. Co., Weedsport, New York, "Executive" model, electric battery-operated clock, brass framework, simple brass rods support the clock w/a brass bezel enclosing the round white dial w/black Arabic numerals & subsidiary seconds dial, slender metal pendulum w/brass disk bob, all on circular molded wooden base on short knob feet, w/original intact glass dome, time-only movement, ca. 1920, 11" h. (ILLUS.).. **364**

Shelf or mantel clock, Bartholomew (Eli) & Co., Bristol, Connecticut, Classical style, carved mahogany & mahogany veneer, a high crest boldly carved w/a large stylized blossom & curled leaves flanked by corner blocks above the case w/leaf-, blossoms & column-carved pilasters flanking a two-pane glazed door, the upper pane over the dial w/Roman numerals, scroll-painted spandrels & a circle of pink roses around the center, the tall lower pane reverse-painted w/a landscape scene w/a large white building on the left & a large tree on the right, an oval pendulum window in the center, flat molded base, ca. 1820, 5 x 17", 34" h...................... **1,680**

Nice Gustav Becker Mahogany Clock

Shelf or mantel clock, Becker (Gustav), Germany, mahogany round-topped case w/a wide glazed door opening to a large silver plated dial w/Arabic numerals, molded base, eight-day movement, time & strike, ca. 1890, 5 3/4 x 8", 10 3/4" h. (ILLUS.)... **300-350**

Early Double-Steeple Mantel Clock

Shelf or mantel clock, Birge & Fuller, Bristol, Connecticut, double-steeple style, mahogany & mahogany veneer, the peaked case w/pointed corner finials & half-round columns flanking the peaked door over the dial w/Roman numerals & a small reverse-painted lower glazed panel flanked by another pair of pointed finials above the stepped-out lower case w/a single long rectangular glazed door reverse-painted w/a bunch of fruits & leaves, on small button feet, eight-day "wagon spring" driven movement, minor imperfections, 1840s, 4 x 13 1/8", 27" h. (ILLUS. on previous page). **3,105**

Early Steeple on Steeple Clock

Shelf or mantel clock, Birge & Fuller, Bristol, Connecticut, steeple-on-steeple model, simple molded mahogany veneer case w/three-quarter round peaked columns, two flanking the upper peaked two-pane glass door, the upper pane over the original dial w/black Roman numerals & open escapement, the lower narrow rectangular pane w/a reverse-painted decoration of stylized leaf designs in greens & greys, the stepped-out lower section w/two finials & columns flanking a similar larger glass pane decorated w/a wreath design reverse-painted in white, green & gold, eight-day "wagon spring" time & strike , knob feet, signed movement, some veneer loss, some loose pieces, label not legible, dial repainted, ca. 1848, 27 1/2" h. (ILLUS.) **3,360**

Shelf or mantel clock, Birge & Fuller, Bristol, Connecticut, steeple-on-steeple style, mahogany veneer, the upper section w/a pointed pedimented door flanked by pointed spires & rounded columns over a dial w/Roman numerals over a lower reverse-painted glass panel w/styl-

ized white & orange florals, the stepped-out lower case w/pointed spires flanking the case above the lower case w/a long rectangular glazed door reverse-painted w/stylized floral decoration in white & orange within a narrow blue border band, ca. 1830s, 4 x 13", 26" h. **2,688**

Rare Early Triple-deck Clock

Shelf or mantel clock, Birge, Mallory & Co., Bristol, Connecticut, triple-deck Classical style, gilt-trimmed mahogany veneer, a high gilded leaf-carved crest flanked by corner blocks w/incised rings above a pair of half-round columns w/gilt capitals & bases flanking the top glazed door opening to a painted wooden dial w/Roman numerals & gilt spandrels above a rectangular center reverse-painted glass panel featuring a colorful landscape w/a large classical home flanked by gilded half-round columns, the lowest section also w/a long rectangular door w/a reverse-painted colorful landscape scene flanked by another pair of short half-round columns, flat blocked base on gilt knob feet, eight-day movement, time & strike, open escapement, 5 x 17 1/2", 38 3/4" h. (ILLUS.) **1,500-1,700**

Shelf or mantel clock, Birge, Mallory & Co., Bristol, Connecticut, upright refinished mahogany double-decker case, the upper section w/a door over the gilt dial, the door in the lower case inset w/a mirror, signed eight-day strap brass movement, first-half 19th c., 35" h. **450-550**

Birge, Peck & Co. Triple-deck Clock

Shelf or mantel clock, Birge, Peck & Co., Bristol, Connecticut, triple-deck style, gilt spread-winged eagle splat flanked by rectangular molded-top chimneys w/molded circular decorations above gilt & faux finish ring-turned columns flanking the door w/three glass panes, top pane over the original square dial w/black Roman numerals, original hands & delicate spandrels of red flowers & green ferns, middle pane w/deep aqua border around grey, silver, green, cream & red design w/star motif, the bottom pane w/green border around grey, silver, green & cream floral design, the base w/gilt knob feet, eight-day time & strike strap brass movement, original weights & pendulum, clean label, some cracks in glass, chip missing from chimney, paint loss to dial, ca. 1855, 36 1/2" h. (ILLUS.) **2,688**

Shelf or mantel clock, Blakesly (M.), Plymouth, Connecticut, upright mahogany ogee case w/gessoed relief detail, the tall two-pane glazed door opening to a paint-

ed wooden dial w/Roman numerals & open escapement, the lower pane reverse-painted w/a landscape scene, 30-hour movement, flaking on scene, veneer damage, crack in glass, partial label inside, ca. 1840-50, 26" h. **197**

Early Bloomer & Sperry Clock

Shelf or mantel clock, Bloomer & Sperry, New York, New York, Empire-style mahogany and/or rosewood case, the wide stepped flat top & frieze supported by four slender turned colonettes flanking a two-pane glazed door, the upper pane over the large painted metal dial w/Roman numerals & floral-painted spandrels, the narrow lower pane reverse-painted w/leaves & floral wreaths, deep molded base, eight-day movement, time & strike, open escapement, ca. 1840, 4 3/4 x 16", 25 3/4" h. (ILLUS.) **350-400**

Shelf or mantel clock, Bourdin, France, black marble rectangular case w/molded pediment topped by bronze sculpture of retriever signed "P.J. Mene," a glass pane over the rectangular decorated gilt dial surround w/round time dial & two oblong dial cartouches w/two subsidiary dials each, all white w/black numerals/text, the time dial w/Roman numerals & subsidiary seconds dial, the panels containing dials w/days of the week, months & dates of the month & moon phases in Arabic numerals, dial signed "Bourdin, Hr. Bté , Rue de la Paix 28, a Paris," the beveled block base on short beveled feet, time & strike movement also signed "Bourdin, a Paris, Nr. 3802," small chip to marble, ca. 1880, 19" h. (ILLUS. top of next page) **5,880**

French Multi-dial Mantel Clock

B & H Iron Mantel Clock

metal dial w/Arabic numerals & a subsidiary seconds dial, the lower section fitted w/a mirror, flat base, good label inside, eight-day time & strike Salem Bridge movement, minor veneer damage, mid-19th c., 26 1/2" h. **2,250**

E.C. Brewster Steeple Shelf Clock

Shelf or mantel clock, Bradley & Hubbard, Meriden, Connecticut, rectangular iron case w/rounded corners on heavy beveled base, gold painted decoration & spandrels, round dial w/black Roman numerals, replaced brass bezel, B&H label inside case, 30-hour time & strike movement, some paint loss, touched-up numerals, ca. 1865, 10 3/4" h. (ILLUS.)........ **140**

Shelf or mantel clock, Bradley (Lucius), Watertown, Connecticut, tall upright rectangular mahogany veneer "Salem Bridge" model clock, a narrow molded cornice above slender side columns flanking the tall, wide two-pane glazed door, the upper pane over the repainted

Shelf or mantel clock, Brewster (E.C.) & Son, Bristol, Connecticut, mahogany veneer steeple case w/molded sides & steeply peaked top flanked by spiked baluster-form corner finials, double-pane glass door also peaked, the upper pane over the original signed dial w/black Roman numerals, the lower pane reverse-painted w/a landscape showing the J.C. Brown residence, 30-hour time/strike/alarm movement w/original brass springs, some veneer chips, some wear on dial, tip of one finial broken off, ca. 1855, 19 1/2" h. (ILLUS.) **448**

Early Beehive-style Shelf Clock

Shelf or mantel clock, Brewster & Ingrahams, Bristol, Connecticut, beehive-style, mahogany molded case on rectangular base, round molding over the glass door over dial w/Roman numerals, rectangular glass door beneath w/cut glass tablet, eight-day time & strike rack & snail movement, Kirk's Patent iron backplate, fading & paint loss to dial, lower panel probably a replacement, ca. 1844, 19" h. (ILLUS.) .. **1,008**

Early Onion-top Shelf Clock

Shelf or mantel clock, Brewster & Ingrahams, Bristol, Connecticut, gothic-style molded mahogany veneer case w/onion top & conical ring-turned finials at corners, a round upper molding over a glass paned round white dial w/wood bezel & Roman numerals, a square lower molding around a frosted glass door cut w/a radiating leaf & berry design, the case w/a ring-turned colonette at each corner, flat base, time-only movement, some veneer chips, original very dark finish, brass springs replaced w/steel, ca. 1850, 20 1/2" h. (ILLUS. bottom left) **1,850**

Early Rosewood Beehive Clock

Shelf or mantel clock, Brewster & Ingrahams, Bristol, Connecticut, Kirk's patent movement, beehive form rosewood case w/molded frame & round molding around the round white signed dial w/black Roman numerals, the lower pane reverse-painted w/an image of Ballston Springs, eight-day time & strike rack & snail movement w/original brass springs, age cracks to dial paint, key escutcheon repaired, pendulum a later Seth Thomas type, hands are old but incorrect for this model, ca. 1845, 19" h. (ILLUS.).................... **560**

Shelf or mantel clock, Brewster & Ingrahams, Bristol, Connecticut, steeple-type, mahogany veneer case w/a pointed crest flanked by pointed finials above half-round columns flanking the two-pane glazed door, the short pointed upper pane over the painted metal dial w/Roman numerals, the tall rectangular lower pane frosted & etched w/flowers & leaves in a vase, flat base, Kirk patent backplate, eight-day movement, good label inside, mid-19th c., 19 1/2" h. **703**

Shelf or mantel clock, Brewster & Ingrahams, Bristol, Connecticut, steeple-type, mahogany case w/a high pointed top flanked by pointed spire finials above half-round side columns flanking the tall two-pane peaked door, the upper pane over the dial w/Roman numerals, the lower pane w/original frosted glass panel cut w/a floral design, small brass knob feet, Kirk patent back plate w/lyre gong support, eight-day movement, good label inside, first half 19th c., 21" h.......................... **2,138**

Bronzed Metal Figural Lion Clock

Brewster Ripple Molded Clock

Shelf or mantel clock, Brewster Manufacturing Co., Bristol, Connecticut, rosewood veneer case w/cut scroll frame extending around ripple molded two-paned door & forming rounded feet & ogee apron, top pane over a square signed dial w/delicate floral spandrels & black Roman numerals, lower pane w/red rose in center, 30-hour time & strike movement, ca. 1852, 17" h. (ILLUS.)............ **784**

Shelf or mantel clock, bronzed metal, a large figural female lion w/a gilt-metal finish resting above a rockwork base inset w/a round clock w/an enameled porcelain dial w/Arabic numerals, all on a red marble rectangular platform w/small brass feet, France, late 19th c. (ILLUS. top of next column).. **360**

J.C. Brown Cottage Clock

Shelf or mantel clock, Brown (J.C.), Bristol, Connecticut, cottage-style, upright rectangular rosewood case on slightly stepped block base, two-pane glazed door, the large upper pane over a signed painted dial featuring Roman numerals & painted spandrels of pink flowers & green leaves, the small narrow rectangular lower glass pane reverse-painted w/a scene of Greek-style columned buildings, some in-painting, good label, eight-day signed time & strike movement, some veneer loss, replacement, hands & doorknob, ca. 1855, 15 1/4" h. (ILLUS.) **560**

J.C. Brown Beehive Ripple Clock

Shelf or mantel clock, Brown (J.C.), Bristol, Connecticut, upright mahogany & rosewood beehive-style case, the pointed top & sides decorated w/rippled molding around the pointed two-pane glazed door, the upper section w/a circle of ripple molding around the signed metal dial w/Roman numerals, the lower rectangular pane w/further ripple molding enclosing the frosted pane w/an engraved landscape, ripple molding around the flat base, partial inside label, eight-day spring time & strike movement, dial paint flaking, mid-19th c., 19" h. (ILLUS.)............ **2,025**

Shelf or mantel clock, Brown (J.C.), Bristol, Connecticut, upright rectangular mahogany veneer case, the flat top w/four short pointed corner finials above half-round columns down the sides flanking the two-pane glazed door, the larger upper pane over the signed painted metal dial w/Roman numerals, the short rectangular lower section w/original frosted glass pane engraved w/a fountain, deep blocked base, partial label inside, eight-day brass time & strike movement, ca. 1840-50, 18 1/4" h. **1,913**

J.C. Brown Ripple Case Shelf Clock

Shelf or mantel clock, Brown (Jonathan C.), Bristol, Connecticut, full-ripple onion-top case w/three-quarter round ring-turned columns at four corners topped by slender knobbed & spired finials, molded base, two-pane glass door, top pane over the round dial w/ripple surround & black Roman numerals, bottom square pane w/original heart-shaped etched & cut design, eight-day time & strike movement, signature rubbed off dial, label missing some pieces, ca. 1848, 19 3/4" h. (ILLUS.) **3,808**

Fine Cast Bronze French Clock

Shelf or mantel clock, cast bronze, figural, the top of the low rectangular body cast w/an ornate hunting scene of a hunter on horseback blowing a horn w/a racing hound beside him & a small tree & fallen stag in front, the platform case cast w/drapery swags flanking the white porcelain dial w/Roman numerals, on a heavy stepped molded base w/ornately scroll-cast feet, French, late 19th c. (ILLUS. on previous page) **3,850**

Shelf or mantel clock, cast spelter, figural case, a large spread-winged eagle atop a rockwork base enclosing a round brass bezel & small dial w/Arabic numerals, Germany, late 19th - early 20th c., 6 x 8 3/4", 13 1/2" h. (ILLUS. bottom left) **250-300**

Figural Bicycle Rider Shelf Clock

Unique Sailor & Griffin Clock

Shelf or mantel clock, cast metal, figural, a standing sailor at a large ship's wheel enclosing the clock w/a copper bezel w/Arabic numerals around a domed glass dial, a large winged griffin on a scrolled banner below the sailor & wheel, gold finish, early 20th c., 10" w., 11" h. (ILLUS.) **159**

Shelf or mantel clock, cast spelter, figural, the case in the form of a man riding a bicycle & tipping his hat w/one hand while holding the handlebars w/the other, the works & dial in cast cascading grapevines above his head, white porcelain dial w/contrasting bezel, black Roman numerals & alarm set hand, the base w/apron & scroll feet w/decoration similar to backdrop, 30-hour time & alarm pendulette movement, small chips & hairlines in dial, one foot repaired, France, ca. 1900, 13" h. (ILLUS.) **784**

Chelsea Clock Co. Marine-style Clock

Shelf or mantel clock, Chelsea Clock Co., Chelsea, Massachusetts, "Marine"-style,

Figural Cast-Spelter German Clock

serial #235736, homemade arched pine bracket on stepped rectangular base, silvered brass dial on brass surround, black Arabic numerals & subsidiary seconds dial, engraved "Sun Shipbuilding & Dry Dock Co. - Chester, PA," hinged bezel & button latch, ca. 1937, 7 11/16" h. (ILLUS. on previous page) **392**

Shelf or mantel clock, Chelsea Clock Company, Boston, Massachusetts, Classical style gilt-bronze, ivory & marble case, a large round gilt-bronze narrow leaf-cast framework topped by a large fruit & leaf finial & enclosing the large marble dial w/overlaid pierced metal Roman numerals, raised on a double C-scroll & leaf pedestal on a leaf-cast rectangular ring over a rectangular white marble platform w/narrow gilt-bronze & thin marble base, retailed by Caldwell & Co., New York, New York, late 19th c., 12" h. **10,350**

Shelf or mantel clock, china case, a high arched case front w/molded scroll border & pierced scroll handles, molded leafy scrolls at the bottom sides above the paneled plinth base, a round metal dial w/Arabic numerals, decorated w/large scattered yellow roses & green leaves, late 19th - early 20th c., 15 1/2" h. **403**

Shelf or mantel clock, Clark (Herman), Plymouth Hollow, Connecticut, double-column style, tall upright two-tier mahogany veneer case, the top w/a narrow flared cornice over the upper tier w/slender columns flanking the large square glazed door over the repainted metal dial w/Roman numerals, the lower tier w/slender columns flanking a horizontal glazed door reverse-painted w/a colorful landscape scene, flat molded base, eight-day Salem Bridge movement, first half 19th c., 26 1/2" h. **2,813**

American Classical Double-deck

Shelf or mantel clock, Classical double-deck-style, mahogany, the high front cornice deeply carved w/acanthus leaves flanking a gilt S-scroll design flanked by carved gilt pineapple corner finials, the two-part case w/a square glazed upper door flanked by turned reeded & leaf-carved pilasters & opening to a white dial w/Roman numerals & gilt painted spandrels, the lower case w/a taller reverse-painted glazed door

Three Varied Mantel Clocks

featuring an oval reserve w/a color bust portrait of George Washington surrounded by black & flanked by carved pilasters matching upper ones, flat base on carved paw feet, original finish, ca. 1830-40, 7 x 16", 36" h. (ILLUS. top of previous page) **900**

Shelf or mantel clock, Classical style triple-deck, mahogany & mahogany veneer, the wide ogee cornice above a two-part glazed door opening to a painted dial w/Roman numerals above a lower reverse-painted glass pane decorated w/a white circle centering flowers & framed by black, the door flanked by bold half-round turned columns, the lower case w/a small glazed door flanked by ogee sides, refinished, ca. 1830, 8 x 18", 30" h. (ILLUS. at bottom center of previous page) **450**

Victorian Papier-mâché Clock

Shelf or mantel clock, Coe & Co., New York, papier-mâché, the scrolled front embellished w/gilt, polychrome & mother-of-pearl floral designs, housing the circular enamel dial inscribed "Saml. S. Spencer" & lever spring-driven movement, all mounted on a decorated oval base on brass ball feet under glass dome, labeled "Botsford's Improved Patent Timepiece manufactured by Coe & Co. 52 Dey Street, New York," 11" h. (ILLUS.) **1,265**

French Pendulum Shelf Clock

Shelf or mantel clock, Dasson (H.), Paris, France, "Conical Pendulum Clock," figural, marble & gilt bronze, a gilt-bronze statue of a figure in classical garb w/right arm aloft holding pendulum stands above the round red & grey marble dial w/bronze bezel, Roman numerals & center & floral crest, dial fitted on the short circular marble plinth resting on a dark red & grey marble circular stepped base on short gilt-bronze ringed tapered side feet, cut-out scroll decoration on either side & floral front foot & floral decorations on either side of statue, signed "Machault," original multi-piece pendulum, time & strike movement, floral mount on front leg repaired, ca. 1880, 25" h. (ILLUS.) **7,840**

Shelf or mantel clock, Dewey-Manila model, an upright cast-iron case w/an arched top centered by an oval bust portrait of Admiral Dewey, the flattened sides & rounded base sections cast w/various military symbols such as cannon, cannon balls, rifles & swords, ca. 1898, 10" h. **315**

French Directoire Mantel Clock

Shelf or mantel clock, Directoire-period mantel regulator, gilt-metal case on marble base, the round dial topped by garlands of leaves w/leaf-filled handled urn crest, the dial connected by shaft decorated w/leaf & ribbon trim to double arched columns ending in spool bases on white marble rectangular base w/gilt trim & round wafer feet, the cobalt blue porcelain dial w/gilt bezel, hands & center w/open escapement, white chapter ring w/Roman numerals, silk thread movement, some loss to bottom edge of marble base, damage to dial, France, ca. 1795, 17" h. (ILLUS.) **5,600**

Art Nouveau "Doorstop" Clock

Shelf or mantel clock, "doorstop" style, cast-iron Art Nouveau-style case sprayed gold, sunburst design frames upper dial section, the base w/relief figural design of woman in diaphanous robes surrounded by relief floral & leaf trim, flanked by cut-out whiplash brackets, round white paper dial w/black Roman numerals & notched bezel, 30-hour fit-up movement w/backwind & center set stem, small chip in crystal, American, ca. 1900, 13 1/2" h. (ILLUS. below left) **134**

Maurice Dufrêne Mantel Clock

Shelf or mantel clock, Dufrêne (Maurice), Art Nouveau mahogany & gilt-bronze case, model 218-v, produced by La Maison Moderne, arched molded hood above a gilt-bronze face cast w/numerals flanked by apostrophic gilt-bronze bosses cast w/flowers above a lower gilt-bronze panel cast w/leafage & flowers, France, ca. 1902 (ILLUS.)............................ **4,025**

Shelf or mantel clock, Empire style, rosewood upright case w/molded crown supported by four columns w/gilt-bronze bases & capitals, on a deep molded rectangular plinth on bun feet, large round brass dial w/scroll-stamped border & Roman numerals, large leaf-stamped pendulum bob, time & strike movement, France, ca. 1840, 7 x 11 1/2", 22" h. (ILLUS. bottom left of next page)... **1,120**

Shelf or mantel clock, Eureka Company, battery-operated electric model, a deep cylindrical brass base supporting a vertical open balance wheel movement below a raised large round dial w/a brass bezel & Arabic numerals, w/original glass dome, early 20th c., 15" h. **900**

"Bonapart's Son" Figural Shelf Clock

French Empire Rosewood Clock

French "Fan on Easel" Clock

Shelf or mantel clock, "Fan on Easel" style, bronze case in the form of a hand fan w/Chinese-style decoration & ribbon-form drop finial, on easel base, bronze dial w/porcelain cartouche Roman numerals, eight-day pendulette movement, some numerals are loose or chipped, France, ca. 1900, 18 1/2" h. (ILLUS.) **476**

Shelf or mantel clock, Federal Revival style, inlaid mahogany case, the pointed arched case w/line inlay above the round glass door opening to the steel dial w/Arabic numerals above a lower line-inlaid panel centered by an inlaid classical paterae, deep molded base w/line inlay, original finish, ca. 1910, sold by Bailey, Banks & Biddle, Philadelphia, 7 x 11", 15" h. (ILLUS. right w/triple-decker clock page 116) **400**

Shelf or mantel clock, figural "Bonapart's Son" model, high stepped ormolu case w/a figure of a seated boy on the top w/his elbow resting on a draped table holding world map & books (one a "Memorial" of Napoleon, the other titled "Code Napoleon"), the table enclosing the round dial w/patterned gilt bezel & black Roman numerals, all on rectangular stepped base w/panels of scroll, floral & shell decoration, notched design & ribbing, wave-form feet & corner decorations, engine-turned time & strike movement, dial w/a stress fracture, ca. 1870, 17" h. (ILLUS. at top of previous page) **1,232**

Figural Eagle Shelf Clock

Shelf or mantel clock, figural, dark patinated cast-metal case, the top section w/wreath frame enclosing the round white porcelain dial w/black Roman numerals & brass bezel, dial raised on a large metal ball enclosing the movement & fitted behind a large model of a spread-winged eagle perched on a branch, ornately decorated base w/low scroll feet, eight-day platform lever time-only , dust cover to movement missing, France, ca. 1890, 15 1/2" h. (ILLUS.) **364**

Shelf or mantel clock, figural, miniature faience model of an ornate grandfather clock w/scrolls around the top round dial section above a tall waisted body on a high scroll-footed base, overall scenic & floral decoration, French eight-day Tiffa-

ny-style movement, 12 1/2" h. (chips, lines in case) **309**

French Double Statue Shelf Clock

Shelf or mantel clock, figural "The Sciences - Ingenuity Rewarded" model, two standing patinated spelter figures on rockwork & half-globe base, one figure holding lightning bolts aloft stands just below the other winged figure w/arm upraised, on a raised platform red marble base centered by the white dial w/gilt-metal scrolling bezel & black Arabic numerals, base on ornate gilt-spelter scroll feet & side scrolls, time & bell-strike movement, France, ca. 1900, 37" h. (ILLUS.) **1,568**

"Column & Cornice" Shelf Clock

Shelf or mantel clock, Forestville Manufacturing Co., Bristol, Connecticut, "Column & Cornice" model, mahogany rectangular molded case w/stepped cornice, three-quarter round columns on body, knob feet, glass panels w/reverse painted decoration in body & base doors, the dial w/Arabic numerals & spandrels, eight-day time & strike weight movement w/24-hour count wheel, some loss on dial, veneer chips, tiny crack in dial glass, ca. 1845, 36 1/2" h. (ILLUS.)............................... **532**

Shelf or mantel clock, Forestville Manufacturing Co., J.C. Brown, Bristol, Connecticut, steeple style mahogany case w/molded peaked top w/corner blocks w/baluster-form finials, the peaked two-pane door w/ripple side molding also used between the two glass panes, the top pane over a dial w/black Roman numerals, the bottom pane reverse-painted w/a scene of Buckingham Palace, eight-day time & strike movement signed "J.C. Brown," minor flaking on tablet, dial needs cleaning, original hands have lost their tips, original brass springs replaced w/steel, ca. 1845, 20" h. (ILLUS. top of next column).. **952**

Forestville Ripple Door Steeple Clock

Forestville Rosewood Shelf Clock

Shelf or mantel clock, Forestville Manufacturing Co., J.C. Brown, Bristol, Connecticut, upright rectangular rosewood case

w/beveled frame & base, delicate gold floral decoration on case, the door w/two
glass panes, the large upper pane over
the dial w/gold floral spandrels & black Roman numerals, the lower reverse-painted
pane w/a center scene of a large building
w/trees in background flanked by two panels of roses, eight-day time & strike signed
movement, legible label, tiny veneer
chips, some paint loss on dial, replacement hands, ca. 1849, 15 1/4" h. (ILLUS.
bottom of previous page) **560**

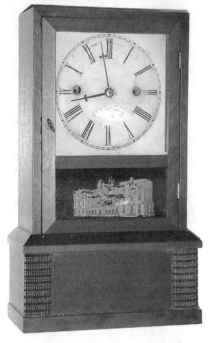

Ripple Cottage Shelf Clock

Shelf or mantel clock, Forestville Manufacturing Co., J.C. Brown, Bristol, Connecticut, wooden ripple cottage style w/origi-
nal glass panels in door, one w/reverse-
painted decoration, round dial w/Roman
numerals, 30-hour time & strike movement, some flaking on tablet, paint loss
on dial, ca. 1849, 15" h. (ILLUS.) **364**
Shelf or mantel clock, Forestville Mfg. Co.,
Bristol, Connecticut, mahogany case
w/ogee molded cornice over two half round
ring-turned columns on either side of the tri-
ple-pane door, upper pane over square
cream-colored signed wooden dial w/Ro-
man numerals & spandrels of red flowers &
green leaves, label w/names of Forestville
partners J.C. Brown, S. Smith & C. Goodrich, center pane w/a reverse-painted
scene of flower-filled urn between two classical columns & drapery, the base w/ogee
side columns flanking bottom door pane in
pale greenish blue w/delicate flower & leaf
decoration, the center w/oval cartouche
framing a flower form, decorated panes by

Wm. B. Fenn, shallow block base, eight-
day time & strike movement, ca. 1845,
34" h. (ILLUS. below) **1,960**

Forestville Mahogany Shelf Clock

Forestville Mfg. Co. Shelf Clock

Shelf or mantel clock, Forestville Mfg. Co., Bristol, Connecticut, tall upright "column & cornice" case in crotch-grained mahogany veneer, a deep ogee molded blocked cornice over tall half-round columns w/ringed capitals & bases flanking a two-pane door, the upper pane over the polychrome wooden dial w/spandrels, black Roman numerals, open escapement & marked "Forestvill [sic], Manufacturing Co. - Bristol, CT. U.S.A.," the lower pane w/an original Wm. B. Fenn monochromatic silver-colored decoration of a vase w/floral stems, bottom ogee-front block feet flank another glass pane w/an original Wm. B. Fenn monochromatic silver-colored decoration of a bird on limb, good label, hand-colored lithograph of Saturday night scene on backboard, time & strike movement, ca. 1850, 34" h. (ILLUS. on previous page) **1,456**

Shelf or mantel clock, Forestville Mfg. Co., Bristol, Connecticut, upright mahogany veneer case-on-case model, the upright rectangular case divided into two sections by the ogee molding, the upper section w/a square glazed door opening to the painted metal dial w/Roman numerals & open escapement, the lower section w/a replaced frosted glass pane engraved w/florals, eight-day time & strike movement, label inside, mid-19th c., 30 1/2" h. **675**

French Marble & Brass Mantel Clock

Shelf or mantel clock, French design, black marble w/gilt brass figural cast lovebirds & fruit clusters on arched top flanked by seated putti figures, dial w/Roman numerals, all raised on stepped rectangular marble base w/incised decoration & gilt banding flanking a central leaf swag & scroll cartouche w/classical mask, raised on scroll cast gilt metal paw feet, last quarter 19th c., some damage (ILLUS.).. **1,025**

Shelf or mantel clock, French Victorian Renaissance Revival-style, gilt-bronze case w/a large swag-draped urn finial on the upright case topped w/ornate

Ornate French Gilt-bronze Clock

scrolls & grape clusters above the round gilt-trimmed enameled dial w/Roman numerals flanked by caryatids, the blocked rectangular base w/leafy scrolls & grapes flanking the case & decorated w/scroll bands & florets, pinwheel movement, third quarter 19th c. (ILLUS. bottom, previous page) **5,200**

Charles Frodsham Shelf Clock

Shelf or mantel clock, Frodsham (Charles), London, England, walnut rectangular case w/molded pediment & base w/square wafer feet, all four sides & top w/glass panels, the silvered brass dial w/delicate engraved spandrels, Roman numerals & beveled reflector mask, marked "By App't to H.M. King" & signature, fusee time-only movement w/Harrison type maintaining power, door key, ca. 1910, 9 3/4" h. (ILLUS.) **3,024**

Gilbert "Curfew" Mantel Clock

Shelf or mantel clock, Gilbert Manufacturing Co., Winsted, Connecticut, "Curfew" model, flat-topped domed wooden case w/ogee sides & aproned base w/small gilt-metal paw feet, the top platform fitted w/an arched scroll-cast metal frame suspending a brass bell, the front of the base w/a fancy brass bezel enclosing the white dial w/Roman numerals, time & strike movement, some discoloration & oxidation, ca. 1910, 17" h. (ILLUS. below left) **420**

Shelf or mantel clock, Gilbert (William L.) Clock Co., Winsted, Connecticut, "Laurel" model, tall pressed oak case w/leafy border designs & four applied wood daisy-form buttons, the tall glass door over the dial w/original hands & stenciled decoration of birds on a branch w/a Greek key border, original pendulum, eight-day time & strike movement, late 19th - early 20th c., 24" h. **175-225**

Wm. Gilbert Acheron Model Clock

Shelf or mantel clock, Gilbert (Wm. L.) Clock Co., Winsted, Connecticut, "Acheron" model, walnut case w/fan-carved crest & line-incised scrolls above the arched molded glazed door opening to a dial w/Roman numerals, the lower door w/original silver stenciled leaves, flowers & a checkerboard design, deep flared platform base, paper label inside, late 19th c., 4 1/2 x 13", 19 1/4" h. (ILLUS.) **200-250**

Gilbert Art Nouveau Shelf Clock

Shelf or mantel clock, Gilbert (Wm. L.) Clock Co., Winsted, Connecticut, Art Nouveau "Standard X," oak case, the rounded upper case composed of entwined looping bands centering the brass dial w/Arabic numerals & copper hands, flat leaf-carved open lower case w/center leaf drop in front of the pendulum, some repairs to case, ca. 1910, 4 x 10", 16 1/4" h. (ILLUS.) **400**

Fancy Gilbert Scroll-cut Clock

Shelf or mantel clock, Gilbert (Wm. L.) Clock Co., Winsted, Connecticut, "Lake No. 5" model, walnut case w/a high ornate

scroll-cut & line-incised crest centered by a roundel above a slender half-round turned rail over the tall rectangular glazed door w/a beaded edging, the glass stenciled in silver w/leafy vines & birds, the large dial w/Roman numerals, the brass pendulum decorated w/grape leaves, the lower case trimmed w/further cut scrolls on the deep flaring platform base, eight-day movement, time & strike, ca. 1890, 4 3/4 x 14", 22" h. (ILLUS. below left) **200-250**

Miniature Gilbert Steeple Clock

Shelf or mantel clock, Gilbert (Wm. L.) Clock Co., Winsted, Connecticut, miniature walnut steeple case, a Gothic arch frame flanked by simple columns w/small metal spires, a round dial w/Roman numerals above a square molding around a glass pane over a print of Victorian women, back of case w/paper label reading "No. 52T English Lancet," original finish, time only, 19th c., 2 1/4 x 4 3/4", 7" h. (ILLUS.) **70**

Shelf or mantel clock, Gilbert (Wm. L.) Clock Co., Winsted, Connecticut, Victorian Renaissance Revival walnut "Lebanon" model, the tall pointed fanned pediment w/roundel above a row of short turned spindles above stepped sides ending in curled-down ears w/roundels over the paneled arched tall door w/reeded molding, decorated w/a fancy silver stencil spider web & grass design below the brass bezel & large dial w/Roman numerals, brass pendulum w/embossed flowers & leaves, rectangular deep platform base w/sawtooth band, eight-day movement, time & strike, ca. 1890, 4 1/2 x 13 1/8", 20 1/2" h. (ILLUS. top, next page) **400-450**

Ornate Gilbert "Lebanon" Clock

Gilbert Eastlake Style Clock

Shelf or mantel clock, Gilbert (Wm. L.) Clock Co., Winsted, Connecticut, walnut kitchen-style case, Victorian Eastlake design, the sawtooth-cut central cornice flanked by tall corner blocks w/knob finials

above reeded sides flanking the tall glazed door w/ornate silver stenciled arches below the dial w/Roman numerals, brass pendulum w/applied grape leaves, molded & blocked base w/line-incised decoration, original varnish, eight-day movement, time & strike, ca. 1885, 4 x 12 1/4", 21 1/4" h. (ILLUS. below left) **450-550**

Gilbert "Necho" Model Shelf Clock

Shelf or mantel clock, Gilbert (Wm. L.) Clock Co., Winsted, Connecticut, walnut "Necho" model, a pointed scroll-carved pediment above scroll-cut & line-incised cornice above the rounded & reeded glazed door w/ornate silver stenciled drapery design over the large dial w/Roman numerals & a brass pendulum w/applied grape leaves, scroll cutouts at the lower sides above the flaring stepped base, eight-day movement, time, strike & alarm, ca. 1890, 5 x 13 1/4", 20 3/4" h. (ILLUS.).. **300-350**

Gilbert Miniature Steeple Clock

Shelf or mantel clock, Gilbert (Wm. L.), Winsted, Connecticut, miniature steeple-type clock, walnut case w/pointed pediment flanked by turned finials above the pointed two-pane glazed door, the upper pane opening to the white metal dial w/Roman numerals & painted spandrels, the lower panel w/a reverse-painted windmill scene, flat base, possibly a salesman's sample, eight-day time & strike movement, mid-19th c., 4 1/2 x 6 1/2", 10 3/4" h. (ILLUS.).. **250**

Ornate Gilt-bronze & Enamel Clock

Shelf or mantel clock, gilt-bronze & enamel, an ornate rococo design w/a scrolling easel-form frame enclosing two porcelain panels h.p. w/18th c. courting scenes, the large lower panel centered by a small clock dial w/Roman numerals, France, late 19th - early 20th c., 4" w., 7 1/2" h. (ILLUS. below left)... **2,450**

Figural Gilt-bronze & Enamel Clock

Shelf or mantel clock, gilt-bronze & enamel, an ornate scrolled lower case on scroll feet enclosing an enameled panel showing a classical maiden & topped by a full-figure seated Victorian lady at the top right, a smaller scrolled case projecting from the top left & enclosing a smaller enameled panel centered by a small clock dial w/Roman numerals, France, late 19th - early 20th c., 3 1/2" w., 5 3/4" h. (ILLUS.)... **2,295**

French Porcelain & Bronze Clock

Shelf or mantel clock, gilt-bronze & porcelain, an upright rectangular case, the temple-form gilt-bronze framework enclosing painted porcelain plaques at the front & sides, each decorated w/romantic scenes, the front w/the raised metal bezel directly over the plaque w/the scene showing through the Arabic dial numerals, heavy base, artist-signed plaques, Monti Works, France, late 19th c., 7 3/4" w., 14" h. (ILLUS. on previous page) **1,955**

Ornate French Bronze Mantel Clock

Shelf or mantel clock, gilt-bronze, the porcelain face mounted in a drum case, works marked "S. Marti Medaille d'Or Paris 1900," the top w/a large bank of gilt-bronze clouds atop which rests an angel blowing a trumpet (presumably Gabriel), above the dial a putto holding a scroll inscribed "Raphael Poussin, Montesquiew, Michelange," 22 1/4" h. (ILLUS.) **1,265**

Shelf or mantel clock, globe model, pre-World War I world globe sits atop a waisted wooden case w/molded top, brass dial & bezel, Arabic numerals in black number cartouches, molded band near bottom, block base w/wafer feet, 30-hour time-only movement, Germany, ca. 1900, 15" h. (ILLUS. top, next column) **1,960**

German Globe Shelf Clock

Asaph Hall Shelf Clock

Shelf or mantel clock, Hall (Asaph), Clinton, Georgia, tall upright mahogany case w/a flat serpentined crestrail above the sides w/inlaid tiger maple square columns, the tall two-pane glazed door w/the top pane over a white dial w/Arabic numerals & gold-painted spandrels, mirror in lower door panel, 30-hour wood time & strike movement, mirror replaced, side returns missing, small piece of veneer missing, ca. 1832, 34 1/2" h. (ILLUS. on previous page) **672**

Late Steeple-type Electric Clock

Shelf or mantel clock, Hamilton-Sangamo Corp., Springfield, Illinois, electric steeple clock, pointed mahogany case w/pointed finials flanking the two-pane pointed door, the upper pane over the dial w/Roman numerals & h.p. floral spandrels, the lower pane w/a reverse-painted landscape, flat molded base, revival of a 19th c. style clock, ca. 1940, 4 7/8 x 9 1/2", 14 3/4" h. (ILLUS.) **150-175**

Shelf or mantel clock, Herschede Clock Co., Cincinnati, Ohio, Style #544, arched mahogany case w/stepped base on short block feet and signed w/Herschede imprint, silvered brass dial w/Arabic numerals signed "The Frank Herschede Co., Cincinnati," unique platform/lever time & strike movement, the hours and half hours struck on a coiled wire gong, ca. 1915, 10 3/4" h. (ILLUS. top, next column) **392**

Frank Herschede Mantel Clock

Shelf or mantel clock, Hills, Goodrich & Co., Plainville, Connecticut, double-deck model, upright tall mahogany case w/a deep ogee cornice above the upper section w/half-round columns flanking the two-pane glazed door, the upper pane over the painted metal dial w/Roman numerals, painted spandrels & open escapement, the lower door w/original frosted glass pane engraved w/a wreath, the slightly stepped-out lower section centered by another rectangular frosted glass pane engraved w/a wreath, flat base, 30-hour upside-down time & strike movement, ca. 1850, 28" h. **619**

Shelf or mantel clock, Hills, Goodrich & Co., Plainville, Connecticut, upright mahogany ogee-style mahogany veneer case, a tall two-pane glazed door, the larger upper pane opening to two slender gilt columns joined at the top by a leaf-carved crest above the round dial w/Roman numerals & open escapement, the smaller rectangular lower pane reverse-painted w/a colorful landscape scene, eight-day Ives brass movement, some loss on lower pane, some veneer damage on case, ca. 1850, 30" h. **506**

Shelf or mantel clock, Ingraham Co., Bristol, Connecticut, cottage-style wooden case w/a scalloped frame w/shallow line-incised decoration & an applied turned wood button, the two-pane door w/the upper pane over the original paper dial, the lower pane stenciled w/a stacked arch design & flowers, leaves & vines, cast-brass pendulum bob w/raised design, signed gong base, eight-day time & strike movement, late 19th c., 22" h. **125-175**

Shelf or mantel clock, Ingraham Co., Bristol, Connecticut, French-style bombé faux marble-painted wood case w/original red & black marbleizing, applied

Fine Ingraham Temple-style Clock

scrolling cast-metal trim, brass bezel & dial w/original hands, original pendulum, eight-day time & strike movement, late 19th - early 20th c., 16" h. **150-200**

Shelf or mantel clock, Ingraham Co., Bristol, Connecticut, "Minerva" model, upright pressed oak case w/scalloped outline & applied C-scroll decoration in the crest, the glass door over the dial w/original hands & pendulum, eight-day time & strike movement, late 19th - early 20th c., 22" h......... **125-150**

Shelf or mantel clock, Ingraham Co., Bristol, Connecticut, shorter cabinet-style pressed oak case decorated w/scrolls & flowers, the glass door over the dial w/original hands & the original pendulum, eight-day time & strike movement, late 19th - early 20th c., 15 1/2" h................. **150-200**

Shelf or mantel clock, Ingraham Co., Bristol, Connecticut, upright oak case w/scalloped borders, three applied oak decorations in pressed fleur-de-lis & medallions, the glass door over the dial decorated w/a stenciled stylized medallion design, cast-brass pendulum bob w/a landscape scene, eight-day time & strike movement, late 19th - early 20th c., 22" h................. **125-175**

Shelf or mantel clock, Ingraham Company, Bristol, Connecticut, temple-style, black enamel over wood, the long, high rectangular case w/applied stamped metal columns & cast-metal paw feet, metal lion head mask end handles, top panels on the front inset w/slag glass framed by metal simulating curtained windows, eight-day movement, time & strike, ca. 1900, 5 1/2 x 20", 10 7/8" h. (ILLUS. top of page)................................. **300-400**

Shelf or mantel clock, Ingraham Company, Bristol, Connecticut, upright pressed oak case w/scalloped sides & deep C-scroll decorations, the tall glass door over the dial w/original hands & original pendulum, eight-day time & strike movement, late 19th - early 20th c., 22" h...... **125-150**

E. & A. Ingraham Shelf Clock

Shelf or mantel clock, Ingraham (E. & A.), Bristol, Connecticut, mahogany & rosewood veneer, contoured miniature lyre-front case w/valanced skirt, glass tablet in door w/reverse-painted scroll & floral decoration, dial w/Roman numerals & spandrels, 30-hour time only movement w/alarm, veneer damage, some flaking to label & tablet, ca. 1853, 11 1/2" h. (ILLUS.)...... **504**

Shelf or mantel clock, Ingraham (E.) Co., Bristol, Connecticut, ornate pressed oak commemorative clock, scenes from the Spanish-American War, the wide three-lobed crest centered by a large profile portrait of Admiral Dewey in a wreath flanked by vignettes of crossed flags & cannon balls above the arched paneled tall door ornately decorated w/gilt stenciling showing the Battleship Maine & crossed American flags, the round dial w/brass bezel & Roman numerals, lower shaped side scroll panels w/flags & cannons, the wide molded base decorated w/a repeating design of stars & anchors, original finish, 1898, eight-day movement, time & strike, 4 1/4 x 14 1/4", 23" h. (ILLUS. bottom of page) **2,000-2,500**

"Small Venetian" Clock

Shelf or mantel clock, Ingraham (E.) & Co., Bristol, Connecticut, "Small Venetian" model, sub-miniature, round-toped rosewood & walnut case w/three-quarter baluster-form gold-painted (over gilt) columns on each side of the case flanking two round wooden moldings, the top molding enclosing a brass bezel & dial w/Roman numerals, the lower molding enclosing a reverse-painted pane decorated w/dark green rings around a red center w/a gilt blossom, a deep molded rectangular base, 30-hour time only movement w/alarm, some wear, bezel w/extra holes, ca. 1870, 11 1/2" h. (ILLUS. at left) **532**

Rare Admiral Dewey Shelf Clock

Handsome Ingraham Eastlake Clock

Shelf or mantel clock, Ingraham (E.) & Co., Bristol, Connecticut, Victorian Eastlake style stained maple case w/applied black trim, the stepped cornice topped by a star-flower & leaf sprig, a tall paneled arched glazed door w/delicate stenciled gilt scrolling, brass bezel around dial w/Roman numerals, scroll-cut side panels w/applied black trim, flaring platform base w/applied black panels & a central starflower, eight-day movement, time, strike & alarm, some black trim missing, ca. 1880, 5 x 13", 20" h. (ILLUS.) **350-400**

Ingraham "Doric" Model Clock

Shelf or mantel clock, Ingraham (E.) & Co., Bristol, Connecticut, walnut "Doric" model figure-eight case, the pointed top above tall molded sides flanking two stacked round molded glazed openings & two roundels, the upper opening over the dial w/Roman numerals, the lower opening decorated w/a colorful floral bouquet on white, molded base, original varnish finish, eight-day movement, time & strike, ca. 1870, 4 1/4 x 9", 16 1/4" h. (ILLUS. below left)... **400**

Nickel & Brass 400-day Clock

Shelf or mantel clock, Jahresuhrenfabrik, Triberg, Germany, Anton Harder patent model 400-day clock, upright square brass frame w/tiny turned brass finials centered by the round white porcelain dial w/black Roman numerals & original hands, all raised on round nickeled columns w/capitals matching the finials, on a stepped circular base, nickel plated disc pendulum, original glass dome, ca. 1883, w/dome 10" h. (ILLUS.) **1,680**

Art Nouveau 400-Day Clock

Shelf or mantel clock, Jahresuhrenfabrik, Triberg, Germany, Art Nouveau style 400-day clock, upright brass frame w/the dial raised on brass columns set on a stepped round base, large round silvered metal dial w/raised chapter ring, beaded brass bezel, contour splat & black Arabic numerals, compensating pendulum, produced for Carp Year-Long Clock Co., adjusting shaft on pendulum broken in center, early gimbal suspension, replacement glass dome, ca. 1902, 11" h. (ILLUS.) **571**

Shelf or mantel clock, Japy, France, Empire-style upright rosewood case, rectangular scroll-inlaid & rib-molded arched crest over a gadrooned molding over an ornately inlaid frieze band, raised on four ropetwist columns w/gilt capitals & bases supporting the wide ornate gilt-brass bezel around the white porcelain dial w/black Roman numerals & the pendulum w/a large brass bob stamped w/a design of a winged cherub & dog, the oblong stepped base on button feet & decorated w/matching scroll inlay & ribbed molding, eight-day time & bell strike movement, comes w/walnut veneer base that supported a dome (now missing), ca. 1880, 19" h. (ILLUS. top of next column) **840**

Empire-style Four-column Clock

Fine French Rococo-style Clock

Shelf or mantel clock, Japy Freres, France, Rococo-style, tortoiseshell & bronze doré case, flattened shield-shaped body w/shaped molded pediment & long bronze leafy scrolls down the sides & across the base, round brass & enameled dial w/Roman numerals, time & strike movement, on small scroll feet, late 19th c., 7 x 14", 23 1/2" h. (ILLUS. on previous page) **2,688**

Shelf or mantel clock, Jefferson Suspense Electric Co., brass & Lucite case, a thin brass frame enclosing an upright flat rectangle of clear Lucite enclosing the clockworks & printed w/Arabic numerals, clock hands rotate on a slender chain, 20th c., 13 1/2" h. **84**

Jennings Art Nouveau Metal Clock

Shelf or mantel clock, Jennings Bros. Mfg. Co., Bridgeport, Connecticut, gilt spelter, the tall Art Nouveau design case bulbous at the top & tapering down to a wide serpentine foot, openwork leaves & cherries at the top & down the front w/loop side handles, the round dial w/Arabic numerals, ca. 1900, 4 3/4 x 5 1/4", 12" h. (ILLUS.) **200**

Chauncey Jerome Mantel Clock

Shelf or mantel clock, Jerome (Chauncey), New Haven, Connecticut, brass-front footed timepiece w/ornate scrolling design on oval base w/brass feet & h.p. decoration, glass dome cover, white dial w/Roman numerals, Botsford Patent 30-hour movement w/mono-metallic balance, some cracks to dial & dome, base decoration worn, ca. 1850, 11" h. (ILLUS.) **616**

Shelf or mantel clock, Jerome (Chauncey), New Haven, Connecticut, miniature upright rosewood rectangular case, a deep ogee cornice above gilt-painted half-round columns flanking the two-pane glazed door, the upper pane over the signed patinated metal dial w/Roman numerals & open escapement, the original lower frosted pane engraved w/florals, deep molded base, eight-day brass spring time & strike movement, good label inside, columns repainted, ca. 1840, 18" h. **259**

Jerome & Co. Cottage Clock

Shelf or mantel clock, Jerome & Co., New Haven, Connecticut, cottage style, wooden rectangular body on rounded rectangular base, w/gutta percha inserts w/gold accented bezel & glass panels on door, white dial w/Roman numerals, label inside door, instructions, eight-day time & strike movement w/alarm, some paint loss, ca. 1860, 13 1/2" h. (ILLUS.) **364**

Shelf or mantel clock, Jerome & Darrow, Bristol, Connecticut, Classical style tall upright painted wood case w/a serpentine crestrail flanked by corner blocks, the sides of the case w/half-round columns flanking the two-pane door, upper pane over a white dial w/Roman numerals & colored spandrels, the lower pane w/an old wavy mirror framed by stenciled gilt leaf bands, original gilt floral stenciling on the crest, original painted graining on the case & columns, 30-hour time & strike movement, hands replaced, ca. 1830, 33 1/2" h. (ILLUS. below left)........................... **364**

Shelf or mantel clock, Jerome & Darrow, Bristol, Connecticut, tall upright rectangular Classical mahogany veneer case, the serpentine flat crestrail decorated w/a stenciled design flanked by corner blocks, painted half-round columns flank the tall two-pane glazed door, the large upper pane over the painted wood dial w/Arabic numerals, the short lower pane reverse-painted w/a landscape w/building, flat base on carved paw front feet, good label inside, 30-hour wood time & strike movement, ca. 1830-40, 28 1/2" h....... **563**

Shelf or mantel clock, Jerome & Darrow, Bristol, Connecticut, tall upright rectangular mahogany case, a stenciled serpentine crestrail above corner blocks over half-round columns down the sides flanking the tall two-pane glazed door, the upper pane over the painted wooden dial w/Roman numerals, lower section fitted w/a mirror, good label inside, 30-hour wooden time & strike movement, ca. 1840, 35" h. **253**

Early Stenciled Shelf Clock

Jeromes, Gilbert, Grant & Co. Clock

Shelf or mantel clock, Jeromes, Gilbert, Grant & Co., Bristol, Connecticut, upright rectangular mahogany case w/molded pediment & rounded sides flanking the tall two-pane door, the upper pane over a zinc dial plate w/Roman numerals around an open escapement all framed by a black reverse-painted border w/gilt scrolls, the lower pane reverse-painted w/a scene of an urn w/flowers flanked by reeded columns & open drapes in gold on a black ground, original card label inside case, original key lock converted to key knob, hands not original, 30-hour time & strike movement, ca. 1840, 22 1/4" h. (ILLUS. on previous page)... **896**

Shelf or mantel clock, Johnson (William S.), New York, New York, double-steeple type, mahogany veneer two-part case, the upper section w/a pointed crest flanked by short turned finials above half-round short columns flanking the two-pane glazed door, the upper pane over the pointed painted metal dial w/Roman numerals & the narrow lower pane etched w/a diamond lattice design, the stepped-out lower case w/turned finials & corner blocks above half-round columns flanking a large rectangular glass door w/a repainted decoration of crossed flags, flat base, good label inside, eight-day brass movement, mid-19th c., 23 1/2" h.................................... **1,013**

Shelf or mantel clock, Johnson (William S.), New York, New York, steeple-on-steeple model, rosewood upright case, the top section w/a pointed top flanked by columns w/pointed spires flanking the two-pane glazed door, the upper pointed pane over the painted metal dial w/Roman numerals, the lower pane reverse-painted w/flowers, the stepped-out lower case w/pointed spires at the front corners above short half-columns flanking a horizontal rectangular door w/reverse-painted pane decorated w/a pinwheel within a rectangular reserve on a colored ground, eight-day time & strike brass movement, label inside, touchup on lower door, ca. 1840-50, 23 1/2" h. **647**

Wm. S. Johnson Shelf Clock

Shelf or mantel clock, Johnson (Wm. S.), New York, New York, tall upright mahogany case w/stepped rectangular top over four round columns flanking the two-pane glazed door, the upper pane over the dial w/Roman numerals & painted gilt spandrels, the bottom pane w/reverse-painted multicolored compass in a center cartouche on an aquamarine background, deep plinth base, original wafer weights, label, time & strike movement, ca. 1855, 26 3/4" h. (ILLUS.) **448**

German Inlaid Mahogany Clock

Shelf or mantel clock, Junghans, Germany, inlaid mahogany arched case w/fine floral marquetry scrolls & blossoms on the crest & around the molded rectangular base on round wafer feet, arched brass dial w/embossed decoration throughout & applied silvered chapter ring w/Arabic numerals & two subsidiary dials for chime-silent & fast-slow, time, strike & chime movement signed "Junghans" & chimes Westminster tune, plaque on rear marked w/name of retailer, "J. Van Wielik, Horologemaker, Gravenahage," ca. 1910, 17 3/4" h. (ILLUS.) **840**

German Mahogany Chiming Clock

Shelf or mantel clock, Junghans, Germany, mahogany arched case on molded block base w/square lozenge feet, silvered dial under beveled glass hinged door, the chapter ring a darker silver w/black Arabic numerals, two subsidiary dials above, one for Chime/Silent & one for F/S regulation, time, strike & chime movement plays Westminster tune & chimes the quarter hours on set of melodious steel rods, rear door painted black, rest of case once painted black but refinished, ca. 1920, 13 3/4" h. (ILLUS. below left) **560**

Junghans German Mantel Clock

Shelf or mantel clock, Junghans, Germany, mahogany rectangular case w/molded arched cornice & stepped base w/lozenge feet, ornately decorated arched brass dial w/Arabic numerals, silvered chapter ring & gilt brass spandrels, eight-day quarter-striking movement, tip of minute hand broken off, ca. 1920, 12 3/4" h. (ILLUS.) **532**

Cased German Skeleton Clock

Shelf or mantel clock, Kieninger, Germany, skeleton movement in an upright walnut case w/beveled glass front door & back, open ring steel dial w/Roman numerals, brass movement & bell, eight-day movement, 7 3/4 x 10 7/8" d., 16" h. overall (ILLUS. on previous page) **600**

Kienzle German 400-Day Clock

Shelf or mantel clock, Kienzle, Germany, 400-day clock, brass framework w/scalloped crest w/three small finials all supported on brass columns w/turned capitals & bases, a brass bezel enclosing the round white dial w/black Arabic numerals, brass disc pendulum, all on circular brass stepped base, gimbal suspension, unit serial number 20825 on both rear plate & pendulum, old glass dome, ca. 1905, 11" h. (ILLUS.) **448**

Shelf or mantel clock, Knox (Archibald), England, Art Nouveau style, enameled pewter upright rectangular case w/a projecting flat border of stylized leafy vines around the large round dial w/brass Arabic numerals against a dark blue enameled ground centered w/a stylized shield design in red, gold & green, produced by Liberty & Company, England & marked "English Pewter - Made for Liberty & Co. - Rd. 46801-0609," ca. 1902-05, 8 1/4" h. (ILLUS. top of next column) **11,500**

Shelf or mantel clock, Kroeber (F.) Clock Co., New York, New York, cast metal statue of bowman on top of metal clock containing Kroeber's eight-day movement & a patented arrangement so hands can be turned backward without harm, eight-day movement, time & strike, 15 x 23" **700**

Fine Pewter Art Nouveau Style Clock

F. Kroeber "Java" Model Shelf Clock

Shelf or mantel clock, Kroeber (F.) Clock Co., New York, New York, "Java" model, ash contoured case w/arched pediment w/palmette crest above rounded sides w/carved decoration, on molded base w/contour apron & bracket feet, arched &

molded glazed door w/original tablet decorated w/a gilt stenciled landscape scene
below the dial w/Roman numerals, glass-
front "slow-fast" indicator pendulum, eight-
day time & strike movement, dial faded &
some numbers missing, ca. 1880,
18 1/2" h. (ILLUS. on previous page) **252**

Ornate "Occidental" Shelf Clock

Shelf or mantel clock, Kroeber (F.) Clock
Co., New York, New York, "Occidental"
model, upright walnut case w/a molded
arched top w/corner urn-form finials & a
large central scroll & shell crest w/a carved
head of classical woman in the center, tall
front molded arch encloses the large brass
bezel around the round white dial w/Ro-
man numerals, the long glass panel below
decorated w/stenciled scroll & geometric
designs, all flanked by mirrored side panels
& turned drop finials w/small quarter-round
side shelves fitted w/gilt cast-metal figures
of cupids, ovoid molded base w/a gilt cartouche on the front, round star-cut glass
pendulum bob, eight-day time & strike
movement, partial label on rear of case, replacement cupids, some wear to dial, ca.
1880, 24 1/2" h. (ILLUS.).................................... **840**

Shelf or mantel clock, Kroeber (Frederic J.)
Clock Co., New York, New York, walnut
cabinet-style case, the top gallery w/a
Gothic design & ball finials, turned corner
columns flank the two-pane glazed door
w/the upper pane over the dial & the lower
pane reverse-painted w/scenes in arches,
signed eight-day movement w/cathedral
gong, late 19th c., 17" h. **300-350**

F. Kroeber "Langtry" Shelf Clock

Shelf or mantel clock, Kroeber (F.) Clock
Co., New York, New York, "Langtry"
model, upright walnut case w/scallop-
bordered peaked crest w/carved decoration & center & corner urn-form finials,
three-quarter round gold-accented ring-
turned colonettes w/carved decoration
flanking the arched door over round dial
w/brass bezel & center ring, Roman numerals, black-scale indicator pendulum
w/beveled crystal, glass door tablet
w/delicate gilt stenciled decoration, block
base w/carved & beaded decoration,
eight-day time & strike movement, ca.
1870, 22 3/4" h. (ILLUS.)................................ **672**

Rare Lalique Glass Clock

Shelf or mantel clock, Lalique glass, "Le Jour et La Nuit," a large front greyish blue disk set upright on a high flaring wood base, the wide side molded on one side of the wide dial w/a nude male representing Day and on the other w/a nude female representing Night, the black central dial w/white Roman numerals, introduced in 1926, inscribed "R. Lalique France," 14 7/8" h. (ILLUS.)...................... **46,000**

Shelf or mantel clock, LeCoultre, Switzerland, "Atmos" model, Art Deco style rectangular upright polished brass case, a background of delicate vertical stripes around a square opening enclosing the white chapter ring w/Roman numerals, open escapement, a narrow presentation plaque below the dial dated 1949, 15 jewel movement, 9" h. **422**

French "La Terre" Statue Clock

Shelf or mantel clock, "La Terre" statue clock, the top w/a bronzed spelter female figure of "Peace" standing next to a child sitting on a short column, she holds a gilt dove in her right hand while her raised left arm supports a bracket-mounted 4" globe made by E. Bertaux, Rue Serpente 25, Paris, all set atop a stepped rectangular base of variegated light violet marble, the front panel set w/a round white decorated porcelain dial w/an ornate brass bezel & black Arabic numerals, raised on ornate gilt-metal scroll feet, time & strike movement that strikes the hours & halves on a bell, France, ca. 1900, 29" h. (ILLUS.) **2,240**

Swiss Perpetual Shelf Clock

Shelf or mantel clock, LeCoultre, Switzerland, "Atmos" model serial number 61279, upright rectangular brass case w/beveled glass front & sides showing round dial w/raised Arabic numerals in quarter hour increments, open escapement, brushed gold chapter ring, shiny bezel, on block base w/bracket feet, perpetual never-wind movement, Atmos book included, ca. 1956, 9" h. (ILLUS. on previous page) **392**

Clock with Limoges China Case

Shelf or mantel clock, Limoges china case, slender upright form w/an ornate scroll-molded top surrounding the dial w/Arabic numerals & a seconds dial above the narrow waist w/molded columns flanking a center panel painted w/a classical maiden reaching up to a flower branch, scroll- and leaf-molded platform base, gilt trim, France, early 20th c., 12 1/2" h. (ILLUS.)...................................... **1,210**

Shelf or mantel clock, Louis XV Boulle clock w/wall bracket, red tortoiseshell & inlaid brass ogee-shaped case w/gilt quatrefoil flattened dome topped w/crest of woman w/trumpet, ormolu scroll decoration framing upper dial & apron, the elaborately decorated cast-brass dial w/white hour cartouches w/black Roman numerals, internal quarter hour divisions & minute divisions on outer chapter, time & pull repeat movement signed "Collier, Paris," two bells mounted on top of case & articulated hammers rising through case top, gilt feet scrolling into heads at base of clock, the tortoiseshell wall bracket w/ornate ormolu decoration at corners & tip of ogee drop & bordering top, some glue blocks renewed, back painted black, minor losses to tortoiseshell veneer, France, ca. 1750, 36" h. (ILLUS. top of next column)............. **7,840**

Early Louis XV Boulle Clock

Late French Boulle Mantel Clock

Shelf or mantel clock, Louis XV-Style Boulle clock w/wall bracket, tortoiseshell & brass-inlaid ogee-shaped case w/qua-trefoil ogee-side flattened-dome top w/or-molu finial, ornate ormolu scroll decoration partially frames dial & base, the dial w/ormolu dial w/white number cartouches w/black Roman numerals & pendulum w/mask bob, ormolu also borders contour glass dial panel, top rim of bracket & ogee-shaped bracket drop, ormolu scroll feet, time & strike movement strikes

hours on delicate bell, marked "J-B. - Paris," France, ca. 1895, w/bracket 17" h. (ILLUS. left) **2,016**

Shelf or mantel clock, Lux Clock Mfg. Co., Waterbury, Connecticut, miniature domed celluloid case, dial w/Arabic numerals, flat molded base, early 20th c., 2 1/4 x 6 1/4", 3 1/4" h. (ILLUS. bottom of page) **40**

French Boulle-type Shelf Clock

Shelf or mantel clock, Mage, Paris, France, Boulle-type clock in the style of Louis XIV, shell & brass inlay cover the ornate rect-angular case, the top w/a raised rectangu-lar platform w/ormolu border & four turned corner finials above an ormolu arched molding below four flame-form ormolu fin-ials, an ormolu-trimmed frieze band & side panels surround the arched glass door w/an ormolu frame over the brass dial cast w/a frieze in the center & white number cartouches w/Roman numerals in cobalt

Lux Miniature Celluloid Clock

blue, the minutes engraved around the flat bezel, a panel w/a black ground & brass scroll decoration below the dial, the sides & base of the case highlighted by ornate brass scroll decoration w/a brass head in relief at the center of the base, all on small ringed knob feet, rectangular time & strike movement strikes the hours & halves on a bell, one top finial not attached, tip of hour hand missing, ca. 1880, 25" h. (ILLUS. on previous page) **5,880**

Marine Clock Mfg. Co. Shelf Clock

Shelf or mantel clock, Marine Clock Manufacturing Co., New Haven, Connecticut, square upright mahogany beveled case on beveled block base, round brass bezel enclosing a white dial w/Roman numerals & marked "C. Kirk Patent," eight-day time & strike movement w/iron backplate, large monometallic balance & double escape wheel patented by Charles Kirk, partial label on back, dial repainted, ca. 1850, 11 3/4" h. (ILLUS.) **924**

Elisha Manross Steeple Clock

Shelf or mantel clock, Manross (Elisha), Bristol, Connecticut, steeple-style mahogany case, two-pane glazed door, top pane over the white dial w/Roman numerals, a frosted glass tablet in bottom pane w/picture of hot air balloon, clean label, 30-hour time & strike movement, hands not original, ca. 1850, 19 3/4" h. (ILLUS.) **476**

German Mini Black Forest Clock

Shelf or mantel clock, miniature Black Forest-style clock, dark carved wood upright case w/cut-out crest of oak leaves around a shield-form plaque, further scrolling oak leaves at the sides & forming feet, the tall door w/wood molding enclosing the white porcelain dial w/brass bezel & center ring, black Roman numerals, the lower door w/a tall glass pane showing the brass three-bar pendulum w/brass-framed bob w/an inset porcelain disk initialed "R - A," eight-day time-only tiny spring movement w/seven wheels in train, hands poorly replaced, porcelain dial damaged at winding hole, Germany, ca. 1890, 13 1/2" h. (IL-LUS. on previous page)................................... **952**

Shelf or mantel clock, miniature, cast gun metal upright case w/Art Nouveau-style serpentine sides & the front set w/rhinestones around the small round porcelain dial w/Roman numerals, early 20th c., 2 1/2" h. **39**

French Silvered Bronze Mantel Clock

Shelf or mantel clock, miniature Middle Eastern-style silvered bronze case cast w/scrolls & leaves, the quatrefoil domed top w/tall finial, notched pediment, crest w/scroll, bead & fleur-de-lis decoration, body w/lion-head side handles, footed aproned base below cove molding, round white porcelain dial w/gilt bronze center & black Arabic numerals in square surround w/spandrels, miniature time-only movement w/platform cylinder escapement, finial slightly bent, France, ca. 1890, 10 3/4" h. (ILLUS.)................................ **560**

Shelf or mantel clock, Mitchell (George), Bristol, Connecticut, tall upright rectangular Classical mahogany veneer case, the arched serpentine crestrail w/stenciled decor flanked by corner blocks w/knob finials, carved front columns flank the tall two-paned glazed door, the large upper pane over the painted wood dial w/Roman numerals, the narrow lower pane reverse-painted w/a repainted landscape scene, partial label inside, 30-hour wood time & strike movement, ca. 1830-40, 29 1/2" h. **1,913**

Shelf or mantel clock, Mountain State No Key Electrical Co., 400-day battery-operated model, a round flaring stepped metal base supporting two columns holding the works & the raised round dial w/brass bezel & Arabic numerals, under a glass dome, early 20th c., 11" h. **619**

German Chiming Shelf Clock

Shelf or mantel clock, Muller GmbH, Germany, Neuchatel-style upright domed burled walnut waisted case w/large round dial & sides curving out to scroll feet, 9" d. white porcelain dial w/black Roman numerals for hours & black Arabic numerals for minutes in outer ring, brass mask bob w/sunburst frame, the body w/contoured glass panel under dial & glass panes inset in sides, carved apron, time/strike/chime three-train movement features solid plates & removable barrels & retains original eight-rod gong set that plays Westminster chime, originally made for Swiss market, ca. 1890, 19" h. (ILLUS.)................. **1,792**

Gallery of Clocks

Left: Elbe model clock, New Haven Clock Co., 24" high, ca. 1880, $280.
R.O. Schmitt Fine Arts

Right: Vienna Regulator rosewood wall clock, 38" high, ca. 1870, $784.
R.O. Schmitt Fine Arts

Left: Waltham Clock Co. miniature banjo clock, 21" high, ca. 1928, $1,176.
R.O. Schmitt Fine Arts

George W. Brown "Briggs Rotary" model clock, 7 3/4" high, ca. 1860, $672.
R.O. Schmitt Fine Arts

Carved folk art maple figural novelty clock, 29" high, early 20th century, $3,450.
Skinner, Inc.

Left: Ansonia Clock Co. Art Nouveau swinging arm clock, 24" high, late 19th century, $3,250.
Slawinski Auction Company

Right: Morbier pressed-brass wag-on-wall clock, French, 54" high, ca. 1890, $672.
R.O. Schmitt Fine Arts

Black Forest-style carved hardwood cuckoo clock, 23" high, probably post-World War II, $200-250.
M. Moran and D. & L. Newquist

Right: Seth Thomas Art Nouveau gilt-metal clock, 12 1/2" high, ca. 1905, $392.
R.O. Schmitt Fine Arts

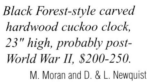

Left: German oak wall clock, plays Westminster chime, 31" high, ca. 1920, $644.
R.O. Schmitt Fine Arts

Gilded brass carriage clock, French, 7 1/2" high, ca. 1905, $2,576.
R.O. Schmitt Fine Arts

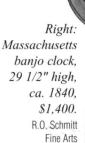

Right: Massachusetts banjo clock, 29 1/2" high, ca. 1840, $1,400.
R.O. Schmitt Fine Arts

Left: Seth Thomas "Office No. 5" model wall clock, 23 1/4" high, ca. 1910, $1,008.
R.O. Schmitt Fine Arts

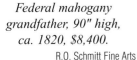

Federal mahogany grandfather, 90" high, ca. 1820, $8,400.
R.O. Schmitt Fine Arts

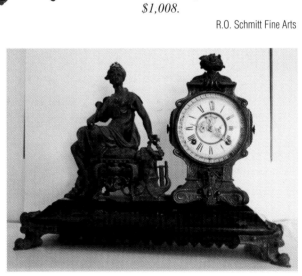

Ansonia Clock Co. "Opera" model cast-metal figural clock, 16 1/4" high, ca. 1885-95, $800-1,000.
M. Moran and D. & L. Newquist

Left: German bracket clock of mahogany and poplar, 17 1/2" high, ca. 1915, $532.
R.O. Schmitt Fine Arts

Right: French cartel wall clock, 28" high, ca. 1890, $532.
R.O. Schmitt Fine Arts

Left: Waltham Clock Co. George Washington banjo clock, 42" high, ca. 1930, $1,120.
R.O. Schmitt Fine Arts

Telechron Clock Co. electric clock with naval motif, 8 1/4" high, 1950s, $125.
M. Moran and E. & J. Schroeder

Haddon Clock Co. electric motion novelty clock, woman in window rocks and fire shimmers when clock is operating, 7 3/8" high, 20th century, $185.

M. Moran and E. & J. Schroeder

Left: E. Ingraham Co. pressed oak Spanish-American War commemorative clock, 23" high, 1898, $2,000-2,500.

M. Moran and D. & L. Newquist

Right: French annular dial clock of bronze, marble and cobalt blue enamel, 9 1/4" high, ca. 1895, $4,592.

R.O. Schmitt Fine Arts

Mantel garniture set with clock and pair of porcelain urns, clock is 15 1/2" high, French, ca. 1880, the set $1,400-1,500.

M. Moran and E. & J. Schroeder

Waterbury Clock Co. "Avignon" model clock, 17 1/2" high, ca. 1903, $599.

R.O. Schmitt Fine Arts

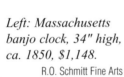

Jonathan C. Brown full-ripple onion-top clock, 19 3/4" high, ca. 1848, $3,808.
R.O. Schmitt Fine Arts

Forestville Mfg. Co. mahogany clock, 34" high, ca. 1845, $1,960.
R.O. Schmitt Fine Arts

Left: Massachusetts banjo clock, 34" high, ca. 1850, $1,148.
R.O. Schmitt Fine Arts

"Sambo" blinking eye novelty clock, painted cast iron, 16" high, ca. 1875, $1,960.
R.O. Schmitt Fine Arts

Tiffany & Company clock of green onyx with enamel-painted scenes, late 19th century, $2,100.
Gene Harris Antique Auction Center

Terry & Andrews mahogany ogee case clock, 26" high, ca. 1845, $280.
R.O. Schmitt Fine Arts

*Right: Waterbury Clock Co.
"Regulator No. 9" oak
model, 76 1/4" high,
ca. 1891, $15,680.*
R.O. Schmitt Fine Arts

*Left: Jennings Bros. Mfg. Co.
Art Nouveau gilt-spelter clock,
12" high, ca. 1900, $200.*
M. Moran and E. & J. Schroeder

*French lyre clock with blue cobalt
enameled case with gilt trim,
22" high, ca. 1785, $12,880.*
R.O. Schmitt Fine Arts

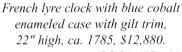

*Ithaca Calendar Clock Co.
"No. 6-1/2 Shelf Belgrade"
upright model, 32" high,
ca. 1880, $2,688.*
R.O. Schmitt Fine Arts

*Right: Austrian
novelty clock with
animated figure of
Tyrolean wood
cutter, 20" high,
ca. 1820, $2,240.*
R.O. Schmitt Fine Arts

Left: Upright mantel regulator with Sevres porcelain front and sides, 11 3/4" high, ca. 1900, $3,696.
R.O. Schmitt Fine Arts

Right: Ansonia Clock Co. "Fisher Swing" swinging arm clock, 22" high, ca. 1883, $3,696.
R.O. Schmitt Fine Arts

French Crystal Regulator, 15 1/2" high, early 20th century, $3,024.
R.O. Schmitt Fine Arts

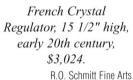

Left: Luman Watson grandfather clock with Federal cherry case with mahogany accents, 94" high, ca. 1820, $4,704.
R.O. Schmitt Fine Arts

Right: Ansonia Clock Co. "La Charny" model with Royal Bonn china case, 11 1/2" high, ca. 1905, $1,848.
R.O. Schmitt Fine Arts

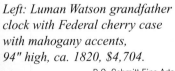

Right: New Haven Clock Co. "Welton" model banjo clock, 25" high, ca. 1940s, $150.
M. Moran and D. & L. Newquist

Waterbury Clock Co. black-painted wooden temple-style clock, 10 5/8" high, ca. 1900, $200-250.
M. Moran and D. & L. Newquist

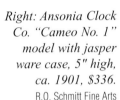

Right: Ansonia Clock Co. "Cameo No. 1" model with jasper ware case, 5" high, ca. 1901, $336.
R.O. Schmitt Fine Arts

Left: English mahogany bracket clock, 18 1/2" high, ca. 1910, $3,584.
R.O. Schmitt Fine Arts

French Victorian Renaissance Revival-style clock, third quarter 19th century, $5,200.
Gene Harris Antique Auction Center

*English walnut burl
wall clock, 31" high,
ca. 1870, $1,008.*
R.O. Schmitt Fine Arts

*Ansonia Clock Co. "La
Mine" model with Royal
Bonn china case,
13 1/2" high, ca. 1900,
$1,000-1,200.*
M. Moran and E. & J. Schroeder

*Seth Thomas Clock Co.
"Fashion No. 5"
calendar clock,
late 19th century, $2,400.*
Gene Harris Antique Auction Center

*Ornate brass French-
made wall clock,
22" high, ca. 1900,
$476.*
R.O. Schmitt Fine Arts

*New Haven Clock Co. Rococo-style gilt-spelter figural
clocks: 10" high, $250-300 (left); 11 1/4" high,
$400-500 (center); 6 1/2" high, $180-250 (right).*
M. Moran and E. & J. Schroeder

Right: New Haven Clock Co. oak long-case wall clock, 37 1/2" high, ca. 1910, $600-700.
M. Moran and D. & L. Newquist

Left: Seth Thomas "King Bee" model oak wall clock, 29 3/4" high, ca. 1905, $868.
R.O. Schmitt Fine Arts

Left: Frank Herschede Clock Co. "Model 215" mahogany grandfather, 80" high, ca. 1950, $2,464.
R.O. Schmitt Fine Arts

Right: Wm. L. Gilbert Clock Co. "Acheron" model clock in walnut, 19 1/4" high, late 19th century, $200-250.
M. Moran and E. & J. Schroeder

Seth Thomas temple-style clock, 13 1/2" high, early 20th century, $700-800.

M. Moran and E. & J. Schroeder

Left: Welch, Spring & Co. Victorian Renaissance Revival mahogany clock, 21" high, ca. 1880, $300-500.

M. Moran and E. & J. Schroeder

Waterbury Clock Co. "Regulator No. 20" wall clock, 38" high, ca. 1905, $1,456.

R.O. Schmitt Fine Arts

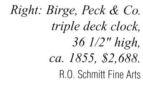

Right: Birge, Peck & Co. triple deck clock, 36 1/2" high, ca. 1855, $2,688.

R.O. Schmitt Fine Arts

Elmer O. Stennes "Massachusetts Shelf Clock" model, 39 1/2" high, ca. 1971, $4,256.

R.O. Schmitt Fine Arts

Left: Seth Thomas "beehive"-style clock, 14 3/4" high, ca. 1920, $600-700.

M. Moran and E. & J. Schroeder

Left: Bradley & Hubbard "Topsy" blinking eye novelty clock, painted cast iron, 17" high, ca. 1870, $2,352.

R.O. Schmitt Fine Arts

Ingraham Co. temple-style clock of black enamel over wood, 10 7/8" high, ca. 190, $300-400.

M. Moran and E. & J. Schroeder

Right: New Haven Clock Co. "Nason" model mahogany wall clock, 35 1/2" high, ca. 1913, $952.

R.O. Schmitt Fine Arts

Left: Elisha Neal pillar & scroll style clock, 31" high, ca. 1830, $2,016.

R.O. Schmitt Fine Arts

Left: Mastercrafter electric motion clocks, plastic cases, ca. 1950s, white church-form clock is 12" high and $125; brown fireplace-form clock is 10 1/2" high and $85.

M. Moran and E. & J. Schroeder

Left: Welsh, Spring & Co. regulator-calendar wall clock, 34" high, ca. 1872, $1,120.

R.O. Schmitt Fine Arts

E. Ingraham & Co. "Doric" model clock, 16 1/4" high, ca. 1870, $400.

M. Moran and D. & L. Newquist

Left: Wm. L. Gilbert Clock Co. "Regulator No. 11" Victorian Eastlake-style wall regulator clock, 50" high, ca. 1885, $2,000-2,2000.

M. Moran and D. & L. Newquist

Brewster & Ingrahams rosewood beehive clock, 19" high, ca. 1845, $560.

R.O. Schmitt Fine Arts

Right: Ansonia Clock Co., black-painted iron temple-style clock, 12 1/4" high, ca. 1900, $300-350.

M. Moran and D. & L. Newquist

Right: Seth Thomas Clock Co. "Regulator No. 2" oak wall clock, 36" high, ca. 1884, $1,000-1,200.
M. Moran and D. & L. Newquist

Left: Attleboro Clock Co. late Victorian Neo-Gothic oak clock, 22" high, $300-350.
M. Moran and D. & L. Newquist

Right: Ansonia Clock Co. "La Layon" model with Royal Bonn china case, 14 1/2" high, ca. 1910, $1,792.
R.O. Schmitt Fine Arts

Mastercrafter electric motion clocks, plastic, 10 3/4" high, ca. 1950s: children swinging (left), $180; girl on swing (center), $165; shimmering waterfall (right), $125.
M. Moran and E. & J. Schroeder

Left: Ansonia Clock Co. iron temple-style clock, 10 1/2" high, ca. 1900, $300-350.

M. Moran and
D. & L. Newquist

Ansonia Clock Co. bank/clock, gilt-spelter, 5 3/4" high, ca. 1920s, $100.

M. Moran and D. & L. Newquist

Left: Hanging oak kitchen-style wall clock attributed to E.N. Welch Mfg. Co., 27 3/4" high, late 19th century, $350-400.

M. Moran and D. & L. Newquist

Left: Victorian Neo-Gothic-style clock attributed to New Haven Clock Co., 22 1/4" high, $350-400.

M. Moran and
D. & L. Newquist

Ansonia Clock Co. "Tunis" model oak clock, 14" high, ca. 1880-1900, $250-300.

M. Moran and D. & L. Newquist

Fancy German Music Box Clock

Shelf or mantel clock, music box clock, fruitwood case w/domed top w/ring-turned finial & crosshatch & scroll carving w/matching corner finials above the stepped flaring cornice, a large brass bezel around the white dial w/Arabic numerals & scrolled brass spandrels flanked by ring-turned finials at each corner, flaring stepped base on small bun feet, eight-day movement, Germany, ca. 1930s, 4 1/4 x 7 1/4", 13" h. (ILLUS.) **250-300**

Shelf or mantel clock, National Electric Clock Co., "Queen" model, large upright flattened rectangular front cast overall w/fancy leafy scrolls & a cartouche at the center of the crest above the figures of standing women flanking the central round dial w/Arabic numerals, raised on a rectangular platform base w/scroll feet, illuminated, early 20th c., 10 1/2" h. **135**

Shelf or mantel clock, Neal (Elisha), New Hartford, Connecticut, pillar & scroll style, bonnet top w/three urn-form finials, body w/two-panel glass door w/dial above & reverse-painted tablet at bottom showing large house set on extensive grounds within a fancy border, oval cut-out in center shows pendulum, body flanked by two slender ring-turned columns, base w/valanced skirt & short tapered feet, square dial w/black Arabic numerals, delicate spandrels & center ring, time & strike movement, new reverse painting, left foot replaced, small veneer repair on skirt, label w/some tears & a missing piece, ca. 1830, 31" h. (ILLUS. top of next column) **2,016**

E. Neal Pillar & Scroll Shelf Clock

Shelf or mantel clock, Neoclassical-style, gilt-bronze, cloisonné & porcelain, the top w/a cloisonné-decorated figural urn finial w/scrolled handles & pedestal foot atop a domed cloisonné top above the upright case w/six cloisonné colonettes w/turned metal finials framing porcelain plaques decorated w/scenes of Neoclassical maidens, the beveled glass front & back showing the suspended works & round enameled dial w/Roman numerals centered by a group of cherubs & ornate metal pendulum, compressed knob metal feet, France, ca. 1900, 16" h. **3,105**

Unusual Victorian Neo-Gothic Clock

New Haven "Bernard Palissy" Clock

Shelf or mantel clock, New Haven Clock Co., New Haven, Connecticut (attributed), Victorian Neo-Gothic style walnut case, a steeply pointed top w/Gothic scroll cut-out border & trefoil finial flanked by sunburst side finials on thin blocks over roundels & shaped side panels w/incised scrolls, the tall steeply pointed door w/heavy molding around the glass decorated w/a fancy gilt stencil border band w/Oriental motifs, the dial w/a brass bezel & Roman numerals printed w/patent date "Feb. 11, 1879," brass pendulum w/unique inset compensating needle indicator, deep rectangular platform base w/incised scrolls, original finish, eight-day movement, time & strike, 4 3/4 x 14 5/8", 22 1/4" h. (ILLUS. on previous page) **350-400**

Shelf or mantel clock, New Haven Clock Co., New Haven, Connecticut, "Bernard Palissy" model, figural w/a cast metal gold-painted figure of a bearded man in Renaissance dress sitting on a stool at a round table w/spool base & reading papers, the upright clock next to figure w/an ornate gold-painted metal case w/footed notched disk-shaped crest w/C-scroll side handles & finial, hanging side decorations, outscrolled decorated base, the white porcelain dial w/brass bezel & center ring, beveled glass & black Arabic numerals, all on a black cast-iron rectangular base w/cast metal gilt leaf-form feet & front scroll decoration w/mask, eight-day time & strike movement, ca. 1900, 16" h. (ILLUS. top of page)....................................... **420**

New Haven Co. "Elbe" Clock

Shelf or mantel clock, New Haven Clock Co., New Haven, Connecticut, "Elbe" model, walnut case w/molded arching cornice featuring beading & urn-form decorations hanging from each side, leaf & scroll carved crest, rectangular body sits on stepped base w/urn-form side decorations sitting on square bases on each side, original painted dial w/Roman numerals, original tri-color glass panel in bottom, Gilbert patent indicator pendulum, eight-day time/strike/alarm movement, some flaking on dial, ca. 1880, 24" h. (ILLUS. on previous page) **280**

Shelf or mantel clock, New Haven Clock Co., New Haven, Connecticut, mahogany veneer, an upright rectangular ogee case surrounding the tall two-part glazed door, the upper section over the painted dial w/Roman numerals, the lower section w/a reverse-painted scene of a beehive, 30-hour movement, mid-19th c., 26" h.. **110**

Victorian Majolica Parlor Clock

Shelf or mantel clock, New Haven Clock Co., New Haven, Connecticut, majolica case w/ornate gilt scroll decoration & cobalt blue insets at top & bottom, pink swirled columns flank dial, clock rests on two scroll feet & apron, case marked "JDB/506" in porcelain, cream-colored porcelain dial w/fancy metal center & bezel, white surround w/gilt leaf border, black Arabic numerals, original hands & pendulum, eight-day time & strike movement w/rack & snail half hour striking, paper label inside rear door w/instructions, ca. 1900, 12" h. (ILLUS.).... **1,064**

Shelf or mantel clock, New Haven Clock Co., New Haven, Connecticut, miniature mahogany veneer ogee case, a two-pane glazed door, the upper pane over the painted metal dial w/Roman numerals & open escapement, the lower pane reverse-painted w/a colorful scene of a large castle against a light background, eight-day time & strike movement, good label inside, some touch-up on painted pane, ca. 1850, 18 1/4" h. **146**

Miniature Rosewood Ogee Clock

Shelf or mantel clock, New Haven Clock Co., New Haven, Connecticut, miniature upright ogee-style rosewood rectangular case, the tall glass door stenciled w/floral & geometric decoration below the round dial, the white dial w/brass bezel & center ring & black Roman numerals, miniature two-weight time & strike movement, some loss to rear label, ca. 1870, 21 1/2" h. (ILLUS.)... **728**

Shelf or mantel clock, New Haven Clock Co., New Haven, Connecticut, oak perpetual-calendar model, w/two parallel dials, inscribed lines, eight-day movement, time only, 14 x 13"....................................... **1,800**

Shelf or mantel clock, New Haven Clock Co., New Haven, Connecticut, Rococo-style gilt-spelter case, an ornate scroll crest above the round dial w/Arabic numerals supported by ornate openwork scrolls flanked by standing putti, on an oblong base decorated w/scrolls & on scroll feet, 30-hour movement, time & alarm, ca. 1900, 3 x 6 1/4", 10" h. (ILLUS. left, top of next page).............. **250-300**

Three Gilded New Haven Clocks

Shelf or mantel clock, New Haven Clock Co., New Haven, Connecticut, Rococo-style gilt-spelter case, an ornate scroll crest above the round dial w/Arabic numerals supported by ornate openwork scrolls on a small platform enclosing a h.p. porcelain plaque all flanked by figures of standing putti, pierced scroll apron & scroll feet, 30-hour movement, time & alarm, ca. 1900, 3 3/4 x 5", 11 1/4" h. (ILLUS. center, top of page) **400-500**

Shelf or mantel clock, New Haven Clock Co., New Haven, Connecticut, Rococo-style gilt-spelter case, an ornate scroll crest above the round dial w/Arabic numerals enclosed by cast flowers & raised on a ribbed stem-form support issuing leaf-form feet, a large standing Cupid at one side, 30-hour movement, time & alarm, ca. 1900, 2 1/4 x 3 1/4", 6 1/2" h. (ILLUS. right, top of page) **180-250**

Shelf or mantel clock, New Haven Clock Co., New Haven, Connecticut, rounded top mahogany case w/simple line inlay, the sides tapering down to a platform base w/brass feet, the brass bezel around a convex glass over the dial w/original moon hands, eight-day round time & strike movement w/cathedral gong, early 20th c., 11 1/2" h. **100-125**

Shelf or mantel clock, New Haven Clock Co., New Haven, Connecticut, spelter Art Nouveau-style case worn to copper color, long tapering bulbous form w/flower crest and cast floral & leaf relief decoration, on short tapering leaf-form feet, the original round paper dial w/brass bezel, black Arabic numerals, New Haven star logo & subsidiary seconds dial, 30-hour backwind movement complete w/winder & setting knob, ticks & stops, ca. 1910, 7 1/2" h. (ILLUS. below) **302**

Art Nouveau Spelter Shelf Clock

French "Bulle Dome" Mantel Clock

Shelf or mantel clock, "No. 100, Bulle Dome" model, unframed round dial raised on a cylindrical brass shaft attached to circular molded wooden base that also holds crossbar to which pendulum is attached, white dial w/open escapement & black Arabic numerals, battery-powered time & strike movement marked w/serial #66920, France, ca. 1935, 15 1/2" h. (ILLUS.) **840**

Shelf or mantel clock, North (Norris), Torrington, Connecticut, Classical mahogany & stenciled style case, the flat cornice above a two-pane glazed tall door w/the larger upper pane over the gilt-trimmed white-painted dial w/Arabic numerals above the lower panel reverse-painted w/a large round central reserve w/a bust portrait of an elegant lady framed by leafy scrolls, engaged black-painted stenciled columns down the sides, flat base, 30-hour movement, ca. 1825, 23 3/4" h. **4,888**

New Haven Clock Co. Majolica Clock

Shelf or mantel clock, New Haven Clock Co., New Haven, Connecticut, tall upright majolica case w/a high pointed palmette crest above a classical face all flanked by outswept scrolls above molded columns down the sides flanking the brass bezel & porcelain dial w/Arabic numerals, original hands & subsidiary seconds dial, molded platform base w/further leafy scroll decoration, case decorated in pale green, pink & brown, 30-hour movement, small re-glued chip on front corner of case, ca. 1904, 10 1/2" h. (ILLUS.) **392**

Shelf or mantel clock, New Haven Clock Company, New Haven, Connecticut, an upright oak framework w/stamped repeating scroll band border design & small block-footed base, the sides & front inset w/pottery tiles embossed w/flying putti under a maroon glossy glaze, the top also inset w/a scroll-molded tile, the front w/a round porcelain dial w/Arabic numerals & a brass bezel, tiles by the J. and J.G. Low Company, designed by Arthur Osborn, late 19th - early 20th c., 6 x 9", 12 1/4" h. (works reconditioned, hairline in front tile, hairlines in dial) **6,050**

Parker & Whipple Mantel Clock

Shelf or mantel clock, Parker & Whipple Mfg. Co., Meriden, Connecticut, tin-plated upright throne-form case w/a shingled slanting roof above ornately decorated sides w/lattice decoration, framing a rounded metal clock case w/Gothic arch trim & paper dial w/Arabic numerals & marked "A.E. Hotchkiss - Patent," on a stepped base, rare original combination winding-setting key, 30-hour backwind balance brass escapement, ca. 1900, 7 1/4" h. (ILLUS.) **336**

French Empire-style Shelf Clock

Shelf or mantel clock, Planchon, Paris, France, early Empire-style upright rectangular mahogany veneer case w/molded cornice, the tall, wide front centered by the signed white porcelain dial w/Roman numerals w/original hands & enclosed by a brass bezel, figural bronze lions lying on each side of the case resting on the deep platform base on bronze square wafer feet, eight-day signed time & strike movement, some cracks in veneer, missing molding above dial, ca. 1850, 14" h. (ILLUS. below left) **1,120**

French Pocket Watch-style Clock

Shelf or mantel clock, pocket watch-style, brass case on brass rococo stand w/scrolling floral legs & gilt finish, winding stem on top, porcelain dial w/Arabic numerals & ornate gilt metal center, eight-day movement, France, ca. 1905 (ILLUS.)................................. **252**

Shelf or mantel clock, portable model w/arched brass "Jump"-style case w/top handle for carrying, arched brass-framed glazed front over a time dial above a smaller round barometer dial, the time dial w/white chapter ring & black Roman numerals & marked "E. Bright - Brighton [England]," the smaller barometer dial w/white chapter ring & black Arabic numerals & text, both dials w/original hands, eight-day time-only key-wind movement, France, ca. 1910, 5 1/4" h. (ILLUS. top of next page) **672**

Portable Clock/Barometer

Shelf or mantel clock, Raingo Freres, Paris, France, Louis XVI-style white marble oblong case topped w/bronze figure of a reclining woman in draped robes looking at a branch of gilded leaves she holds in her hand, the body of the case w/panels decorated w/gilt bronze ornamentation, the center round dial bordered w/gilt swags & wreaths flanked by bronze figures of children, one reading a book, the other holding a globe, the white porcelain signed dial w/cobalt blue Roman numerals & finely chased & gilded hands, original signed time & strike movement w/silk thread suspension & count wheel strike on a bell, minor repairs to dial, ca. 1830, 20" h. (ILLUS. bottom of page) **4,480**

Shelf or mantel clock, Richmond Fabri, France, bronze & gilt-bronze, a tall rectangular plinth in bronze w/gilt-bronze scroll feet & applied band & pierced scroll mounts supporting a round gilt-bronze case enclosing the movement topped by a gilt-bronze figure of Cupid leaning on a bow, marked "Richmond Fabri," France, late 19th c., 4 1/2 x 8 1/4", 15 1/4" h. **1,430**

Shelf or mantel clock, "Ridgeway" walnut reproduction calendar shelf clock, eight-day movement, time & strike, 15 1/2 x 27" **300**

French Marble & Bronze Shelf Clock

French Rococo Gilt-metal Clock

Shelf or mantel clock, Rococo-style, gilt cast-metal case, upright rounded case w/a figural putto w/flowers at the top above a cartouche & slender scrolls down the sides framing the round porcelain dial w/Roman numerals, a porcelain panel in the lower case w/h.p. figural scenes, cast cartouche at apron continuing to incurved scroll feet, France, late 19th - early 20th c., 5 x 8", 16" h. (ILLUS.) **450**

Ornate French Clock with Figures

Shelf or mantel clock, Rococo-style, gilt cast-metal upright case, a small pierced urn finial & tall leafy scrolls on the pediment above the brass bezel enclosing the porcelain dial w/Arabic numerals above a lower inset h.p. porcelain plaque decoration w/an 18th c. courting scene, fitted at each side w/a large cast figure of a seated putto, one holding a bird's nest, the other a bird, the high blocked base centered by a cartouche & scrolls, France, late 19th c., 6 x 11 1/2", 18 1/4" h. (ILLUS. below left) **1,000-1,200**

French Art Deco Marble Shelf Clock

Shelf or mantel clock, Scherraus & Co., St. Gall, France, Art Deco mottled tan & black marble rounded arch case on square brass lozenge feet, long arched brass bezel around a beveled glass conforming pane over the conforming brass dial w/heavy stylized Roman numerals, original hands, signed "Gg. Scherraus & Co., St. Gall," time-only lever movement, hinged back door also made of marble, ca. 1930, 6 1/2" h. (ILLUS.) **784**

Shelf or mantel clock, Sessions Clock Co., Bristol, Connecticut, temple-style, hardwood case w/honey-colored varnish, serpentine top above the deep brass bezel & glass door opening to an ornate brass dial w/Arabic numerals flanked by pairs of celluloid half-columns w/brass capitals & bases, deep molded base w/gilt-metal scroll feet, lion head & ring end handles, incised line decoration on case, eight-day time & strike movement, ca. 1900, 7 1/4 x 18 3/4", 12 1/2" h. (ILLUS. top of next page) **200**

Sessions Temple-style Mantel Clock

Sessions "Unique #1" Model Clock

Shelf or mantel clock, Sessions Clock Co., Forestville, Connecticut, "Unique #1" model, oak paneled arched case w/conforming door w/glass pane w/silver pastoral scene w/windmill, the door frame w/beaded border, stepped base w/sawtooth band, round dial w/brass bezel & black Arabic numerals, sliver missing on back of case, door snap clip broken, ca. 1908, 17 1/4" h. (ILLUS.) **235**

Solomon C. Spring Shelf Clock

Shelf or mantel clock, Spring (Solomon C.) & Co., Bristol, Connecticut, tall upright rosewood veneer column-and-cornice case w/cove molded cornice & base accented w/darker wood, half-round front columns in darker wood w/gilt bases & baluster-form capitals flank the tall two-pane door, upper pane over the white dial w/delicate floral-painted spandrels, gilt center & black Roman numerals, original hands, the bottom tall pane reverse painted w/a landscape of a river w/trees & rocks along its banks in yellows, greens & browns, weights & pendulum, eight-day time & strike strap brass movement, inside paper label reads "From Smith's Clock Warehouse, Extra Eight Day Rolling Pinion Brass Clocks manufactured by S.C. Spring, successor to Birge, Peck & Co., for A.D. Smith, No. 12 East Fifth Street, Cincinnati, Ohio," center alarm disc & follower missing, paint flaking on dial, ca. 1865, 30 1/4" h. (ILLUS. on previous page).. **784**

merals & gold vining ornamentation of raised gesso underneath dial surrounding the signature, the tall, wide base section w/valanced skirt & French feet, numbered 18, time-only weight movement, weight & movement signed, ca. 1971, 39 1/2" h. (ILLUS. below left)...................... **4,256**

L. & J.G. Stickley Mission Oak Clock

Shelf or mantel clock, Stickley (L. & J.G.) Mission Oak rectangular case, the front w/a paneled opening for the copper dial w/Arabic numerals above a small six-pane glazed panel & a simple knob, early 20th c. (ILLUS.)... **9,200**

Elmer Stennes Federal-style Clock

Shelf or mantel clock, Stennes (Elmer O.), Weymouth, Massachusetts, "Massachusetts Shelf Clock" model, modern Federal-style mahogany case w/molded cornice, cut-out crest & finial, the tall upper section of the case w/an arched opening over white painted dial w/black Arabic nu-

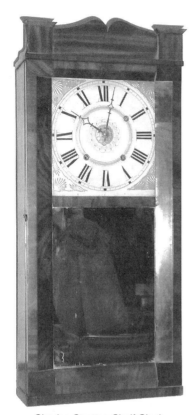

Charles Stratton Shelf Clock

Shelf or mantel clock, Stratton (Charles), Holden, Massachusetts, tall upright mahogany veneer rectangular case, the tall two-pane door w/the upper pane over the dial w/Roman numerals & gold-painted spandrels, long lower pane fitted w/a mirror, superb label, three-train internal alarm time & strike movement w/small weight, professionally refinished case, label dated 1836, 34 1/2" h. (ILLUS. left) **336**

Shelf or mantel clock, Telechron Clock Co., electric, the stained wood case center w/a large ship's wheel w/brass pegs enclosing the dial w/Arabic numerals, tapering sides & flat base w/metal ropetwist trim, 1950s, 4 1/4 x 16", 8 1/4" h. (ILLUS. bottom of page) **125**

Terry & Andrews Shelf Clock

Telechron Ship's Wheel Clock

Shelf or mantel clock, Terry & Andrews, Bristol, Connecticut, ogee mahogany veneer case w/a two-pane glazed door, the upper pane over the painted wood dial w/Roman numerals, the lower glass tablet w/reverse-painted floral decoration in diamond-shaped border, surrounded by floral spandrels on black background, 30-hour time & strike movement, original hands, weights & pendulum, some flaking, chips, dirt, ca. 1845, 26" h. (ILLUS. on previous page) **280**

Shelf or mantel clock, Terry & Andrews, Bristol, Connecticut, steeple model, the upright mahogany veneer case w/a pointed top flanked by small pointed finials above half-round columns flanking the two-pane glazed door, the upper pointed pane over the painted metal dial w/Roman numerals, the lower pane reverse-painted w/a scene of a hot air balloon & American flags, eight-day time & strike brass movement, ca. 1840, 20" h. **647**

Terry Clock Co. "Cottage" Clock

Shelf or mantel clock, Terry Clock Co., Pittsfield, Massachusetts, "Cottage" model, upright walnut case w/molded peaked pediment & carved decoration at top & sides, the glass door w/molded frame & squared-arch top over the signed luminous dial w/copper-color bezel & black Roman numerals, the lower glass w/gold stenciled decoration of a building in country setting w/"Cottage" stenciled across the top, beveled notched base w/molded bracket feet, time & strike movement, brown label on inside bottom of clock, luminous dial no longer active, ca. 1885, 21 3/4" h. (ILLUS.).. **560**

Shelf or mantel clock, Terry (E.) & Son, Plymouth, Connecticut, upright rectangular Classical mahogany veneer case, the flat serpentine crestrail stenciled w/fruit basket flanked by corner blocks above the case w/slender colonettes flanking the tall two-pane glazed door, the large upper pane over the painted wood dial w/Arabic numerals, the lower smaller pane reverse-painted w/a repainted landscape w/building, on carved paw front feet, partial label inside, 30-hour wood time & strike movement, minor veneer damage, ca. 1830-40, 28 1/2" h. **478**

Shelf or mantel clock, Terry (Eli) and Sons, Plymouth, Connecticut, pillar-and-scroll mahogany veneer case, the scrolled pediment w/three small brass urn-form finials above a wide two-pane glazed door opening to a white dial w/Roman numerals above a lower églomisé panel decorated w/a landscape of a small white house by a road w/trees & an oval central pendulum window, flanked by slender colonettes, on a narrow molded base & serpentine apron w/slender French feet, wooden 30-hour movement, paper label, ca. 1810-15, 31 1/4" h. (some restoration) **1,955**

Fine Classical Eli Terry Clock

Shelf or mantel clock, Terry (Eli) & Co., Plymouth, Connecticut, Classical style mahogany veneer stenciled case, the flat scalloped pediment stenciled w/a fruit-filled compote & leaves flanked by corner blocks above half-round columns flanking the tall two-pane door, the top glazed pane over a wooden painted dial w/Arabic numerals & gilt spandrels, the lower pane w/a mirror, flat base w/stenciled corner blocks, ivory keyhole escutcheon, eight-day movement, time & strike, ca. 1845, 5 3/8 x 16 1/2", 35" h. (ILLUS. on previous page) **900-1,000**

Shelf or mantel clock, Terry (Eli) Jr., Plymouth, Connecticut, carved mahogany Classical style case w/a carved eagle crest above a two-pane long door opening to a painted dial w/Roman numerals flanked by leaf-carved half-columns, small paw-carved front feet, label inside, eight-day wooden works, first half 19th c., 37" h. (finials missing)...................................... **440**

Early Eli Terry Shelf Clock

Shelf or mantel clock, Terry (Eli), Plymouth, Connecticut, mahogany case, a flat rectangular cornice above a glazed two-section door w/the upper large section over a painted & gilt wooden dial & a 30-hour wooden weight-driven movement w/outside escapement, the lower pane of the door reverse-painted w/a landscape w/buildings, the door flanked by freestanding colonettes on a flat molded base, engraved label inside reads "Patent invented, made and sold by Eli Terry, Plymouth Connecticut," ca. 1817-18, old finish, imperfections, 16" w., 20 3/4" h. (ILLUS.)...................................... **4,255**

Shelf or mantel clock, Terry (Eli), Plymouth, Connecticut, miniature pillar-and-scroll mahogany case, the swan's-neck cresting above a two-pane glazed door, the upper pane over the painted dial w/Arabic numerals & decorated spandrels, the lower pane reverse-painted w/a landscape showing a classical building, slender colonettes down the sides, molded base, shaped apron & slender French feet, old refinish, 30-hour movement, minor imperfections, ca. 1822, 22 1/2" h. **7,455**

Eli Terry Outside Escapement Clock

Shelf or mantel clock, Terry (Eli), Plymouth, Connecticut, rare outside escapement pillar-and-scroll clock, mahogany veneer on butternut secondary wood case, broken-scroll crest w/urn finial & matching smaller corner finials, slender ring-turned columns flanking door w/two old glass panes & original brass door turn, top pane over the dial w/black Roman numerals & delicate pale pink & green floral spandrels & cartouche w/decorations in similar colors, the lower pane w/metallic scalloped border around reverse-painted pastoral scene w/house, bordered oval window in center for pendulum, molded base w/ogee apron & slender tapered legs, top of door is stamped "XXI," original label, time & strike movement, lower pane repainted, left scroll cracked & repaired, tip of right scroll replaced, three mahogany wood finials old but probably replaced brass finials, edge of both dial stiffeners & inside of bottom door stretcher shaved, one section of the backboard behind the movement replaced, ca. 1817, 28 3/4" h. (ILLUS.)...................................... **10,080**

Shelf or mantel clock, Terry (Eli) & Son, Plymouth, Connecticut, Classical style carved mahogany case, a large carved spread-winged eagle & leaves cornice flanked by corner blocks above half-round acanthus leaf-carved & ring-turned columns flanking a two-pane door, the upper pane over the dial w/Arabic numerals & painted flowers in the spandrels, time & strike movement, the lower door pane reverse-painted w/a landscape w/a large white building & trees framed w/a black geometric border band, an oval pendulum window above the building, on small paw front feet, ca. 1830s, 4 x 18", 31" h.. **2,240**

Shelf or mantel clock, Terry (Eli) & Sons, Plymouth, Connecticut, Classical style upright mahogany veneer case, the top w/a serpentine splat w/original stenciled decoration flanked by corner blocks above half-round columns flanking the tall, wide two-pane glazed door, the large upper pane over the painted wood dial w/Roman numerals, the shorter rectangular lower pane repainted w/a landscape scene, on carved paw front feet, good label inside, 30-hour wood time & strike movement, minor damage to foot, ca. 1830-40, 28 1/2" h......................... **1,575**

Shelf or mantel clock, Terry (Eli) & Sons, Plymouth, Connecticut, pillar-and-scroll style, mahogany veneer, the broken-scroll crest fitted w/three replaced brass urn finials above the case w/two slender colonettes flanking the two-pane glazed door over the upper dial w/Arabic numerals, the lower short pane w/worn reverse-painting, molded base on scalloped apron & small French feet, original paper label on interior, w/weights, key & pendulum, early 19th c., 32" h. (refinished, professional restoration).................................... **1,430**

Shelf or mantel clock, Terry (Henry), Plymouth, Connecticut, miniature upright ogee model, the rectangular mahogany veneer case w/a tall two-pane glazed door, the upper pane over the repainted wood dial w/Roman numerals, the larger lower pane reverse-painted w/a colorful landscape w/building, partial label inside, 30-hour brass time & strike movement by S.B. Terry, lower pane cracked, mid-19th c., 19 3/4" h... **759**

Shelf or mantel clock, Terry (S.B.) & Co., Terryville, Connecticut, simple upright oak rectangular case w/molded cornice & base, round dial w/molded brass bezel & white paper dial w/black Roman numerals & subsidiary seconds dial, small lower round glass-paned panel w/brass frame shows decorated pendulum bob, double-spring eight-day time-only movement w/springs behind the backplate, some wear to dial, ca. 1855, 12 1/4" h. (ILLUS. below left) **672**

Shelf or mantel clock, Terry (Samuel), Bristol, Connecticut, upright mahogany veneer Classical transitional case, carved eagle crest above applied half-columns flanking the tall two-pane glazed door, the upper pane over the paper dial, the lower pane w/original reverse-painted decoration, original pendulum, weights & moon hands, paper label inside, 30-hour wood works, early 19th c., 29" h.................... **750-1,000**

Shelf or mantel clock, Terry (Samuel), Plymouth, Connecticut, Federal pillar-and-scroll type, mahogany, scroll-cut cresting joining three brass urn finials above the glazed door enclosing a 30-hour wooden weight-driven movement & a polychrome & gilt-decorated dial w/Roman numerals, the lower door tablet decorated w/a colorful églomisé landscape, slender free-standing columns at the sides, molded base w/scalloped apron & slender bracket feet, old refinish, ca. 1825, 32" h. (minor restorations) **4,255**

S.B. Terry Oak Shelf Clock   *Terryville Mfg. Steeple Clock*

Shelf or mantel clock, Terryville Manufacturing Co., Terryville, Connecticut, rosewood steeple-style case w/two-pane glazed door, upper pane over the white dial w/Roman numerals, the lower pane decorated w/an etched center rectangular scene of a fountain framed by scrolls, clean label, 30-hour time & strike movement features springs behind the backplate, some restoration, tips on steeples have been replaced, ca. 1855, 19 1/2" h. (ILLUS. on previous page) **308**

Shelf or mantel clock, Thomas (Seth) Clock Co., Plymouth, Connecticut, Art Nouveau style, upright bronzed cast-metal case decorated up one side w/a standing nude female w/leafy vines continuing around the sides, a shell design below the dial, brass bezel around the dial w/Arabic numerals, eight-day time & strike movement, early 20th c., 11 1/4" h. **315**

Seth Thomas "Atlas" Parlor Clock

French "Astronomer" Figural Clock

Shelf or mantel clock, "The Astronomer" figural clock, bronze & ormolu case, a cast & gilded round dial w/floral center & cast blossom bezel w/black Roman numerals & signed "LeRoy, Paris," raised atop a bronze column w/ormolu ribbon & fruit-filled urn trim, standing next to a rose-garlanded cherub standing beside a telescope & globe on columnar base, all atop a deep rectangular platform base w/a blossom & leaf band across the front, the beveled base molding on ornate triangular feet, silk thread time & strike movement bears number "123," some repairs, compass missing from figure's hand, France, ca. 1830, 14" h. (ILLUS.) **2,520**

Shelf or mantel clock, Thomas (Seth) Clock Co., Plymouth, Connecticut, Art Nouveau style, gilt-metal, figural, a female figure in a flowing gown resting on a foliate-form standard w/round clock face, white enameled dial w/black numerals, Seth Thomas works, early 20th c., 10 3/4" h. (minor spotting & gilt wear) **173**

Shelf or mantel clock, Thomas (Seth) Clock Co., Plymouth, Connecticut, "Atlas" model, walnut case w/molded arched crest & corner ringed finials on pediment, three-quarter round ring-turned columns at each corner of body flank the door w/bronze decoration on glass over the white dial w/black Roman numerals, nickel-plated gong base & pendulum, cove molding to beveled rectangular base w/square wafer feet, original black label inside, eight-day time & strike movement, gong striking on the quarter hour, hour hand replaced, ca. 1886, 22 1/2" h. (ILLUS.) **1,792**

Shelf or mantel clock, Thomas (Seth) Clock Co., Plymouth, Connecticut, "Bee" model, upright ebonized wood case w/inlaid flowers & bees, embossed flowers & vines in friezes above & below the face, cast brass bezel w/beveled glass over the signed porcelain dial, interior key & pendulum storage area, fifteen day movement w/cathedral gong, late 19th c., 15 1/2" h. **400-450**

Fine Thomas Late Beehive Clock

Shelf or mantel clock, Thomas (Seth) Clock Co., Plymouth, Connecticut, "beehive" style, the upright peaked walnut case w/a glass door opening to a steel dial w/Arabic numerals & small speed & chime adjustment dials all backed by ornately scroll-incised gilt brass, molded base, eight-day movement w/Westminster chimes, ca. 1920, 7 3/4 x 10 1/2", 14 3/4" h. (ILLUS.) **600-700**

Shelf or mantel clock, Thomas (Seth) Clock Co., Plymouth, Connecticut, bird's-eye maple & mahogany veneer, upright ogee case w/maple front sides & mahogany banding, a single tall two-pane glazed door, the upper glass over the painted dial w/Roman numerals, the lower pane reverse-painted in color w/a scene of the Baltimore cemetery, 30-hour works, mid-19th c., 26" h. **121**

Shelf or mantel clock, Thomas (Seth) Clock Co., Plymouth, Connecticut, "Chime Clock No. 1" model, temple-style adamantine mahogany case w/slightly arched molded pediment engraved w/scrolling line decoration, the inset dial section flanked by gold-painted brass reeded Corinthian columns, the signed white porcelain dial w/brass bezel & black Arabic numerals, on a molded block base w/tiny brass ball feet, time & strike movement w/four-bell Sonora chime that plays Westminster tune, some tiny chips & splits on case, ca. 1910, 12 1/2" h. (ILLUS. below left) **487**

Seth Thomas Chiming Shelf Clock

Shelf or mantel clock, Thomas (Seth) Clock Co., Plymouth, Connecticut, "Chime Clock No. 11" model, unadorned simple domed mahogany case, silvered dial w/brass bezel & black Arabic numerals, molded base on small button feet, eight-day time/chime/strike movement w/five-bell Sonora chime, ca. 1915, 13 1/4" h. (ILLUS.) **756**

Seth Thomas "Chime Clock No. 1"

Seth Thomas "Chime Clock No. 51"

Shelf or mantel clock, Thomas (Seth) Clock Co., Plymouth, Connecticut, "Chime Clock No. 51" model, temple-style quarter-sawn oak case w/molded pediment & cornice w/gentle dome & molded sides, the silvered metal round dial w/brass bezel & black Arabic numerals, the body w/ribbed panels on either side of dial, on stepped molded base on square wafer feet, time/chime/strike movement w/four-bell Sonora chime that plays Westminster tune, ca. 1913 (ILLUS. on previous page) **532**

Thomas Classical Revival Clock

Shelf or mantel clock, Thomas (Seth) Clock Co., Plymouth, Connecticut, Classical Revival mahogany veneer case, the deep blocked ogee cornice above a long door w/a large pane over a short rectangular mirrored pane, the large repainted dial w/Roman numerals, door flanked by colonettes w/gilt capitals & bases, ogee blocks at the base flanking a set-back panel w/a round pendulum window, eight-day movement, strike & alarm, ca. 1900, 4 7/8 x 10 3/4", 16" h. (ILLUS.)............ **175**

Seth Thomas Classical Revival Clock

Shelf or mantel clock, Thomas (Seth) Clock Co., Plymouth, Connecticut, Classical Revival tall case, mahogany veneer, the deep ogee cornice w/blocked corners above a pair of gilt columns flanking the two-pane door, the large upper pane over the worn painted metal dial w/Roman numerals, clear lower pane, the lower section w/ogee corner blocks flanking a panel w/a small round pendulum window, eight-day movement, time & strike, some veneer damage, last quarter 19th c., 4 1/2 x 8 1/2", 16" h. (ILLUS.)......................... **225**

Thomas Late Classical Shelf Clock

Shelf or mantel clock, Thomas (Seth) Clock Co., Plymouth, Connecticut, Classical-style ogee rosewood veneer case, the front w/rounded molding around the two-pane long door w/rounded molding, the upper pane over the painted metal dial w/Roman numerals, the lower pane showing the pendulum & works, eight-day movement, time, strike & alarm, face wear, ca. 1880, 4 x 10 3/4 x 16 1/2" h. (ILLUS. on previous page) **200-250**

Fine Early Thomas Two-deck Clock

Shelf or mantel clock, Thomas (Seth) Clock Co., Plymouth, Connecticut, Classical-style two-deck decorated mahogany veneer case, the deep ogee blocked top above large gilt-decorated half-round columns flanking the tall two-pane door, the upper pane over the dial w/Roman numerals, the lower pane decorated w/elaborate reverse-painted gilt decor of a scalloped frame enclosing lattice centered by a colored urn of flowers, the deep lower case w/heavy ogee scrolls flanking a small glazed door reverse-painted w/further gilt stencil decoration centering a diamond & bowl of colored flowers, flat base, dated 1863, eight-day movement, time & strike, original finish, 5 1/8 x 18 1/2", 32 1/2" (ILLUS.) **1,200-1,500**

Shelf or mantel clock, Thomas (Seth) Clock Co., Plymouth, Connecticut, Federal pillar-and-scroll type, mahogany, scroll-cut cresting joining three brass urn finials above the glazed door enclosing a 30-hour wooden weight-driven movement & a polychrome & gilt-decorated dial w/Roman numerals, the lower door tablet decorated w/a colorful landscape, slender free-standing columns at the

sides, molded base w/scalloped apron & slender bracket feet, old refinish, ca. 1825, 32" h. (minor imperfections) **2,185**

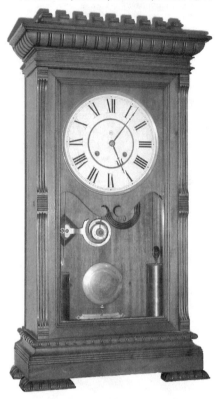

Seth Thomas "Garfield" Clock

Shelf or mantel clock, Thomas (Seth) Clock Co., Plymouth, Connecticut, "Garfield" model, tall upright walnut case w/crenelated cornice on notched molding, a tall door w/glass pane w/ogee contour over the dial w/brass bezel & center ring & black Roman numerals above the pendulum & bob w/damascene pattern, the case w/ribbing at sides & notched border at bottom, molded base w/notched wafer feet, original weights & pendulum, two-weight eight-day time & strike movement, ca. 1880, 29" h. (ILLUS.) **2,464**

"Good Luck" Mantel Clock

Shelf or mantel clock, Thomas (Seth) Clock Co., Plymouth, Connecticut, "Good Luck" metal clock framed by horseshoe, 30-hour movement, time only, 7 1/2 x 9" (ILLUS. on previous page) **50**

Thomas Domed Mahogany Clock

Shelf or mantel clock, Thomas (Seth) Clock Co., Plymouth, Connecticut, mahogany, the angled domed case top above a conforming glazed door opening to a dial w/Roman numerals above a brass & silvered metal pendulum w/inset brass star, rectangular stepped base, paper label inside, eight-day movement, time & strike, 1850-80, 4 3/4 x 10 3/8", 16" h. (ILLUS.) **150**

Seth Thomas "Lincoln" Shelf Clock

Shelf or mantel clock, Thomas (Seth) Clock Co., Plymouth, Connecticut, "Lincoln" model, tall upright walnut case w/molded pediment w/small knob corner finials, the tall glass-paned door w/contour top edge over the white dial w/brass bezel & center ring & black Roman numerals above the pendulum & bob w/damascene pattern, the case w/ribbed sides & the stepped base w/scrolled floral decorations at the sides, original weights, about 2/3 of label remains in case bottom, two-weight eight-day time & strike movement, ca. 1880, 27" h. (ILLUS.).................................... **2,464**

Seth Thomas Columned Shelf Clock

Shelf or mantel clock, Thomas (Seth) Clock Co., Plymouth, Connecticut, mahogany case w/stepped cornice & base, gilt half-round columns flanking dial & tablet, the white dial w/Roman numerals & delicate spandrels, the lower tablet w/reverse-painted earth-tone bird in border of rust & gold scallops, 30-hour time & strike signed movement, label, some wear & minor flaking to tablet, ca. 1860, 25" h. (ILLUS.).............. **280**

Fine Quality Chiming Thomas Clock

Shelf or mantel clock, Thomas (Seth) Clock Co., Plymouth, Connecticut, metal-front, nickel plating over brass, minute hand, time & alarm, 7 x 9" **145**

Seth Thomas "Orchid No. 4" Clock

Shelf or mantel clock, Thomas (Seth) Clock Co., Plymouth, Connecticut, "Orchid No. 4" model, brass rectangular case w/stepped cornice & beveled base w/block feet & apron, beveled glass front & side panels, porcelain dial w/Arabic numerals & original hands, simulated mercury pendulum, eight-day crystal regulator movement, left glass panel appears to be replacement, chip on one glass vial on pendulum, ca. 1909, 10 3/4" h. (ILLUS. left) **280**

Shelf or mantel clock, Thomas (Seth) Clock Co., Plymouth, Connecticut, "Prospect #1" model, Gothic-style mahogany case, time & strike, ca. 1910, 13 1/2" h. **190**

Thomas Rosewood Cottage Clock

Shelf or mantel clock, Thomas (Seth) Clock Co., Plymouth, Connecticut, round-topped rosewood veneer case, the front forms a door w/a molded ring around the dial w/Roman numerals, eight-day movement, time & strike, ca. 1865, 4 x 8 3/8", 12 1/4" h. (ILLUS.) **200**

Fine Seth Thomas Temple Clock

Shelf or mantel clock, Thomas (Seth) Clock Co., Plymouth, Connecticut, simulated adamantine wood finish on temple-style case, gently arched top w/flat cornice above the blocked case centering a brass-framed glass door over the porcelain dial w/Arabic numerals, deep platform base on tiny brass knob feet, eight-day movement, time & strike w/Sonora chimes, early 20th c., 7 x 15 1/4", 13 1/2" h. (ILLUS. top of previous page) **700-800**

Shelf or mantel clock, Thomas (Seth) Clock Co., Plymouth, Connecticut, tall upright painted wood Classical style case, a rounded crestrail w/original basket & leaf stenciling flanked by corner blocks over half-round painted columns flanking the tall, wide two-pane glazed door, the larger upper pane over the painted wooden dial w/Roman numerals, floral-painted spandrels & a painted ring of flowers in the center, the short horizontal lower pane reverse-painted w/a colorful landscape scene, on carved paw front feet, good label inside, 30-hour wooden time & strike movement, ca. 1830-40, 29" h. **563**

Shelf or mantel clock, Thomas (Seth) Clock Co., Plymouth, Connecticut, tall upright rosewood case w/square molded pediment, paneled half columns at the sides flanking an octagonal glass over the dial w/black Roman numerals, two lower glass panes, a central rectangular one & a large octagonal lower one, each decorated w/gilt leaf & scroll designs on black, weight time & strike movement, some veneer loss & chips to case, long scratch across top pane, ca. 1863, 30 1/2" h. (ILLUS. next column) **700**

Shelf or mantel clock, Thomas (Seth) Clock Co., Plymouth, Connecticut, temple-style case, beige marbleized wood w/cast-metal scroll feet & lion heads at each end, flat rectangular top w/a stepped cornice over the blocked center w/an ornate brass bezel & dial flanked by stepped-back side panels w/applied gilt-metal scroll cartouches, a deep molded

flat base, eight-day movement, time & strike, ca. 1890, 7 x 16 1/2", 10 3/4" h. (ILLUS. at top of page) **250-300**

Seth Thomas Rosewood Shelf Clock

Shelf or mantel clock, Thomas (Seth) Clock Co., Plymouth, Connecticut, "The Whistler" model, gilt-finished metal, eight-day movement, time only, 14" h. **500**

Seth Thomas "Tory" Shelf Clock

Shelf or mantel clock, Thomas (Seth) Clock Co., Plymouth, Connecticut, "Tory" model, upright mahogany case w/molded arched top, the signed white porcelain dial w/Arabic numerals within a brass bezel & beveled glass, the sides of the case w/pierced brass frets, floral & line inlay below dial, molded base on brass ball feet, eight-day time & strike movement strikes on a coiled flat wire cathedral gong, minor corner abrasion, original silk needs replacing in side frets, ca. 1909, 13 1/2" h. (ILLUS.) **420**

Shelf or mantel clock, Thomas (Seth) Clock Co., Plymouth, Connecticut, "Whitby" model, mahogany case w/rounded arch top, a cast-brass bezel & beveled glass over the dial, cast brass feet, eight-day time & strike movement, late 19th c., 12" h. **300-350**

Shelf or mantel clock, Thomas (Seth) Clock Co., Plymouth Hollow, Connecticut, simple upright rectangular rosewood case w/heavy ogee base, a two-pane glass door w/a large square pane over the white dial w/delicate floral spandrels & black Roman numerals, original hands w/"S" & "T" tips, a narrow horizontal lower rectangular pane decorated w/a stylized mask & shell flute design, signed 30-hour time-only movement, minor chips, some paint loss to dial, ca. 1863, 9" h. (ILLUS. top of next column) **459**

Seth Thomas Ogee-base Shelf Clock

Seth Thomas "Arch Top" Shelf Clock

Shelf or mantel clock, Thomas (Seth) Clock Co., Thomaston, Connecticut, "Arch Top" model, mahogany case w/stepped rectangular top over arched molding, round upper molding enclosing the round white dial w/brass bezel & center & black Roman numerals, lower body w/raised rectangular molding panel, base w/squat ogee bracket feet, eight-day time & strike movement w/alarm, some paint loss to dial, veneer chips, ca. 1885, 15 1/2" h. (ILLUS.) **700**

Fine Thomas Black Onyx Clock

Shelf or mantel clock, Thomas (Seth) Clock Co., Thomaston, Connecticut, black onyx case w/stepped top mounted w/a brass compote finial, the body of the case w/rounded sides & gilt-trimmed incised scrolls flanking the brass bezel & white dial w/Roman numerals, long base w/brass scrolls flanking the dial, raised on low gilt-brass feet w/a gilt-brass apron boss, made for Mitchell, Vane & Co., New York, eight-day time & strike movement, ca. 1900, 4 5/8 x 15 3/4", 13 3/4" h. (ILLUS. top of page)...................... **400**

Shelf or mantel clock, Thomas (Seth) Clock Company, Plymouth, Connecticut, arched & angled rosewood veneer case, the front door w/an octagonal frame enclosing the worn painted dial w/Roman numerals above a narrow panel enclosing a mirror, deep molded flat base, 30-hour movement, time & strike, ca. 1840-60, 3 3/4 x 7", 9 1/2" h. (ILLUS.) **200-250**

Nice Seth Thomas Cottage Clock

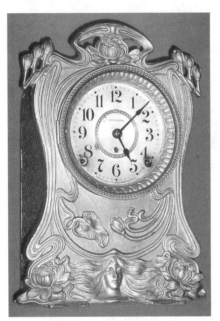

Art Nouveau Mantel Clock

Shelf or mantel clock, Thomas (Seth) Clock Company, Plymouth, Connecticut, gilt white metal case heavily embossed w/Art Nouveau floral & whiplash decoration, the head of a woman w/long flowing hair forming the base, white dial w/Arabic numerals & ribbed bezel, eight-day time & strike movement w/gong sounding on the hour & bell on the half hour, gold paint not original, ca. 1905, 12 1/2" h. (ILLUS.) **392**

Carved Seth Thomas Shelf Clock

Shelf or mantel clock, Thomas (Seth), Plymouth, Connecticut, Classical style mahogany veneer upright rectangular case w/ornately carved scroll pediment & molded corner blocks, the case w/elaborately carved half-round columns flanking the two-pane door, the large upper pane over the dial w/gold spandrels & center gold ring of leaf decoration surrounding a basket w/flowers, black Arabic numerals, the rectangular lower pane reverse-painted w/a scene of sailing ships at sea within a gilt sawtoothed border, molded flat base w/carved front paw feet, 30-hour short-pendulum time & strike movement, the bell replaced w/an early heavy gong, only fragment of label remains, ca. 1830, 29 3/4" h. (ILLUS. below left) **1,232**

Seth Thomas "Column" Clock

Shelf or mantel clock, Thomas (Seth), Plymouth, Connecticut, "Column" model, rectangular wooden case w/stepped cornice & base, two three-quarter round faux shell columns flanking the two-pane glazed door, the upper pane over the white dial w/Roman numerals & delicate spandrels, the lower pane w/reverse-painted design in blue, green & gold, movement & label signed "Plymouth Hollow," two-weight 30-hour time & strike movement, ca. 1860, 25" h. (ILLUS.) **308**

Federal-style Mahogany Mantel Clock

Shelf or mantel clock, Thomas (Seth), Plymouth, Connecticut, Federal-style, mahogany pillar-and-scroll case, the scrolled cresting joining three plinths & brass urn finials above the glazed door & églomisé tablet showing a town green flanked by freestanding columns, the gilt & polychrome dial w/a basket of flowers decoration housing the wooden 30-hour weight-driven movement, all resting on cut-out bracket feet, old finish, ca. 1825, tablet w/paint loss, 31 1/2" h. (ILLUS.) **2,415**

Rare Eli Terry Patent Box Clock

Shelf or mantel clock, Thomas (Seth), Plymouth, Connecticut, rare Eli Terry patent "Box Clock," simple rectangular wooden frame w/single band of molding at edges, door w/glass reverse-painted w/dial w/Ar-

abic numerals & floral spandrels, the works visible through the dial, engraved label stating that the clock was patented by Eli Terry but made & sold by Seth Thomas visible through lower part of door beneath dial, rack & snail strap wood movement, original weights w/integral pulleys, numerals & spandrels repainted, ca. 1816, 20" h. (ILLUS. below left) **58,240**

Seth Thomas "Turin" Mantel Clock

Shelf or mantel clock, Thomas (Seth), Plymouth, Connecticut, "Turin" model, mahogany temple-style case w/a flat top w/molded cornice above the front w/chamfered front corners flanking a brass bezel & round glass door over the white porcelain dial w/black Arabic numerals, ogee molding connecting body to beveled base, lozenge feet, time & strike movement, ca. 1909, 8 3/4" h. (ILLUS.) **392**

Seth Thomas Eagle Crest Shelf Clock

Shelf or mantel clock, Thomas (Seth), Plymouth, Connecticut, upright mahogany & mahogany veneer case w/carved spread-winged eagle crest flanked by molded corner blocks, the case w/two half-round columns w/baluster-form capitals & ringed knob bases flanking the two-pane door, the large upper pane over the cream dial w/delicate pink & green floral spandrels, decorative center ring & black Arabic numerals, the horizontal smaller lower pane reverse-painted w/a central landscape showing a columned building w/tree in foreground, an oval center opening for viewing the pendulum, the scene framed by a leaf border on a black ground, carved front paw feet, 30-hour time & strike movement, clean label, dust cover to back of movement missing, minor flaking on lower pane, ca. 1830, 29 1/4" h. (ILLUS. on previous page) **896**

Thomas "Ding Dong" Mantel Clock

Shelf or mantel clock, Thomas (Seth), Thomaston, Connecticut, "Ding Dong" model, Adamantine veneer w/rosewood finish, rectangular case w/slightly arched top & beveled base, dial w/Arabic numerals & "Seth Thomas - Ding Dong Strike" under the 12, partial label on rear cover, time & strike movement, strikes on two cupped bells mounted to the side of the movement, ca. 1910, 11 1/4" h. (ILLUS.) **470**

Seth Thomas "Flautist" Clock

Shelf or mantel clock, Thomas (Seth) & Sons Co., New York, New York, "Pattern #8228 'The Flautist'" model, gilt-metal case, the top set w/a tall figure of a woman in classical robes sitting in a chair & holding a flute, the central case enclosing the signed dial w/brass bezel & black Roman numerals, the case sides flaring toward the base & embellished w/applied masks on sides & scroll design on front all flanked by serpents whose bodies scroll downward, the rectangular stepped-out case base tapering in at the sides & raised on scroll & block feet, time & strike round movement, hands replaced, ca. 1875, 18" h. (ILLUS.) **560**

Fine Enamel & Onyx Clock

Shelf or mantel clock, Tiffany & Company, New York, New York, an upright rectangular case w/a stepped green onyx top mounted w/a gilt metal spread-winged eagle, the base also of green onyx, the sides of the case w/h.p. enamel-painted romantic scenes, dial w/Roman numerals & the Tiffany name, artist-signed panels, late 19th c. (ILLUS. on previous page) **2,100**

Gothic Revival Shelf Clock

Shelf or mantel clock, Victorian Gothic Revival style, carved mahogany, the case carved in the form of a Gothic arch w/three spires enclosing a glazed arch door over the engraved silver dial w/Roman numerals & a small seconds dial, blocked base, French two-train half-strike movement, retailed by Shreve, Crump & Low, late 19th c., 19 1/2" h. (ILLUS.) **805**

Shelf or mantel clock, Victorian temple-style, black marble case w/peaked pediment line-incised decor & mother-of-pearl inlay above a round dial w/open escapement & Roman numerals flanked by further inlay, wider platform base w/line-incised decor & central roundel, ca. 1880, 6 x 8", 10" h. (ILLUS. left with triple-decker clock on page 116) **400**

Shelf or mantel clock, Vincenti, France, white marble & bronze portico clock topped by footed urn-form crest w/C-scroll side handles & lyre-form bronze finial, the dial supported between two marble columns w/bronze ring-turned capitals & bases, the round white porcelain dial w/bronze bezel & surrounded w/bronze ribbon & garland decoration & w/black Roman numerals for hours, minutes in Arabic numerals in outside ring in increments of 5, all above the pendulum & pendulum bob in the form of mask w/sunburst frame, beveled marble rectangular platform base w/bead border & panel of bronze floral decoration on front, on bronze ringed knob feet, time & bell-strike movement, F/S rod missing from top of the movement, minor abrasion to dial, ca. 1885, 16 1/2" h. (ILLUS.) **448**

Marble & Bronze Portico Clock

Shelf or mantel clock, Vosburgh (Wm. C.), New York, New York, rosewood rounded Gothic form case, door w/upper pane over the dial & the lower pane w/a re-painted scene, paper label inside, eight-day time & strike movement, 19th c., 18 1/2" h. **200-275**

Shelf or mantel clock, Waltham Clock Co., Waltham, Massachusetts, rounded-top mahogany case w/light satinwood inlay tapering down to a platform base, cast-brass bezel w/convex beveled glass over the signed silvered metal dial, eight-day time & strike movement w/cathedral gong, early 20th c., 14" h. **250-300**

Gold-plated "Avignon" Shelf Clock

Shelf or mantel clock, Waterbury Clock Co., Waterbury, Connecticut, "Avignon" model, gold-plated case w/beveled glass side panels, ornate scroll & floral pierced decoration at top, corners & feet, large urn-form finial, white dial w/gold-tone bezel & Arabic numerals, eight-day time & strike crystal regulator movement, some

decorative elements missing from rear, some wear to plating, ca. 1903, 17 1/2" h. (ILLUS. left) **599**

Shelf or mantel clock, Waterbury Clock Co., Waterbury, Connecticut, black-painted wood temple-style case, flat rectangular top above the projecting central section w/an ornate brass bezel enclosing the dial w/Roman numerals, small creamy celluloid column w/gilt-metal capitals & bases at each side, deep stepped base w/rounded corners, raised on scrolling gilt-metal feet, eight-day movement, time & strike, ca. 1900, 7 1/4 x 15 1/2", 10 5/8" h. (ILLUS. at bottom of page)...................... **200-250**

Pretty Waterbury China Case Clock

Shelf or mantel clock, Waterbury Clock Co., Waterbury, Connecticut, china case, upright form w/flared shell-form crest & serpentine scroll sides & case, purple trim on

Waterbury Wooden Temple Clock

white w/a transfer-printed panel of yellow & purple flowers below the round brass bezel & floral-decorated porcelain dial w/Arabic numerals, eight-day time & strike movement, late 19th - early 20th c., 4 3/4 x 9", 11 1/4" h. (ILLUS. on previous page) **500-600**

Shelf or mantel clock, Waterbury Clock Co., Waterbury, Connecticut, "Clifton" model, upright walnut case w/rounded profile w/Art Nouveau influences, the tall glass door over the dial & stenciled line decoration, regulator pendulum, paper label inside, eight-day time & strike movement plus alarm, late 19th c., 20" h. **155-170**

Shelf or mantel clock, Waterbury Clock Co., Waterbury, Connecticut, "Fenwick" model, upright oak base w/scalloped frame w/shallow line-incised decoration in a fan motif, applied turned half-bar over the dial, the glass door over the repainted dial, door w/stenciled decoration of entwined lines, eight-day time & strike movement, late 19th - early 20th c., 22"h. **200-250**

Gilt Spelter Clock with Cupids

Shelf or mantel clock, Waterbury Clock Co., Waterbury, Connecticut, gilt-spelter rococo style case, the upper dial frame heavily cast w/ornate floral & scroll decoration & high top finial & smaller drop finial, an ornate brass bezel surrounds the white round porcelain dial w/Arabic numerals & subsidiary seconds dial, the case held aloft by two gilt-spelter cupids standing on an oblong base w/ornate scroll decoration & short scroll feet, 30-hour backwind time-only movement w/winder & setting knob, some gilt wear, seconds hand missing, ca. 1910, 10 3/4" h. (ILLUS.) **258**

Shelf or mantel clock, Waterbury Clock Co., Waterbury, Connecticut, "Hobart" model, upright walnut case w/scallop-cut sides & line-incised decoration, three pressed applied buttons w/stylized florals, the tall glass door over the dial & pendulum, eight-day time & strike movement, late 19th c., 22 1/2" h. **125-175**

Louis XV-Style Waterbury Clock

Shelf or mantel clock, Waterbury Clock Co., Waterbury, Connecticut, Louis XV Revival-Style, gilt-metal, the upright domed case w/ornate leafy scrolls & arches & a loop top handle above the round glass door w/bezel opening to a painted porcelain dial w/Arabic numerals & time & strike keyholes, the dial above an inset porcelain plaque decorated w/putti, scroll-framed mask at the front bottom, ornate leafy scroll legs, ca. 1900, w/key (ILLUS.) **200**

Waterbury Classical Revival Clock

Shelf or mantel clock, Waterbury Clock
Co., Waterbury, Connecticut, mahogany
veneer Classical Revival case, the deep
ogee cornice above a pair of large grain-
painted columns flanking the two-pane
door, the large upper pane over the worn
painted metal dial w/Roman numerals, the
lower pane decorated w/a decoupaged
color print of white doves in a basket of
pink roses, deep ogee base, eight-day
movement, time & strike w/alarm, ca.
1880, 4 1/4 x 12 1/4", 16 1/4" h. (ILLUS.
on previous page).. **350**

Waterbury Round-top Clock

Shelf or mantel clock, Waterbury Clock
Co., Waterbury, Connecticut, round-top
walnut case, an arched top molding continuing to tapering gilt spearpoints at the
front flanking the tall glazed door w/gilt
scroll decoration & opening to the replaced dial face w/Roman numerals,
rectangular molded base, eight-day
movement, strike & alarm, adjustable
mercury pendulum, late 19th c.,
4 3/4 x 11 1/4", 17 1/4" h. (ILLUS.)......... **200-300**

Shelf or mantel clock, Waterbury Clock
Co., Waterbury, Connecticut, upright
walnut case w/a scalloped outline & shallow incised circular designs, the glass
door over the painted dial & stenciled
decoration w/a checkerboard design,
scrolls & vines, original brass pendulum
bob & regulator scale, label inside, eight-
day time & strike movement, late 19th c.,
18" h. **175-250**

Waterbury "Steeple" Clock

Shelf or mantel clock, Waterbury Clock
Co., Waterbury, Connecticut, mahogany
veneer "steeple" clock, pointed top
flanked by turned tapering finials above a
pointed two-pane glazed door, the top
pane over the dial w/Roman numerals,
the replaced pane w/a frosty & etched
leafy vine design, half-round columns
down the sides, stepped base, one finial
replaced, eight-day movement, strike &
alarm, ca.   1860-80,   4 3/8 x 11 1/4",
19 1/4" h. (ILLUS.).................................... **250-300**

Waterbury Clock Co. Chiming Clock

Shelf or mantel clock, Waterbury Clock Co., Waterbury, New York, "Chime Clock 501" model, upright mahogany case w/molded arched top above three-quarter round columns inset at front corners & flanking the signed white porcelain dial w/brass bezel & black Arabic numerals, stepped block base on short square wafer feet, eight-day time/chime/strike movement signed "Waterbury" & w/patent dates, chimes the quarters on four steel rods, label on bottom of case, ca. 1917, 16 3/4" h. (ILLUS.)............... **364**

Waterbury "Spider" Clock

Shelf or mantel clock, Waterbury Clock Co., Waterbury, New York, "Spider" model, cylindrical gold-plated case on four outcurved feet, ring handle, white dial w/Arabic numerals & subsidiary

seconds dial, Waterbury mark under the 12, beveled glass cover, jeweled eight-day movement, much of the gold has been polished away, ca. 1911, 3" high (ILLUS. below left) **224**

Classical Revival Rosewood Clock

Shelf or mantel clock, Welch (E.N.) Mfg. Co., Bristol, Connecticut (attributed), Classical Revival rosewood veneer case, the arched paneled top above a conforming glazed door opening to a dial w/Roman numerals centered by an embossed brass disc, brass pendulum w/pierced scroll trim, rectangular base w/ogee border, eight-day movement, time, strike & alarm, ca. 1880, 4 3/4 x 10 1/2", 16" h. (ILLUS.).. **250-300**

E.N. Welch "Jewel" Shelf Clock

Shelf or mantel clock, Welch (E.N.) Mfg. Co., Bristol, Connecticut, "Jewel" model, octagonal amber cut-glass case w/white porcelain signed dial w/black Roman nu-

merals & subsidiary seconds dial, 30-hour
time & strike lever movement, minute
hand needs replacing, ca. 1889, 3 1/2" h.
(ILLUS. on previous page) **392**

Shelf or mantel clock, Welch (E.N.) Mfg.
Co., Bristol, Connecticut, miniature "Dan-
delion" model, walnut upright case w/a
scallop-cut outline & thistle-like sawtooth
design across the top w/shallow line-incised decoration, applied turned half-bar
over the dial, the glass door over the dial
& decorated w/a stenciled bird design,
30-hour time, strike & alarm movement,
late 19th c., 17" h. **150-200**

Welch Walnut Eastlake Clock

Shelf or mantel clock, Welch (E.N.) Mfg.
Co., Bristol, Connecticut, Victorian Eastlake style walnut case, the high two-tier
pediment w/a palmette top over a turned
roundel flanked by reeded blocks &
pierced designs, similar lower tier above
the tall molded glazed door decorated
w/ornate gilt stenciling over the dial
w/Roman numerals, cut-out & line-incised side panels, wide reeded rectangular flat base, eight-day movement, time,
strike & alarm, ca. 1890, 4 3/4 x 15 1/4",
24 1/2" h. (ILLUS.).................................... **350-400**

Welch Clock with Unique Vignettes

Shelf or mantel clock, Welch (E.N.) Mfg.
Co., Bristol, Connecticut, oak kitchen-
style clock, the wide flat cornice w/an
elaborate pierced & scroll-cut crest
above a tall glazed door flanked by similar scroll cutting, the glass ornately stenciled w/various figural vignettes including
black minstrel figures, a woman playing a
harp, a violinist & trumpeter, brass pendulum w/a black weight w/the raised let-
ter "W," original finish w/ebonized trim,
eight-day movement, time & strike, ca.
1890, 5 1/4 x 14 1/2", 22" h. (ILLUS.).... **600-700**

Welch, Spring & Co. Classical Clock

Shelf or mantel clock, Welch, Spring & Co., Forestville, Connecticut, Classical Revival rosewood veneer case, the paneled arched top above conforming molding framing a round molding around the dial w/Roman numerals & two roundels over a trapezoidal glass panel showing the pendulum, rectangular base w/ogee border, label inside, ca. 1880, 5 x 11 1/4", 16 1/4" h. (ILLUS. on previous page) **200-250**

Rare Early Aaron Willard Mantel Clock

Fancy Victorian Walnut Clock

Shelf or mantel clock, Welch, Spring & Co., Forestville, Connecticut, walnut case, Victorian Renaissance Revival style, peaked pediment w/dentil-cut crestrail centered by a block w/a carved classical bust above a molded cornice & a line-incised frieze above the arched, molded glazed door decorated w/a silver stenciled design of stalks of wheat & small desert & seascape vignettes, rectangular platform base w/flaring sides & line-incised decoration, dial w/Roman numerals, brass pendulum w/inset glass medallion, paper label on the back, eight-day movement, time & strike, ca. 1880, missing top finial, 5 x 13 1/2", 21" h. (ILLUS.) **300-500**

Shelf or mantel clock, Willard (Aaron), Boston, Massachusetts, Federal style mahogany & mahogany veneer case, a broken-scroll crest centering a large pointed gilt finial above a tall rectangular églomisé door w/a gold-ground border w/red & gold ovals & scrolls in each corner above a lower white band w/gilt scrolls & a central red oval inscribed "Aaron Willard - Boston," the door opening to the dished white enamel dial w/Roman numerals, the stepped-out lower case w/a large square églomisé panel w/a gold border band & gilt leaftip border around a central panel w/a gilt scene of Father Time, a narrow serpentine apron on French feet, ca. 1805, wear to églomisé, 5 3/4 x 12 3/4", 36 1/2" h. (ILLUS.) **23,000**

Shelf or mantel clock, Willard (Aaron) Jr., Boston, Massachusetts, Federal mahogany & mahogany veneer case, the tall upright case w/a pierced fretwork centering a fluted plinth & brass ball finial above the flat half-round molded cornice & glazed door w/half-round molding framing the églomisé tablet w/shield spandrels inscribed "Aaron Willard Jr. Boston," opening to an iron concave white & gilt dial w/Roman numerals & a brass eight-day weight-driven striking movement, the lower mahogany hinged door on rounded base band & small ball feet, refinished, early 19th c., 36 1/4" h. (restored) **2,990**

Miniature Yale Shelf Clock

Shelf or mantel clock, Yale Clock Co., New Haven, Connecticut, miniature, rectangular upright wood case w/side molding and stepped base, original white dial w/Roman numerals, spandrels & brass surrounds, bottom compartment shows pendulum bob, minor losses, bottom dust cover & some screws missing, ca. 1880, 3" high (ILLUS.)... **168**

Shelf or mantel clock, Year Clock Co., tambour model, Series No. 1025, a brass case w/a large round upright frame enclosing the brass bezel & white dial w/Arabic numerals, w/a narrow stepped rectangular base, early 20th c., 7" h. **591**

Seth Thomas Ship's Bell Clock

Ship's bell clock, Thomas (Seth) Clock Co., Plymouth, Connecticut, "Merrimack" model, simple brass case, white dial w/black Arabic numerals & subsidiary seconds dial,

one-day time & strike movement, ca. 1935, 7" d. (ILLUS. below left)..................................... **364**

Ship's bell clock, Waterbury Clock Co., Waterbury, Connecticut, Model No. 10, w/twin-train movement striking on gong, Arabic numerals, silvered metal dial, & lacquered brass case & glazed door in the form of a ship's wheel, patent dated 1910, 8 1/4" d.. **288**

Waterbury Ship's Bell Clock

Ship's bell clock, Waterbury Clock Co., Waterbury, Connecticut, "Ship's Bell No. 17" model, polished brass case in the form of a ship's wheel enclosing the white dial w/black Arabic numerals, on ogee shaft connected to rectangular base, small button feet, original bottom label, eight-day jeweled time & strike movement, ca. 1929, 8" h. (ILLUS.).............. **532**

Rare Victorian Skeleton Clock

Skeleton clock, Blackhurst, England, brass, the round pierced dial w/flanges marked w/Roman numerals mounted in front of the open works framed by pierced scrolls & raised on tall flat scrolls above the stepped oval white marble base w/bun feet, ca. 1855 (ILLUS. on previous page)................... **3,740**

Rare Monumental Store Clock

French Le Roy Skeleton Clock

Skeleton clock, Le Roy, Paris, France, double-deck brass model, each rectangular deck w/a beveled base & four ringed columns at the corners, the top columns support the signed dial w/open escapement below a top domed bell, the white chapter ring w/black Roman numerals, the brass pendulum & bob suspended through the top deck to just above the base, time & strike movement w/dead beat escapement, gridiron pendulum & articulated strike hammer that rings the bell from the rear, crack in bell glued, ca. 1845, 20" h. (ILLUS.) **4,760**

Store floor clock, Victorian Renaissance style, walnut & burl walnut, the top stepped breakfront pediment above a conforming case, the central stepped-out section w/carved columns flanking a tall arched door glazed at the top over the round dial w/Roman numerals & w/four long raised burl panels below centering a roundel, the narrow setback side sections fitted w/long glass doors, one enclosing a thermometer measured in centigrade, the other w/a thermometer measured in Fahrenheit, all on a conforming base w/a heavy molded band supported by four large carved seated winged lions on the deep platform base on compressed bun feet, possibly French, ca. 1880, original finish, 20 x 44", 99" h. (ILLUS.) **35,000**

Swinging arm clock, Ansonia Clock Co., Ansonia, Connecticut, bronzed spelter w/a standing figure of a classical maiden holding aloft a free-swinging torch topped by a brass sphere enclosing the works & w/a band of applied numbers, late 19th c., overall 31" h. (loss to the suspension).. **1,210**

Tall Ansonia Swinging Arm Clock

Swinging arm clock, Ansonia Clock Co., Ansonia, Connecticut, figural, a tall bronzed metal figure of a classical maiden on a socle base holding aloft in one hand the clock w/a brass bezel & ribbon crest over the round dial w/Arabic numerals suspending the bar-form pendulum w/stamped brass bob, clock & works swings w/the pendulum, ca. 1880s, 28" h. (ILLUS.).. **3,640**

Swinging arm clock, Ansonia Clock Co., Ansonia, Connecticut, "Juno" model, standing figure of a classical woman holding aloft the clock dial & movement, bronze-finished metal, gilded pendulum, eight-day movement, time only, 4 1/2" dial, 28" h. **3,500**

Ansonia Swinging Arm Clock

Swinging arm clock, Ansonia Clock Co., Ansonia, Connecticut, patinated cast metal, a figure of an Art Nouveau maiden standing on rockwork & holding the swinging clock up w/one arm, late 19th c., 24" h. (ILLUS.).. **3,250**

Ansonia "Huntress Swing" Clock

Swinging arm clock, Ansonia Clock Co., New York, New York, "Huntress Swing" model, gold patinated metal figure of a standing woman in clinging gown w/raised left arm holding aloft the brass-framed dial w/original white paper face w/Roman numerals & brass bezel, gilt-brass ribbon scroll trim around dial & above the long three-bar brass pendulum & bob decorated w/a stamped bust portrait, on a stepped round molded base, time-only movement, ca. 1883, 25" h. (ILLUS.).. **3,808**

Ansonia "Fisher Swing" Clock

Swinging arm clock, Ansonia Clock Co., New York, New York, "Fisher Swing" model, bronze figure of a man in Renaissance attire, one arm raised to hold the large brass-framed dial & long pendulum, the dial w/Roman numerals, brass bezel & ribbon crest, further brass scrolls at the top of the three-bar pendulum ending in an ornate bob w/a stamped classical portrait bust, on stepped circular base, time-only movement, some discoloration to dial, ca. 1883, 22" h. (ILLUS.) **3,696**

Ansonia's "Juno Swing" Clock

Swinging arm clock, Ansonia Clock Co., New York, New York, "Juno Swing" model, brass, figure of woman in classical dress standing on embossed waisted pedestal on circular base, the right arm holding a baton, the left raised to hold the ball dial w/decorative articulated crest & brackets & Arabic numerals suspending the bar-form pendulum w/orb-shaped bob w/drop finial, original patina, some pitting, dirt & oxidation, ca. 1895, 28 1/2" h. (ILLUS.) **3,864**

"Brise d'Automne" Swinging Arm Clock

Swinging arm clock, bronzed spelter figure of "Brise d'Automne" (Autumn Breeze), a standing woman in diaphanous robes & flowing hair, on circular stepped wooden base painted to simulate marble, her upraised left arm holding the dial piece, the dial on 6" d. forest green ball trimmed w/gilt ribbon & scroll decoration, gilt hands & Roman numerals, long pendulum w/orb-shaped bob, statue & brass plaque on base signed "Moreau," time-only movement, ball professionally refinished, minute hand repaired, France, ca. 1890, 38 1/2" h. (ILLUS.) **4,760**

Japanese Copy of Swinging Arm Clock

French Fluted Pillar Swing Clock

Swinging arm clock, "Fluted Pillar" model, rectangular linden wood base supporting a wooden fluted pillar w/cast-metal capital & base, rectangular wood pediment supports the round brass clock w/a round white dial w/black Arabic numerals, slender straight brass rod pendulum holds the ringed orb bob, time-only movement, France, ca. 1915, 11" h. (ILLUS.) **1,232**

Swinging arm clock, Fuji, Japan, brass & spelter, a tall brass figure of a classical woman holding up the dial & swinging pendulum in one arm, on a black plastic base, a copy of a late Victorian design, ca. 1960s, 13 3/4" h. (ILLUS.) **200**

Swinging arm clock, gilded cast spelter figure of a young boy in tattered clothes holding fruit in one arm & holding the round movement & dial aloft w/the other, Junghans, German-type movement, late 19th c., 12" h. (regilded, on replaced wood base) **394**

"Barmaid" Swinging Arm Clock

Glass Dial Swinging Arm Clock

Swinging arm clock, gilt spelter figure of a standing woman in draped attire w/right arm raised to hold the unframed 7" d. glass white dial w/gold leaf Roman numerals & hands & marked "Robert Houdin - Paris," the long open bar pendulum ending in a dark orb decorated w/gilt decoration & stars enclosing the movement, the movement suspended by a normal suspension spring w/a separate miniature gravity movement in the center of the glass dial w/a tiny pendulum & ratchet that advance the hands w/each swing of the arm, all atop a rectangular white marble base raised on a scalloped gilt-metal frame w/scroll feet, old crack near base of statue, professionally restored, France, ca. 1880, 24 1/2" h. (ILLUS.)....... **14,560**

Swinging arm clock, Junghans, Germany, "Barmaid" model, metal figure of barmaid w/a ribbon in her hair wearing a low-cut blouse w/sleeves pushed up, skirt falling to just below knees & short, puffy overskirt, standing w/left hand on hip & holds clock in her extended right hand, the round brass clock case w/ribbon crest & scroll decoration under the dial encloses a white dial w/black Arabic numerals, a multi-rod brass pendulum & spherical brass bob, on a stepped circular base, original patina, time-only movement, gilt polished off clock case, ca. 1910, 13 1/2" h. (ILLUS.).. **1,680**

Swinging arm clock, Junghans, Germany, "Batboy" model, cast patinated metal figure of a standing barefoot boy wearing rolled-up pants & undervest, holding short bat in his right hand & the clock in his upraised left hand, ornate brass case enclosing the white porcelain dial w/black Arabic numerals, brass bezel, multi-bar pendulum w/spiked orb bob, on oblong base, original dark greenish bronze patina, time-only movement, ca. 1910, 18" h. (ILLUS. top of next page)............................. **2,016**

"Batboy" Swinging Arm Clock

Kangaroo Swinging Arm Clock

Swinging arm clock, Junghans, Germany, cast metal figure of a kangaroo standing on hind legs & holding clock arm in its mouth, brass case w/ribbon crest encloses the white dial w/black Arabic numerals, multi-bar brass pendulum w/spiked ringed orb bob, time-only movement, ca. 1910, 12" w. x 12" h. (ILLUS.) **2,576**

Swinging arm clock, Junghans, Germany, "Diana" model, tall bronze-finished cast spelter classical figure w/one arm holding the round clock movement & dial continuing to the long pierced pendulum w/bob, on a round wood base, late 19th c................. **900**

Swinging arm clock, Junghans, Germany, figural, round movement & dial w/long pendulum held aloft on the raised trunk of a later cast metal walking elephant on an oval base **591**

"Onion Boy" Swinging Arm Clock

Swinging arm clock, Junghans, Germany, "Onion Boy" model, bronze finished cast-spelter figure of a barefoot boy w/rolled up pants holding bunch of onions over left shoulder & holding clock in his up-raised right hand, brass clock case w/ornate decoration at top & bottom of white porcelain dial w/black Arabic numerals, single-shaft pendulum tapering to spiked ringed orb bob, time-only movement, some wear, ca. 1900, 15 1/2" h. (ILLUS.).. **1,456**

"Onyx Pillar" Swinging Arm Clock

Swinging arm clock, Junghans, Germany, "Onyx Pillar" model, brass clock case attached to a green onyx column w/rings of gilt spelter, case w/ribbon crest & floral decoration beneath dial, brass bezel enclosing the white dial w/black Arabic numerals, ladder-style brass pendulum w/ringed orb bob, circular green onyx base, time-only movement, ca. 1900, 10" h. (ILLUS.)... **1,568**

Swinging arm clock, patinated metal, figural, a tall classical maiden holding one arm out & grasping small wreaths & holding the other arm aloft supporting the orbed clock dial & movement w/a long pendulum, figure after a work by Auguste Moreau, on a socle base, France, late 19th - early 20th c., restorations (ILLUS. top of next column)............ **1,955**

French Swinging Arm Clock

Swinging arm clock, painted cast-metal, a round foot supporting the figure of a standing classical maiden in flowing gown holding one arm up & supporting the round clock dial & free-swinging pendulum in the other, late 19th c., 14" h. **440**

E. Howard Tower Clock

Tower clock, Howard (E.) & Co., Boston, Massachusetts, from a stand in Closter, New Jersey, upright cast-iron frame retains original two-tone green paint w/pin striping & serial number 3587, replaced wood dial w/Roman numerals & sweep seconds hand, hard-to-find set of compression motion works suitable for glass dial, meter pendulum, premium renewable bushing, time-only movement, ca. 1880, 16" h. (ILLUS. without dial on previous page) **3,388**

German Vienna Regulator Clock

Vienna Regulator wall clock, Becker (Gustav), Germany, tall wooden case w/molded pediment w/band of geometric carving topped w/a high, ornately carved crest w/scrolls, columns & mask, the tall arched glass door flanked by three-quarter round reeded columns w/ring-turned tops & Ionic-type capitals & turned baluster-form bottoms on rectangular bevel-carved bases, the dial w/silver chapter ring w/black Arabic numerals, simple brass bezel & center ring, the dial, weights & pendulum bob all w/matching scroll en-

graving, the molded & carved base drop w/incised decoration, three-weight time, strike & chime movement strikes grand sonnerie sequence on two steel rods, carved top is new, bottom finial missing, chapter ring w/some oxidation, bezel loose, ca. 1890, 46" h. (ILLUS. left) **1,400**

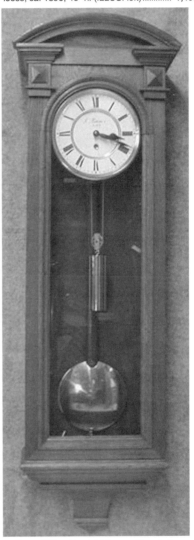

Post Office Model Vienna Regulator

Vienna Regulator wall clock, post office model, tall oak case w/an arched molded cornice above raised blocks above the tall arched molding enclosing the glass front, brass bezel around the white porcelain dial w/Roman numerals, a long brass weight & pendulum w/large brass bob, molded base w/tapering, stepped drop, eight-day single weight movement, Austria, ca. 1900, 13" w., 41" h. (ILLUS.) **2,000-2,250**

German Vienna Regulator

Vienna Regulator wall clock, rosewood case w/barley twist columns, stepped arched top, drop finial, white dial w/Roman numerals, one weight, eight-day time-only movement w/dead beat escapement, some veneer loss, hairline cracks to chapter ring, dial chipped, Germany, ca. 1870, 38" h. (ILLUS.) **784**

Pretty Walnut Vienna Regulator

Vienna Regulator wall clock, tall light walnut case w/molded pediment arching at center, urn-form center & corner finials & rectangular black panel accents, three-quarter round reeded columns at sides w/ring-turned capitals & bases flanking the tall arched glass door showing the round dial w/brass bezel & center ring, black Roman numerals & cut-out hands above the weights & pendulum, the base w/an ogee drop w/ringed knob finial & conforming corner finials, the case accented w/blocks of dark color, door warp caused cracking in the glass, Austria, ca. 1880, 53" h. (ILLUS.) **952**

Fancy Vienna Regulator

Vienna Regulator wall clock, tall walnut-veneered case w/a broken-arch pediment centered by a large urn finial over a paneled block over tall reeded columns w/carved capitals & turned bases flanking the tall arched glass front, brass bezel enclosing the enameled dial w/Roman numerals, three plain brass weights & large brass bob on pendulum, blocked & molded base over turned corner drop finials & a rounded drop section w/finial, eight-day time & strike movement, Austria, ca. 1880-90, 50" h. (ILLUS.) **3,800-4,200**

Vienna Regulator wall clock, walnut, the high arched crest centered by a carved relief eagle above a flaring stepped cornice above the tall case w/a glazed front panel over the round dial w/Arabic numerals & the long two-weight pendulum w/large brass bob, the panel flanked by columnar sides w/urn-turned supports on blocks, molded base w/tapering ogee paneled drop w/finial, Austria, ca. 1880, 6 x 16 1/4", 46" h. (ILLUS. top of next column) **840**

Vienna Regulator with Eagle Crest

Vienna Regulator Wall Clock

Vienna Regulator wall clock, walnut, the high scroll-cut crest w/a flat top over a shell carving flanked by corner blocks w/turned urn finials above a molded cornice over a long glazed panel showing the round dial w/Roman numerals & the long wooden pendulum w/large brass bob, the side columns w/ring- and knob-turned top & bottom sections centered by a narrow reeded colonette, ogee molded fluted base drop w/finial flanked by corner drop finials, Austria, ca. 1880, 7 x 16 1/2", 48" h. (ILLUS.) **728**

Early Dutch Friesland Wag-on-Wall

Wag-on-wall clock, early "stoelklok," the carved & painted case w/a pointed & pierced painted arch crest above a wide painted backboard w/scalloped sides h.p. w/large mermaids flanking the clock works w/a high arched & pierced metal crest over the dial plate w/painted angels above the painted metal dial w/a white chapter ring w/Roman numerals, a wooden platform shelf above the long free-hanging weights & pendulum, time & strike movement w/turned angle posts, Dutch Friesland, damage to mounts, case 27" h. (ILLUS.) **844**

German Wag-on-Wall Clock

Wag-on-wall clock, flat decorated metal shield-shaped dial w/red & gold-leaf trim & full-color scene of village above dial, the round dial w/raised chapter ring & black Roman numerals, period hands, pendulum engraved w/image of horse, 30-hour time & strike movement, strike hammer improperly replaced but functioning, Germany, ca. 1860, 14" h. (ILLUS.) **420**

Wag-on-wall clock, Mercier-Hupel, France, embossed brass, the oval embossed upper case decorated w/ornate scrolls & flowers surrounding a white-enameled round dial w/Roman numerals, a short bar connecting to the very large & long pendulum w/tapering scroll-embossed sides & a large rounded bottom, embossed overall w/ornate scrolling & a small floral bouquet on the upper section & a large bouquet on the lower section, polychrome japanning & gilding, dial labeled "Mercier-Hupel - à Bain de Bretagne," France, 19th c., w/weights & key, overall 55" h. **770**

Pressed-brass Wag-on-Wall Clock

Wag-on-wall clock, Morbier "2-Weight Prayer" repeat model w/calendar, pressed-brass dial surround features four cherubs at harvest time, the lyre-form pendulum w/detailed embossing of Helios, the sun god, & ornately decorated bob, white dial w/black Roman numerals & concentric calendar & 1-31 dates just inside numeral ring, sawtooth bezel, time & strike movement w/large deep-toned bell at top, repeats hour strike at one minute past, France, ca. 1890, 54" h. (ILLUS.) **672**

Wag-on-wall clock, Neugart (Juan), Volladolid, France, embossed brass dial surround decorated w/scene of figures in field of wheat, round white dial w/Roman numerals, old cast-iron weights, lyre-form grid pendulum, eight-day time & strike Morbier movement w/anchor escapement w/gong strike, the gong attached to board on the rear, small dent to

French Embossed Wag-on-Wall Clock

pendulum, some oxidation, ca. 1890, 53" h. (ILLUS. below) **476**

Wag-on-wall clock, pinwheel type, a round white porcelain convex dial w/engine-turned brass bezel, black Roman numerals & sweep seconds hand above the large reeded brass pendulum w/large round bob, eight-day time-only weight & pendulum movement, France, ca. 1860, 52" h. (ILLUS. top of next page) **1,904**

French Convex Dial Wall Clock

Early French Wag-on-Wall Clock

Wag-on-wall clock, Spéth (André), France, embossed brass, the square upper section w/a sheet steel frame w/an arched stamped brass cornice, the open enameled dial w/Roman numerals signed "André Spéth à la Charité," the large long ta-

pering rounded pendulum of ornate stamped brass w/C-scrolls, flowers & a classical urn, the dial w/hairlines & yellowed repair, w/weights & key, wrought-iron shelf a late replacement, Normandy, France, late 18th - early 19th c., overall 56" h. (ILLUS. below left) **935**

Decorative German Wag-on-Wall Clock

Wag-on-wall clock, square dial plate w/arched top, the arch painted w/a polychrome scene of a bullfighter being gored by bull, the spandrels around the round dial decorated w/polychrome images of children at play, the dial w/heavy black Roman numerals & a stamped brass center ring & brass hands, brass weights & pendulum, 30-hour time/strike/alarm movement, Germany, ca. 1900, 13 1/2" h. (ILLUS.) **392**

Wall clock, a wide brass plate frame cast in relief w/various animals including a deer, dog & snake, a central red plush dial w/inset porcelain number shields w/Roman numerals, eight-day time & strike movement w/alarm, American-made, late 19th - early 20th c., 12" d. **90**

Ansonia "Eclipse" Model Wall Clock

Wall clock, Ansonia Clock Co., Ansonia, Connecticut, "Eclipse" model, oak Victorian Eastlake style case, the high pierce-carved pediment w/a palmette finial over a roundel & reeded blocks & corner ears above a lower rail w/cut-out spearpoints & corner ears above long notch-cut & line-incised side brackets flanking the tall glass door w/delicate gilt stencil decoration, brass bezel & dial w/Roman numerals, the base w/a deep scallop-cut & line-incised apron, eight-day movement, time, strike & alarm, ca. 1885-90, 5 x 15", 27 1/2" h. (ILLUS.) **350-450**

Wall clock, Ansonia Clock Co., New York, New York, "Capital" model, long mahogany case w/molded arched crest w/a large center finial centered by a gilt-metal portrait medial & flanked by ring-turned corner finials, three-quarter round colonettes flank the long arched glass door over the dial w/brass bezel, center ring, black Roman numerals & subsidiary seconds dial, the wood pendulum w/large brass bob, bottom of case w/an ogee drop w/large drop finial & two smaller corner drop finials, eight-day time & strike weight movement, bottom finial loose, re-papered chapter ring, ca. 1901, 54" h. (ILLUS. top of next column) **2,072**

Ansonia "Capital" Wall Clock

Ansonia Octagonal Wall Clock

Wall clock, Ansonia Clock Co., New York, New York, "Drop Octagon Extra Cal" model, oak case, octagonal top section embossed w/scroll & floral decoration enclosing the round dial w/black Roman numerals for time & smaller Arabic numerals for date, brass bezel & center ring, original hands, the short pointed drop case molded & embossed w/geometric border around a shaped glass pane w/gilt design around oval pendulum window on black ground, eight-day time & strike movement, dial darkened from age & wear, case refinished, glass pane restored to proper design, ca. 1901, 24 1/2" h. (ILLUS.) **308**

Ansonia "Queen Elizabeth" Clock

Wall clock, Ansonia Clock Co., New York, New York, "Queen Elizabeth" model, long oak case w/a stepped pediment, the center raised section w/two urn-form corner finials over a narrow rectangular panel flanked by two larger turned corner finials, the long arched glass front over a white round dial w/brass bezel & center ring, black Roman numerals & long pendulum w/large brass bob, the sides of the case w/a short & tall slender ring-turned column, the base w/corner drop finials connected by a ring-turned bar & carved peaked apron, a matching carved backboard, eight-day time & strike movement, good label on rear of clock, replacement drop finials, ca. 1901, 37" h. (ILLUS.) **784**

Ansonia "Queen Jane" Wall Clock

Wall clock, Ansonia Clock Co., New York, New York, "Queen Jane" model, long rectangular oak case w/flaring crown-form pediment over a flaring cornice w/a carved ropetwist border molding, matching molding frames the tall glass door opening to the white paper dial w/brass bezel & center ring & black Roman numerals, the base w/further ropetwist molding over serpentine side brackets flanking the scalloped & ribbed baseboard, eight-day time & strike movement, ca. 1901, 41" h. (ILLUS.) **2,128**

French Art Deco Wall Clock

Wall clock, Art Deco box-type, rectangular walnut veneer case w/step-carved bands & geometric designs along the outer edges flanking an upper octagonal opening over the silvered metal dial w/Arabic numerals & a lower octagonal opening w/vertical bands of leaded glass over the pendulum w/octagonal chrome bob, eight-day time & strike movement w/Westminster chimes, France, ca. 1930s, 14" w., 29" h. (ILLUS.) **1,000-1,200**

Wall clock, Atkins (Alden A.), Bristol, Connecticut, rectangular upright ogee case w/mahogany veneer, two-pane glass door, the upper pane over the painted dial w/Roman numerals & floral-painted spandrels, the lower pane reverse-painted w/a color landscape scene of a large white classical home w/a large tree in the foreground, some flaking, original dark, dirty finish w/some veneer chips, pendulum bob an old replacement, 30-hour movement, time & strike, ca. 1845, 26 1/2" h. (ILLUS. top of next page) **280**

Alden Atkins Early Ogee Clock

case, large round molded top around the white dial w/Roman numerals & original moon hands, the drop case w/a square glass tablet w/gilt center decoration on black background, eight-day time & strike movement, label, veneer chip, repainted dial, tablet replaced long ago, ca. 1865, 24 1/2" h. (ILLUS. below left)........................... **672**

Atkins Cottage Clock with Alarm

Wall clock, Atkins Clock Co., Bristol, Connecticut, rosewood veneer cottage-style, arched paneled top over a conforming door w/two glass panes, upper pane over the original painted dial w/Roman numerals, lower pane w/original gilt-stenciled rose & wreath decor, interior label coming loose, 30-hour movement, time & alarm, ca. 1865, 10 1/4" h. (ILLUS.).............. **252**

Drop Regulator Wall Clock

Wall clock, Atkins Clock Co., Bristol, Connecticut, drop regulator style, rosewood

1850s Drop Octagon Wall Clock

Wall clock, Atkins, Whiting & Co., Bristol, Connecticut, rosewood veneer ripple molded drop octagon case w/original ivory knobs for bezel & lower door locks, the large white dial w/Roman numerals, small panel in drop w/gilt decoration, round 30-day wagon-spring time & strike movement mounted in later iron frame, dial repainted, some flaking & minor abrasion, ca. 1855, 25" h. (ILLUS.) **3,360**

Wall clock, Badger (W.), Ltd., Lowell, England, mahogany case, gallery-type, single-fusee eight-day movement, time, 12" d.. **945**

German Art Nouveau Wall Clock

Wall clock, Becker (Gustav), Germany, Art Nouveau style walnut case w/high arched cut-out crest over a wide molded cornice above a frieze band w/incised whiplash designs, reeded & blocked side panels flank an arched onion-form panel w/glass over the white porcelain dial w/brass bezel & center ring & black Arabic numerals & subsidiary seconds dial, brass weights & pendulum show below the dial, incised ogee side base blocks above the rectangular molded base platform above scroll-cut brackets flanking a cut-out scroll drop panel centered by a bull's-eye medallion, time & strike movement w/serial #2,208,282, minor dings to pendulum, ca. 1908, 49 1/2" h. (ILLUS.) **1,400**

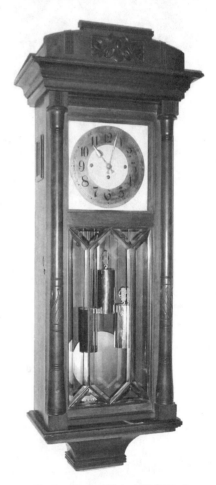

turned spindles between molded bands, a stepped & ribbed base drop w/molded drop finial, three-weight time & strike movement strikes the hours & quarters on steel rods mounted to separate iron standard at the top of the back, ca. 1890, 49" h. (ILLUS. left).. **3,696**

German Three-weight Wall Clock

Wall clock, Becker (Gustav), Germany, grand sonnerie type, ornate carved walnut Victorian Baroque Revival case, the top w/a high pierced scroll-carved finial above an arched double S-scroll cornice above a dial panel w/carved scrolls at each corner, a brass bezel around the inset round dial w/Roman numerals & an engraved brass center ring, the case w/a narrow mid-molding over the tall lower panel enclosing a glass pane within a molding w/notched corners, the glass shows the row of three weights & large brass pendulum bob decorated w/Art Nouveau-style appliqué, the deep base section w/a panel of half round ring-

Gustav Becker Walnut Wall Clock

Wall clock, Becker (Gustav), Germany, long walnut case w/flat-topped arched crest w/panel of carved flowers, the sides of the case w/half round columns w/incised decoration & ring-turned capitals flanking the long two-pane glazed door, the square upper pane over the dial painted yellow except for chapter ring, black Arabic numerals, the long lower section composed of seven heavily beveled clear glass panes over the weight & pendulum w/large brass bob, small inset side panels, molded base & tapering drop, three-weight time/strike/chime movement striking grand sonnerie on eight rods, iron gong standard signed "GB," normally blue hands have been painted gold, yellow paint on dial plate incorrect, ca. 1920, 43" h. (ILLUS. on previous page)............ **739**

G. Becker Art Nouveau Wall Clock

Wall clock, Becker (Gustav), Germany, walnut Art Nouveau "Berliner" case w/carved openwork cornice w/fleur-de-lis crest, molded pediment & scroll side trim, the top section that overhangs base w/cartouche-shape glass pane in door, the contour base flanked by delicate whiplash brackets, w/curved cut-out wood design over spring-loaded glass panel protecting Art Nouveau-style pendulum, metallic dial w/Arabic numerals & spandrels, the dial center w/lily motif, the pendulum bob depicting sun setting into the ocean, time & strike movement, some losses to finish & minor dry splits in door, ca. 1910, 30" h. (ILLUS.) **1,092**

Gustav Becker Walnut Wall Clock

Wall clock, Becker (Gustav), Germany, tall box-style walnut case w/rounded corners, glass panels in the sides, the tall door w/an upper wooden panel enclosing the white porcelain dial w/black Roman numerals & brass bezel & center ring, a long glass lower panel composed of seven geometric beveled clear panes of glass over the weight & pendulum w/large brass bob, the movement number dates to 1880 so the works have been recased to fit a 1920s decor, non-matching replacement minute hand, ca. 1920, 33" h. (ILLUS.) **392**

Very Ornate Black Forest Wall Clock

Wall clock, Black Forest-type, ornate carved walnut case w/a large carved crest of a spread-winged eagle attacking a mountain goat, the wide sides of the rounded case finely carved w/evergreen trees & roots entwining around the round black glass dial w/white Roman numerals, two further carved goats at the bottom of the case, eight-day movement, Germany, late 19th - early 20th c., dial possibly replaced, overall 47" h. (ILLUS.) .. **3,600**

Black Forest Clock with Eagle Finial

Wall clock, Black Forest-type, ornately carved walnut case w/a large spread-winged eagle at the top above spreading leafy branches & acorns across the top & around the sides centering the wood dial w/Roman numerals, a stag & hunting dog carved at the bottom, eight-day movement, some damage to case, Germany, late 19th - early 20th c., 37" h. (ILLUS. below left) **1,181**

French Box Wall Clock with Chimes

Wall clock, box-style, long walnut case w/a spindled top gallery trimmed w/a scroll-cut crest & flanked by turned finials, pairs of slender colonettes down the sides flanking the long door w/a round opening over the silvered metal dial w/Arabic numerals, the lower door w/three narrow vertical glass panes showing the pendulum & brass bob, molded base w/corner drop finials & short center drop, eight-day time & strike movement w/Westminster chimes, France, ca. 1910-20, 15" w., 36" h. (ILLUS.) **1,800-2,000**

Wall clock, Bulova, electric, round, marked w/"Sable's Jewelry" on face, 16" d. **110**

U.S. Navy Radio Room Wall Clock

Large Ornate Cartel-style Wall Clock

Wall clock, cartel-style, gilt-bronze Louis XVI-Style case, the lyre-form case flanked by putto terms holding a wreath, the tall neck centered by a sphinx term below a domed canopy & scrolls, the lower case cast also w/delicate floral bands around the round dial w/enameled Roman numerals, probably France, ca. 1900, retailed & signed by J.E. Caldwell & Co., Philadelphia, overall 55" h. (ILLUS.) **2,875**

Wall clock, Chelsea Clock Co., Boston, Massachusetts, U.S. Navy Radio Room model, round black Phenolic resin case, hinged door over 24-hour black dial w/white Arabic numerals, sweep seconds hand & marked "U.S. Navy - Ser. No. 83913E," time-only movement, ca. 1942, 10 1/2" h. (ILLUS.) **532**

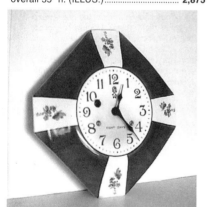

Decorative Ceramic Wall Clock

Wall clock, ceramic case, squared form w/cut corners, wide dark blue panels alternating w/small white panels w/pink flower sprigs, round dial w/Arabic numerals, eight-day movement, time only, ca. 1935-55, 9 3/4" w. (ILLUS.) **50-60**

English Drop Octagon Wall Clock

Wall clock, drop octagon-style, brass-inlaid mahogany veneer, the large octagonal top frame enclosing a large brass bezel around the dial w/Roman numerals, the short rectangular drop case flanked by carved reed & cattail brackets & decorated w/inlaid brass lines around a narrow glazed shaped window showing the brass pendulum bob, eight-day time-only movement, England, ca. 1900-10, 16 x 26" (ILLUS.) **950-1,150**

French Picture Frame Wall Clock

Wall clock, Dugas, Paris, France, picture frame style, square molded wood frame enclosing a brass-inlaid & enameled panel w/a round opening over the glass dial w/Roman numerals, dial signed "Dugas à Paris," eight-day spring-wound time & strike movement w/silk thread pendulum, ca. 1870s, 19 1/2" sq. (ILLUS.) **800-1,000**

English Walnut Burl Wall Clock

Wall clock, English walnut burl case w/large round top section framing the brass bezel & white dial w/black Roman numerals, original hands, middle case section w/a carved cartouche panel flanked by scroll & floral cut-out brackets, "double rolling pin"-type ogee base, eight-day time & strike movement marked "E.N. Welch," dial re-painted on original pan, ca. 1870, 31" h. (ILLUS.) **1,008**

1930s English Wall Clock

Wall clock, Empire Clock Co., England, round gallery timepiece, oak frame w/stripped finish, white painted dial w/some chips, Roman numerals, movement marked "Made in England," cylindrical pendulum, ca. 1930, 16" d. (ILLUS.) **123**

Furtwangler German Wall Clock

Wall clock, Furtwangler (Lorenz) & Sohne, Germany, Berliner style solid & veneered oak case w/Art Nouveau detailing, a high crestrail pierced & carved w/scrolls & stylized leaves above a flaring molded cornice above the molded sides enclosing a square glass front over an engraved silver & gold metal dial w/Arabic numerals, a simple scroll apron above shaped side brackets & a long scroll-pieced backboard framing the free-hanging pendulum w/shaped & stamped brass bob, eight-day time & strike movement strikes the hours & half hours on a gong, ca. 1900, 17" w., 36" h. (ILLUS.) **2,000-2,500**

Gilbert Mfg. Co. Calendar Wall Clock

Wall clock, Gilbert Manufacturing Co., Winsted, Connecticut, "Maranville Patent Octagon Drop Calendar" model, rosewood case w/large octagonal frame enclosing the dial w/brass bezel, black Roman numerals for time, Arabic numerals for dates in outside ring, month in window at top of dial, & days of the week in narrow ring between time & date numerals, over a short drop case w/a reverse-painted glass pane w/floral & scroll design, time & strike movement, full legible label, ca. 1870, 24" h. (ILLUS.) **1,092**

Gilbert Octagon Drop Calendar Clock

Wall clock, Gilbert Manufacturing Co., Winsted, Connecticut, "Maranville's Patent Octagon Drop Calendar" model, rosewood case w/large octagonal frame around the dial w/black Roman numerals for time, dates in Arabic numerals in outside ring, month appearing in window at top of dial, days of the week in ring between time & date numerals, brass bezel, lower short drop section w/glass pane decorated in gold stenciling w/the English royal crest, time & strike movement, label reads "Maranville Calendar clock manufactured for N.C. Hyde and Co., by Gilbert Manf'g Co., Winsted, Conn.," glass loose in bezel, dial dark from age, numbers, hands & trademark info touched up, ca. 1868, 24" h. (ILLUS. on previous page) **672**

Wall clock, Gilbert (William L.) Clock Co., Winsted, Connecticut, "Hollywood" model, mahogany finished case w/a low arched crest on rectangular cornice, long two-pane glass front w/beveled glass covering square silvered metal dial w/Roman numerals marked "Gilbert" & lower pane over the silvered metal pendulum, flattened ogee bottom splat w/floral decoration, eight-day time & strike movement, clock strikes on duo-tone steel rods, ca. 1925, 24 1/2" h. (ILLUS. below left) **308**

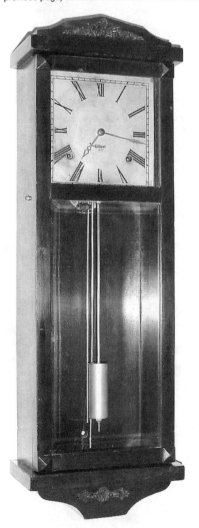

Gilbert Mahogany Wall Clock

Wall Clock with Arts & Crafts Case

Wall clock, Gilbert (William L.) Clock Co., Winsted, Connecticut, "No. 3040 Limerick" model, oak Arts & Crafts case w/stepped cornice & peaked column crest supported by two curved brackets, scalloped splat depending from base, tall glazed door w/the top pane over the silvered metal dial w/Arabic numerals &

original hands, lower pane w/two vertical slats over the original nickel-covered pendulum, label on back of case, eight-day time & strike movement signed w/Gilbert trademark, ca. 1925, 33" h. (ILLUS. on previous page).. **280**

Wall clock, Gilbert (Wm L.), Winsted, Connecticut, dark stained wood, advertising "Saucer's Flavoring Extracts," glass etched & gold leafed coins, eight-day movement, time only, spring-driven, 40" h... **2,000**

Austrian Grand Sonnerie Clock

Wall clock, grand sonnerie type, Biedermeier style case in dark wood w/scalloped cornice over long rectangular body highlighted in upper corners w/ornate gilt metal trim, base w/rounded corners & notched band, waisted base drop w/articulated gilt metal decoration, the glass front over a round two-piece dial w/ornate cast bezel w/original gilding & chapter ring w/very slender Roman numerals, 56-hour time & strike movement, powered by a weight on the time train &

springs on the quarter & hour strike, crest on case missing, Austria, ca. 1845, 39" h. (ILLUS. left) **1,960**

Wall clock, Guimard (Hector), Paris, France, Art Nouveau style gilt-bronze & copper case, a rounded border frame of gilt-bronze pointed loopings around a copper border around the large round dial w/Arabic numerals surrounded w/a band of small leaf & berry sprigs, the center signed "Pardieu - Agen.," designed by Guimard, ca. 1900, 19" h. **23,000**

Vienna-style Carved Wall Clock

Wall clock, Hamburg American Clock Co., Vienna-style dark stained softwood case, a gilt cast-metal spread-winged eagle finial on the high central crest w/a dentil band & applied carved swag flanked by corner blocks w/turned finials, heavy half-round ring-turned spindles flank the tall two-pane front, the upper pane over the square brass dial w/brass spandrels & an applied Roman numeral chapter ring, the lower pane showing the pendulum & brass bob, spring-wound eight-day time & strike on a rod movement, ca. 1910, 13" w., 36" h. (ILLUS. on previous page) **850-950**

Wall clock, Hamilton Sangamo Company, electric model, a molded round frame enclosing a white dial w/Arabic numerals, w/a brass tag marked "Penn Central 3999 LT and PR Co.," from the Altoona, Pennsylvania Power House, 20th c., 14" d... **158**

Wall clock, hooded "staartklok" model, the arched pediment centered by a cast-metal figure of Atlas holding a globe & w/figural metal angel finials at each corner, an arched glazed frame around the arched dial plate w/painted scene in the top above the painted metal dial w/Roman numerals framed by embossed metal spandrels all within a brass bezel, scroll-cut tapering brackets flank the long flat drop board w/a three-lobed end, large decorative pierced brass pendulum bob, time & strike one-bell movement, Dutch, 19th c., 44" h. **1,575**

Dutch Hooded "Staartklok"

Wall clock, hooded "staartklok" model, the broken-scroll pediment above an inset landscape painted panel above a heavy arch molded around the glass front, another painted landscape in the arch above the painted metal dial w/Roman numerals & embossed brass spandrels & bezel, a long flat board base drop w/tri-lobed end backs the long pendulum w/a large oval pierced brass bob, weight-driven movement striking two bells, Dutch, 19th c., 60" l. (ILLUS. below left) **1,800**

E. Howard & Co. Marble Dial Clock

Wall clock, Howard (E.) & Co., Boston, Massachusetts, "No. 20 Marble Dial" model, square cartouche shaped marble dial w/heavy bronze Roman numerals & markers, eight-day time-only weight movement, minor edge nicks, mark of E. Howard almost worn off, ca. 1923, 28" h. (ILLUS.) **3,296**

E. Howard & Co. Engine Room Clock

Wall clock, Howard (E.) & Co., Boston, Massachusetts, "No. 69" engine room timepiece, simple round brass molded case w/silvered brass dial signed "W.W. Lindsay & Co., Philadelphia" & marked "H. Belfield & Co, Phila." (possibly the vendor), w/black Roman numerals & subsidiary dial, eight-day time-only movement w/jeweled escapement & chronometer balance, ca. 1900, 13 3/4" d. (ILLUS. on previous page) **4,256**

L. Hubbell Octagonal Wall Clock

Wall clock, Hubbell (L.), Bristol, Connecticut, thick octagonal rosewood case w/rounded front, original glazed dial w/brass bezel, black Roman numerals, subsidiary seconds dial & marked "Patent Lever Escapement," signed 30-hour time-only movement, ca. 1870, 6" h. (ILLUS.) **252**

Unusual Ingraham Oak Wall Clock

Wall clock, Ingraham (E.) Co., Bristol, Connecticut, ornate oak kitchen-style, the peaked scroll crest w/an applied pressed

shell & scrolls above applied trefoils & scallop-cut side panels w/an overall small block design flanking the angled arched tall glass door w/egg-and-dart trim & ornate gilt stenciling w/a courtyard scene of ferns, palms & pillars, the dial w/badly worn numbers, shelf-style base w/scallop-cut apron w/further block design above the pointed scroll-cut back drop, eight-day movement, time, strike & alarm, late 19th c., 4 1/8 x 14 1/8", 25 1/2" h. (ILLUS. below left).................. **350-450**

International Time Wall Clock

Wall clock, International Time Recording Co., Master electric Model 16, a tall rectangular mahogany case w/a flat top & base, the tall arched glass door over the large white dial w/Arabic numerals, two long brass weights & a long pendulum w/a large brass disk bob, self-winding movement, 20th c., 63" h. (ILLUS. on previous page) **2,081**

Simple Junghans Box Wall Clock

Wall clock, Junghans, Germany, box-style, walnut veneer case w/a thick flat top w/beveled front corners above a conforming case & a long door w/an upper wood panel cut to show the round silvered metal dial w/Arabic numerals, the lower door divided into three vertical panes of glass showing the pendulum & brass bob, molded base, eight-day time & strike movement, ca. 1910-20, 10" w., 19" h. (ILLUS.).. **700-800**

Wall clock, Junghans, Germany, box-type, solid & veneered walnut case w/an arched top w/a floral-carved frieze & floral-carved swag below the face, silvered metal dial w/Arabic numerals, the lower door w/beveled glass w/an oval center, eight-day time & strike movement w/Westminster chime, ca. 1920-30, 12 1/2" w., 32" h................................. **1,500-1,750**

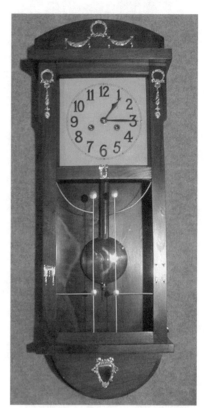

Junghans Wall Box Clock with Trim

Wall clock, Junghans, Germany, mahogany-finished hardwood box-style, arched pediment w/applied brass classical wreath & swags above top corner blocks w/similar brass trim flanking the two-pane glass front, the top pane over the celluloid dial w/Arabic numerals, the lower long pane w/slender brass wire overlay showing the pendulum & large brass bob, half-round base apron w/applied brass wreath, eight-day time & strike movement, ca. 1920, 12" w., 33" h. (ILLUS.)..................................... **900-1,000**

F. Kroeber "Grandfather" Wall Clock

Wall clock, Kroeber (F.) Clock Co., New York, New York, "Grandfather" model, molded nickel-plated case in the form of a large pocket watch, bottom-hinged glass door over the dial w/black Roman numerals & concentric panels that indicate minutes, seconds & quarter seconds, sweep seconds hand & subsidiary time dial, start & stop button on right side, ring handle at top, 30-hour lever movement, ca. 1885, 6" h. (ILLUS.) **392**

Kroeber Neo-Gothic Wall Clock

Wall clock, Kroeber (Frederick J.) Clock Co., New York, New York, Model No. 46, Victorian Neo-Gothic style walnut case, the pointed pediment w/blossom finial flanked by matching corner finials above shaped sides w/applied half-round bobbins flanking the rounded tall glass door opening to the dial w/Roman numerals & pendulum w/large brass bob, deep base drop w/Gothic-style curved bracket trim, eight-day movement, time & strike, original finish, ca. 1890, 4 3/4 x 9 1/2", 33 1/2" h. (ILLUS.)................................ **800-1,000**

columns & finials matching those at the top, corner disks at the base w/ring-turned drop finials, ogee base drop w/drop finial, time-only movement, some new finials, some hairlines in dial, Austria, ca. 1870, 38" h. (ILLUS. left)... **1,456**

Mauthe Clock Co. Berliner Clock

Wall clock, Mauthe Clock Co., Germany, Berliner style, walnut & softwood case, a cast-metal spread-winged eagle finial atop the high stepped pediment w/shell carving flanked by corner blocks w/urn-turned finials over the stepped flat cornice above boldly ring-and-baluster-turned half-columns flanking the dial panel w/leaf carvings in each corner around the wide brass bezel enclosing the celluloid chapter ring w/Arabic numerals centered by an embossed brass Art Nouveau floral center disk, turned drop finials at the front base corners backed by a large, long scroll-cut board behind the free-hanging ornate floral-stamped pendulum bob, eight-hour time & strike movement w/hour & half hour gong strike, ca. 1895-1910, 15" w., 36" h. (ILLUS.)................................... **1,200-1,500**

Austrian Walnut Wall Clock

Wall clock, long rectangular walnut case w/an arched top crest w/turned finial flanked by projecting disk corners w/matching finials above rounded reeded drops & drop finials above the sides flanking a tall arched glass door over a brass bezel & round white dial w/black Roman numerals & brass center ring, a long pendulum w/large brass bob & a single cylindrical brass weight, bottom corners short

Mauthe Berliner Fancy Wall Clock

Wall clock, Mauthe Clock Co., Germany, Berliner-style, carved light walnut case , the high carved & pierced central crestrail w/a molding over a carved iris flanked by corner blocks & turned finials over a flat stepped cornice above half-round ring-turned columns flanking the wood dial frame w/carved leaves at each corner around the brass bezel enclosing the dial w/a celluloid chapter ring w/Arabic numerals around an embossed brass center, a narrow scalloped front apron & short turned corner drop finials, scalloped brackets & a long pierce-carved backboard framing the pendulum & embossed brass bob, eight-day time & strike movement, ca. 1890-1900, 15" w., 35" h. (ILLUS.).............. **1,400-1,500**

German Box Clock with Leaded Glass

Wall clock, Mauthe (F.), Schwenningen, Germany, box-type, tall oak-veneered case w/a simple arched crest above a case w/a thin beaded band at each side flanking the tall door, the upper wood door panel w/a round opening for the silvered metal dial w/Arabic numerals, the lower door glazed w/clear beveled glass segments showing the pendulum & large brass bob, eight-day spring-wound time & strike movement, ca. 1910-20, 12 1/2" w., 30" h. (ILLUS.) **800-1,000**

Wall clock, Mauthe (F.), Schwenningen, Germany, R-A-type, softwood & walnut-veneered case in a dark finish, the gallery crest carved w/leaves, turned supports & turnip-form finials, reeded side columns w/turned capitals & bases flank the long door over the porcelain dial w/Roman numerals & a brass gridiron pendulum w/large brass bob, drop pendants at the bottom corners of the case, eight-day spring-wound time & strike movement, ca. 1900-10, 15" w., 37" h. **800-950**

Herman Miller Brand Wall Clock

Wall clock, Miller (Herman) Clock Co., Zeeland, Michigan, Herman Miller brand ceramic wall clock, white hexagonal shape printed in blue on four sides w/Dutch scenes, hexagonal dial w/Arabic numerals, eight-day movement, time-only, ca. 1950s, 9" w. (ILLUS.) **70-80**

Miniature German Wall Clock

Wall clock, miniature "retard-advance" model, wooden-backed brass case w/molded arched top bordered w/floral decoration & topped w/ribbed urn-form finial, the case w/side brass panels flanking the arched glass front over the brass dial w/steel chapter ring w/black Roman numerals, the dial center & pendulum bob ornately decorated w/florals, the base w/elaborate scroll decoration & ribbed drop, time-only movement w/seven-wheel train to get week's duration out of quarter second pendulum, marked w/Meyer foundry stamp, Germany, ca. 1890, 17" h. (ILLUS. below left)................... **2,240**

French Picture Frame Clock

Wall clock, Morbier, France, metal picture frame-style, the squared iron case w/molded serpentine sides w/mother-of-pearl inlaid decoration around the round glazed white dial w/black Roman numerals & original hands, iron framed spring prayer repeat movement strikes the hour, then repeats it two minutes later, ca. 1880, 19" h. (ILLUS.) **588**

Wall Clock with Leaded Glass Door

Wall clock, New Haven Clock Co., New Haven, Connecticut, "Nason" model, mahogany case, round molded top around the original white paper dial w/black Arabic numerals, long drop base w/molded scroll sides flanking a leaded glass door panel, knobbed drop finial, pendulum w/original lacquer, good rear label, some wear to paper dial, ca. 1913, 35 1/2" h. (ILLUS.)... **952**

French Morbier Brass Wall Clock

Wall clock, Morbier, France, square narrow repoussé brass frame w/high arched embossed ornate floral & leaf crest, the round white porcelain dial w/black Roman numerals & pierced brass hands above the original folding pendulum, mounted on open black iron wall bracket w/scroll side braces, eight-day two-weight prayer repeat movement that strikes the hour on large bell, then repeats the strike again at two minutes past the hour, iron weights copies of originals, hand tension device needs adjusting, ca. 1840, 15" h. (ILLUS.) **728**

New Haven "Saxon" Figure-eight

Large New Haven Oak Wall Clock

Wall clock, New Haven Clock Co., New Haven, Connecticut, oak long-case type, the arched crest decorated w/a pressed design of lappets & scrolls above the tall two-pane door w/egg-and-dart molding, the upper pane over a large dial w/Roman numerals, the lower pane over the large brass pendulum bob & printed in gold "Standard Time," flat base, original finish, ca. 1910, 5 1/4 x 15 1/2", 37 1/2" h. (ILLUS.).................................. **600-700**

Wall clock, New Haven Clock Co., New Haven, Connecticut, "Saxon" model w/figure-eight case, rosewood w/a large brass ring around the upper dial w/Arabic numerals, brass roundels at the center above another large brass ring around a glass pane w/a stenciled lacy silver ring framing the pendulum, eight-day movement, time & strike, late 19th c., 4 x 11", 19" h. (ILLUS.) **300-400**

Wall clock, New Haven Clock Co., New Haven, Connecticut, "Thistle" model, porcelain-cased hanging wall clock w/brass surround & wall chain, 15-day, time only, 10 x 14" **600**

Novelty German Landscape Clock

English Short-drop Oak Wall Clock

Wall clock, New Haven Clock Co., New Haven Connecticut (works only), English oak short-drop case, large round frame around the dial w/Roman numerals & the printed name of the English retailer, pierced leafy scroll side brackets flank the small rectangular glazed door w/beaded edge trim over the decorative brass pendulum bob, long coved base drop w/slender horizontal rods w/finials, refinished, late 19th c., 5 x 16", 26 1/2" h. (ILLUS.) **600-700**

Wall clock, novelty movement, hand-carved landscape w/a waterwheel & stream, trees & an onion-dome church w/the clock dial set in the tower, framed, eight-day seven-jewel movement, string on reverse runs from waterwheel to clock & is wound by turning the wheel, Germany, ca. 1950s, 15 x 31" (ILLUS. at bottom of previous page) **300**

Ornate Carved Walnut Wall Clock

Wall clock, Peyron Castille, Dijon, France, carved cartouche-form walnut case w/molded notched pediment w/broken arch pediment centered by heavily carved shell-top crest, the case w/carved reeded pilasters & florets flanking the round notched wood bezel & wooden dial w/white porcelain number cartouches w/black Roman numerals & signed "Peyron Castille a Dijon," gadrooned base band over the ornate drop w/scroll drop finial & conforming corner drop finials, eight-day time & strike movement striking the hours & halves, France, ca. 1890, 22" w. x 29" h. (ILLUS.) **616**

French Picture Frame Wall Clock

Wall clock, picture frame-style, cartouche-form Morez iron frame enclosing a repeating movement that automatically repeats the strike at two minutes after the hour, black frame centered by a brass bezel & white round enamel dial w/black Roman numerals & signed "Petiot Guichard à Louhans," frame decorated w/inlaid mother-of-pearl scrolls, striking on a coiled wire gong, only minor losses, France, ca. 1870, 25" h. (ILLUS. on previous page) **543**

Picture Frame Wall Clock

Wall clock, picture frame-style, oblong undulating heavy outer molding around a mother-of-pearl inner border enclosing the brass bezel & glass dial w/Roman numerals, eight-day time & strike movement, France, ca. 1900, 16 x 20" (ILLUS.) **900-1,100**

Daniel Pratt Jr. Ogee Shelf Clock

Shelf, Pratt (Daniel Jr.), Reading, Massachusetts, upright rectangular mahogany veneer ogee case w/two-paned door, smaller upper pane over the dial w/delicate painted spandrels, black Roman numerals & open escapement, the lower pane of frosted glass w/floral & leaf garland engraving, good label w/image of Pratt's Boston showroom, 30-hour time/strike/alarm movement, replacement frosted tablet, some veneer chips, ca. 1850, 26" h. (ILLUS.) **196**

Ornate French Brass Wall Clock

Wall clock, rectangular pressed-brass case w/ornate ropetwist, shell, & floral decoration, open brass dial w/enameled inset Roman numerals & rococo hands, sunburst pendulum bob, made in France for Roehm & Wright, Detroit, Michigan, ca. 1900, 22" h. (ILLUS.) **476**

Ornate German Wall Clock

Wall clock, Renaissance-style walnut case, a high arched & petal-carved crest above a blocked & scroll-carved rail w/a small turned knob (one missing) above a cornice overhanging the round dial w/Arabic numerals flanked by leaf carvings & heavy turned column supports above a lower compartment w/column supports flanking a spindled gallery, scroll- and block-carved base section w/turned drops, Germany, late 19th c. (ILLUS. below left)... **1,550**

Wall clock, Sangamo Company, electric model, a square flat walnut frame centering a large white dial w/Arabic numerals & subsidiary seconds dial, 20th c., 19 sq....... **135**

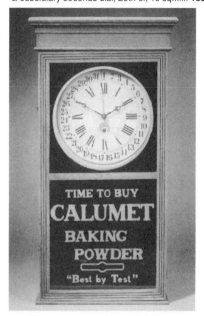

Sessions Advertising Wall Clock

Wall clock, Sessions Clock Co., Bristol, Connecticut, advertising-type, tall simple oak case w/flat cornice above a two-part glazed door framed w/reeded molding, the upper door opening to a white dial w/Roman numerals framed w/month numerals, the lower door w/gold reverse-painted advertising reading "Time To Buy - Calumet - Baking Powder - 'Best by Test,'" late 19th - early 20th c., 34" h. (ILLUS.)... **690**

Sessions Mission Oak Wall Clock

Wall clock, Sessions Clock Co., Bristol, Connecticut, miniature "Aztec" model Mission Oak case, a square molded frame enclosing the square wood dial face w/applied brass Arabic numerals, the free-hanging pendulum w/brass bob backed by a lattice framework, eight-day time & strike movement, ca. 1915-20, 10" w., 19" h. (ILLUS.) **500-600**

Sessions Oak Wall Clock

Wall clock, Sessions Clock Co., Bristol, Connecticut, oak case w/a flat top & deep cornice above a large square reeded glazed door w/black reverse-painted ground & gold ring over the large dial w/Arabic nu-

merals, angled side brackets flank a backboard at the bottom, eight-day movement, time only, ca. 1900, 4 3/4 x 18", 24 1/2" h. (ILLUS. below left) **200-300**

Wall clock, Sessions Clock Co., Bristol, Connecticut, oak cased schoolhouse-type, the octagonal upper section w/a pressed design around the dial w/original hands, the drop case w/a glass door showing the pendulum, original dark varnished finish, eight-day time-only movement, late 19th - early 20th c., 27 1/2" h. **250-275**

Sessions Octagonal Drop Wall Clock

Wall clock, Sessions Clock Co., Bristol, Connecticut, octagonal short-drop model, golden oak case, the octagonal top w/a large brass bezel over the dial w/Roman numerals, the drop case w/a pointed base & small glazed pointed door w/gilt banding, original finish, replaced eight-day time-only movement, ca. 1900, 5 1/4 x 17", 28" h. (ILLUS.) **300-400**

Sessions "Home No. 1" Clock

Wall clock, Sessions Clock Company, Forestville, Connecticut, "Home #1" miniature model "Regulator," mahogany finished poplar case w/flaring stepped cornice over a glass front w/gilt line decoration, dial w/Roman numerals, worn paper label on back, time & strike movement, some discoloration, ca. 1915, 19 1/2" h. (ILLUS.).............................. **336**

Anglo-American Short-drop Clock

Wall clock, short-drop style, walnut burl veneer case, the large round molded top enclosing the brass bezel & painted dial w/Roman numerals, the short drop case flanked by pierce-carved grapevine brackets, centered by a small rectangular glass pane showing the brass pendulum bob, short curved base drop, Anglo-American, eight-day spring-wound time & strike movement, ca. 1870s, 15" w., 28" h. (ILLUS.) **1,100-1,500**

Commemorative Gallery Clock

Wall clock, Smith (A.D.), Cincinnati, Ohio, Marine movement gallery-style clock made to commemorate Civil War, S.B. Jerome patented round case, a flat simulated leather over pine round frame w/brass trim featuring pressed-brass stars, bugles & crossed swords bordered in brass, the central round dial w/Roman numerals, missing seconds hand, Hubbel eight-day time-only movement, original label, ca. 1868, 13" d. (ILLUS. on previous page) **728**

Terry Clock with Iron Case

Wall clock, Terry Clock Co., Waterbury, Connecticut, round-topped black iron case w/a deep rectangular base, most of the original gold scroll & line decoration remains, original brass bezel around the dial w/Roman numerals, some paint chips on sides of case, 30-hour movement, time-only, ca. 1875, 8 1/4" h. (ILLUS.)..................................... **190**

Biedermeier Period Wall Clock

Wall clock, tall rectangular Biedermeier-style rosewood veneer case w/beveled pediment on band of beaded molding, body w/rounded corners flanking the tall glass door w/cast pierced gilt-metal trim over the white dial w/fancy brass bezel, black Roman numerals & subsidiary seconds dial, a long iron pendulum w/brass bob & weight, the inset sides & base w/beaded molding & waisted base drop w/drop finial, the base & drop finial decorated w/cast pierced gilt-metal trim, 30-day time-only 72-beat movement w/five-wheel train, original mounting bracket, top trim missing, mounting bracket repaired, Austria, ca. 1845, 40" h. (ILLUS.).. **4,760**

Seth Thomas Box Wall Clock

Wall clock, Thomas (Seth) Clock Co., Plymouth, Connecticut, box-type, mahogany-stained hardwood case, flat top w/narrow cornice over a simple square frame w/a glass door reverse-painted in black w/a gold band around the large old replaced dial w/Roman numerals, flat molded base, eight-day movement, time only, ca. 1900, 4 1/4 x 15 1/4", 15 1/4" h. (ILLUS.).. **250-300**

Seth Thomas "Eclipse" Wall Clock

Wall clock, Thomas (Seth) Clock Co., Plymouth, Connecticut, "Eclipse" model, Victorian Eastlake style walnut case, the high pierce-carved pediment w/a half-round wheel molding w/top knobs over a sunburst device on a blocked molding w/cut-out spearpoints & corner arches over a molded cornice & angular line-incised brackets flanking the tall glass door w/elaborate gilt stencil leaf & lacy net decoration, the dial w/Roman numerals, stamped brass pendulum bob w/a sunflower design, the lower molding w/scroll-cut brackets flanking the lower case & w/a deep double-arch cut apron w/a central sunflower device above spearpoint & block drops, eight-day movement, time, strike & alarm, ca. 1880s, 4 3/8 x 14 1/2", 26" h. (ILLUS.).. **400-500**

"King Bee" Clock with Gingerbread

Wall clock, Thomas (Seth) Clock Co., Plymouth, Connecticut, "King Bee" model, oak case w/extensive gingerbread decoration & metal ornaments including a tall crown crest above wide rounded & notched top sides, panel-topped arched front w/original tablet reverse-painted w/gilt fern & floral decoration, white dial w/brass bezel & center & black Roman numerals, original pendulum, label on back notes it was made for the L.B. Price Co. of Kansas City, Missouri, eight-day time & strike movement w/alarm, ca. 1905, 29 3/4" h. (ILLUS.) **868**

"No. 1 Marble Dial Clock" Model

Wall clock, Thomas (Seth) Clock Co., Plymouth, Connecticut, "No. 1 Marble Dial Clock" model, large unframed circular marble dial w/original bronze Arabic numerals & brass hands, 15-day double wind spring movement w/dead beat escapement, some roughness, small chips around circumference, ca. 1905, 20" d. (ILLUS.)... **1,176**

Thomas Oak Schoolhouse Clock

Wall clock, Thomas (Seth) Clock Co., Plymouth, Connecticut, oak short drop schoolhouse-style case, wide octagonal top framing the heavy brass bezel & painted dial w/Arabic numerals, the short pointed drop w/a small conforming glass window showing the brass pendulum bob, eight-day time-only movement, ca. 1920s, 15" w., 22" h. (ILLUS.) **500-600**

Thomas "Office No. 11" Wall Clock

Wall clock, Thomas (Seth) Clock Co., Plymouth, Connecticut, "Office No. 11" model, square flat oak frame enclosing a brass bezel & painted dial w/Arabic numerals & sweep seconds hand, 30-day movement, ca. 1920-25, 15" w. (ILLUS.) **1,200-1,500**

Seth Thomas "One Day Lever" Clock

Wall clock, Thomas (Seth) Clock Co., Plymouth, Connecticut, "One Day Lever" model, gallery-type, 10-sided rosewood veneer molded case, a large brass bezel enclosing glass over the painted dial w/subsidiary seconds dial ring & black Roman numerals, good label on back, 30-hour time & strike lever movement, some paint loss on dial, ca. 1880, 13" h. (ILLUS.)... **308**

Seth Thomas Oak Wall Clock

Seth Thomas "World" Wall Clock

Wall clock, Thomas (Seth) Clock Co., Plymouth, Connecticut, "World" model, oak case w/a large octagonal top framing the brass bezel enclosing the dial w/Roman numerals & sweep seconds hand, the long pointed drop base enclosing a pointed glass door over the pendulum w/a brass bob, double spring 15-day movement w/Graham dead beat escapement, ca. 1905-15, 17" w., 32" h. (ILLUS.) **1,500-1,750**

Wall clock, Thomas (Seth) Clock Co., Thomaston, Connecticut, "Office No. 1" model, square oak case, round white dial w/Arabic numerals & "Seth Thomas" over the 6, clean label on back, eight-day time only movement, ca. 1922, 16" h. (ILLUS. top of next column) **476**

Seth Thomas "Flora" Wall Clock

Wall clock, Thomas (Seth) Clock Company, Plymouth, Connecticut, "Flora" model, long cherry case w/rectangular flat top raised on a deep decorated ogee molding flanked by small corner blocks w/tiny knob finials over the tall two-pane door, the top section w/a square panel w/corner fan-carving around the white painted dial w/black Roman numerals & sunburst spandrels, the large lower pane over two weights & wood pendulum w/brass damascene bob, the sides of the case carved w/floral designs, scroll brackets flank the base backboard, eight-day time & strike movement, small repair by hanging hole, warning lever needs adjusting, ca. 1880, 38" h. (ILLUS. on previous page).............. **5,264**

sidiary seconds dial, original hands & pendulum, 15-day double-spring time-only movement, some crazing to dial, ca. 1910, 38 1/2" h. (ILLUS. left) **1,176**

"Office No. 5" Wall Clock

Wall clock, Thomas (Seth), Plymouth, Connecticut, "Office No. 5" model, square oak case w/flat top w/molded flaring cornice, the wooden front panel decorated w/Eastlake-style incised lines & centered by a large brass bezel around the white dial w/black Roman numerals, a molded base band above short curved brackets flanking a scalloped back panel, eight-day time-only movement, ca. 1910, 23 1/4" h. (ILLUS.)....................................... **1,008**

Wall clock, Wallace Company, electric miniature schoolhouse-style clock, battery-operated, the mahogany case w/a rounded top enclosing the large dial w/Arabic numerals, the short drop case w/beveled bottom corners, 20th c., 11" h. **146**

Seth Thomas "Umbria" Clock

Wall clock, Thomas (Seth) Clock Company, Plymouth, Connecticut, "Umbria" model, tall molded oak case w/broken arch pediment w/finial, stepped base w/carved skirt, white dial w/Roman numerals & sub-

French Clock with Weather Station

Wall clock, walnut case w/a top gallery w/turned bobbins & urn-form corner finials above a narrow flared cornice above the case w/turned & reeded colonettes flanking a round molding enclosing the dial w/enameled plaques w/black Roman numerals, the tapering lower case carved w/ornate leaf scrolls at the sides flanking a small rectangular thermometer over a round brass bezel enclosing a barometer dial, eight-day German time & strike movement, France, ca. 1900, 16" w., 35" h. (ILLUS.)..................................... **1,900-2,200**

Waltham Gaslight Wall Clock

Wall clock, Waltham Watch Co., Waltham, Massachusetts, wall-mounted gaslight timepiece w/period gas fixture & valve assembly w/a narrow upright rod supporting the original round brass clock case enclosing the white dial w/blue Arabic numerals & original hands, time only movement, balance intact, runs for about one hour, deterioration to cloth covering case, Waltham trademark slightly worn, ca. 1890, 5 1/2" h. (ILLUS.) **650**

Fine Classical Revival Wall Clock

Wall clock, Waterbury Clock Co., Waterbury, Connecticut, Classical Revival style rosewood veneer case, the flat stepped cornice over an ogee panel flanked by end blocks above half-round maple columns w/gilt capitals & bases flanking the two-pane door, the large upper pane over the painted tin face w/Roman numerals & green-stenciled leaves, the lower door pane reverse-painted w/a bluebird in a gilt ring surrounded by flowers on a tan ground, deep blocked ogee base, open escapement, paper label inside, ca.

1890, 4 3/8 x 14 3/4", 24 3/4" h. (ILLUS. on previous page) **600-700**

Waterbury "Drop Octagon" Clock

Wall clock, Waterbury Clock Co., Waterbury, Connecticut, "Drop Octagon 10 Inch" model, large mahogany veneer octagonal top enclosing a large brass bezel over the original dial w/Roman numerals & original hands, short pointed drop case w/a small window w/gilt stenciled rings showing pendulum & brass bob, label inside case, eight-day signed time & strike movement, ca. 1895, 21 1/2" h. (ILLUS.)......... **392**

Waterbury "Galesburg" Model Clock

Wall clock, Waterbury Clock Co., Waterbury, Connecticut, "Galesburg" model, long oak case, the molded arched crest centered by a block w/turned urn finial flanked by turned corner finials, short reeded columns & turned drops flank the top sides above the tall arched & glazed door, a wood molding encloses the brass bezel & original paper dial w/Roman numerals, the long lower pane shows the pendulum & large brass bob, short reeded columns & finials flank the bottom of the door, a long stepped & tapering base drop w/a turned finial, two drop finials at the bottom case corners, original finish, late 19th - early 20th c., eight-day time & strike movement w/half-hour gong strike, 52" h. (ILLUS.) **1,069**

Sample Size Waterbury Wall Clock

Wall clock, Waterbury Clock Co., Waterbury, Connecticut, short-drop salesman's sample, stained softwood, dial w/Arabic numerals, eight-day movement, time-only, ca. 1920, 4 3/8 x 8", 12 1/2" h. (ILLUS.) **200-300**

Waterbury "Galesburg" Wall Clock

Wall clock, Waterbury Clock Co., Waterbury, Connecticut, "Galesburg" model, tall oak case w/a high arched crest centered by a block & turned finial flanked by turned corner finials on the molded cornice, short blocks & turned finials at the top & bottom corners of the front flanking the tall arched & glazed door w/wood molding enclosing the brass bezel & paper dial w/Roman numerals, the glass showing the long pendulum & large brass bob, original label inside case, eight-day spring-wound time & strike movement, ca. 1900-10, 15" w., 52" h. (ILLUS.) **1,900-2,250**

Waterbury Drop Octagon Clock

Wall clock, Waterbury Clock Co., Waterbury, New York, "12 Inch Drop Octagon" model, rosewood veneer short drop case w/octagonal upper section framing the painted dial w/brass bezel w/hinge at top of dial, black Roman numerals for time & Arabic numerals for date, the short polygon molded drop w/hinged glass door decorated w/a gilt floral & scroll design around an oval pendulum window on black ground, partially legible label inside case, eight-day time-only movement, glass over dial replaced, lower glass pane reblacked from reverse, ca. 1895, 23" h. (ILLUS. on previous page)................. **476**

E.N. Welch Octagonal Wall Clock

Wall clock, Welch (E.N.) Mfg. Co., Bristol, Connecticut, octagonal drop model, oak case, the octagonal upper section w/a stamped star band around the brass bezel over the dial w/Roman numerals & an outer calendar date band & sweep seconds hand, the pointed drop base w/matching glass door w/stamped star band trim, large stamped brass pendulum bob, original finish, eight-day movement, time only, ca. 1880, 4 x 17 1/2", 33" h. (ILLUS.) **400-500**

Elaborate Oak Hanging Clock

Wall clock, Welch (E.N.) Mfg. Co., Bristol, Connecticut (attributed), hanging oak kitchen-style, the high arched crest w/a carved shell above scrolls & blocked corners above carved scrolls & notch-cut sides flanking the angled arched door w/beaded edging & ornate gilt stencil decoration, dial w/Roman numerals, flat built-in shelf above a scroll-stamped apron centered by an inset level above the pointed scallop-cut drop, eight-day movement, strike & alarm, old case refinish, late 19th c., 4 1/2 x 14 3/8", 27 3/4" h. (ILLUS.) **350-400**

Welch Short Drop Octagonal Clock

Wall clock, Welch (E.N.) Mfg. Co., Bristol, Connecticut, octagonal drop wall case, original dark varnish finish, the stepped octagonal top w/a large brass bezel enclosing the dial w/Roman numerals, sweep seconds hands & an outer day-of-the-month band, the short pointed drop case w/a small glass door w/gilt trim, eight-day movement, time, strike & calendar, open escapement, minor wear on face, ca. 1890, 4 1/2 x 17", 22" h. (ILLUS. on previous page)............................ **350-400**

German Chiming Clock

"Gale Drop Model No. 3" Clock

Wall clock, Welch, Spring & Co., Forestville, Connecticut, "Gale Drop Model No. 3," by Daniel J. Gale, mahogany case w/a large round molded frame enclosing a brass bezel & large single slightly yellowed dial w/Arabic numerals for the time & four subsidiary date dials w/Roman numerals for days of the week, months & lunar phase, day dates in Arabic numerals around the edge, the rectangular drop case w/a square door glass pane w/a gilt band border & delicate gilt-stenciled band decoration framing the pendulum & brass bob, cove-molded base drop, ca. 1879, 30" h. (ILLUS.) **11,760**

Wall clock, Westminster Chime "box" clock, oak case w/arched cornice & stepped base, beveled glass in lower panel in brass frame, silvered brass dial w/Arabic numerals, the gong set w/heavy cast-iron base, time & strike movement, Germany, ca. 1920, 31" h. (ILLUS.).............. **644**

Papier-mâché Gallery Clock

Wall gallery clock, Litchfield Manufacturing Co., Litchfield, Connecticut, papier-mâché scalloped scroll-cut flat frame decorated w/gilt scroll decoration, red & gold flowers & mother-of-pearl inlay on a black ground, a brass bezel encloses the cream dial w/black Roman numerals, 30-hour time-only lever movement, minor chip at bottom of case, extra set of four holes that line up with bezel, some dial discoloration, ca. 1860, 10" h. (ILLUS.) **1,456**

Ansonia "Regulator A" Wall Clock

Wall regulator clock, Ansonia Clock Co., Ansonia, Connecticut, "Regulator A" model, walnut veneer case w/a large octagonal top section w/molded black ring around the brass bezel enclosing the paper dial w/Roman numerals & an outer calendar date ring w/Arabic numerals, the long drop case w/a pointed bottom w/conforming molding framing the glazed door printed w/"Regulator A," pendulum w/large brass bob, eight-day time & strike movement, ca. 1900-10, 17" w., 32" h. (ILLUS.).. **900-1,000**

Ash Ansonia "Regulator A" Model

Wall regulator clock, Ansonia Clock Co., Ansonia, Connecticut, "Regulator A" model, ash case, the large octagonal top w/a molded black band around the brass bezel & paper dial w/Roman numerals, the pointed drop case w/a molded & pointed glazed door w/"Regulator A" over the pendulum & large brass bob, eight-day time & strike movement, ca. 1905-10, 17" w., 32" h. (ILLUS.)................. **1,000-1,250**

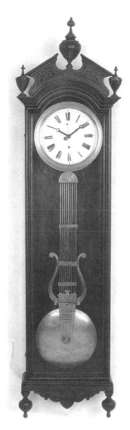

Ansonia Wall "Regulator No. 4"

Wall regulator clock, Ansonia Clock Co., Ansonia, Connecticut, "Regulator No. 4," walnut Renaissance Revival-style long case, the broken arch pediment w/a large turned central urn finial & smaller turned corner finials above an arched glazed front over a large round dial w/wide brass bezel & Roman numerals suspending a large brass pendulum w/a band of thin strings continuing into a lyre design above the large brass disk pendulum bob, molded base w/pointed scalloped apron & turned corner drops, ca. 1880 (ILLUS.) **5,880**

Ansonia "Office Regulator"

Wall regulator clock, Ansonia Clock Co., New York, New York, "Office Regulator" model, black walnut molded case w/octagonal top over long drop, white dial w/Roman numerals & subsidiary seconds dial, glass door w/"Regulator" decal in bottom through which pendulum shows, eight-day time & strike movement, new decal, some replacement/restoration, ca. 1901, 32" h. (ILLUS.) **588**

Austrian Walnut Regulator Clock

Wall regulator clock, Austrian one-weight model, tall walnut case w/molded arched pediment w/two finials, tall arched glass front over the brass bezel & white porcelain dial w/Roman numerals, a single small cylindrical brass weight & long pendulum w/a large brass bob, stepped base w/drop finial, time-only movement, replacement finials, spider web in porcelain dial, ca. 1890, 43 1/2" h. (ILLUS.) **840**

Gustav Becker Walnut Regulator

Wall regulator clock, Becker (Gustav), Germany, tall walnut case in Viennese style, arched pediment above the arched glass door w/molded frame over the white dial w/black Arabic numerals, a brass bezel, center ring, weight, pendulum & bob, ogee base drop w/beveled drop finial, one-weight time-only movement signed w/Becker's medal of honor seals, ca. 1895, 44" h. (ILLUS.) **504**

Chelsea Clock Co. Wall Regulator

Wall regulator clock, Chelsea Clock Co., Chelsea, Massachusetts, "No. 1 Pendulum" model, long oak case w/a large round top molding enclosing the white dial w/black Roman numerals, the long rectangular drop case w/a glass door over the pendulum & large brass bob, short cove-molded base drop, time-only movement signed w/Chelsea trademark & "A-142," dial repainted, movement restrung, ca. 1920, 34" h. (ILLUS.) **1,568**

English Wall Drop Regulator

Wall regulator clock, drop-style hardwood case, the large round molded top centering the dial w/Roman numerals & an outer month calendar ring, the lower case w/a small glazed door printed in gold "Regulator," scroll cut-outs at the sides, the deep ogee scroll base drop w/horizontal rods & finials at the top & base, England, late 19th - early 20th c., 4 1/2 x 12 1/4", 22" h. (ILLUS.) **200-250**

Eastman Clock Co. Wall Regulator

Wall regulator clock, Eastman Clock Co., Boston, Massachusetts, "Pendulum No. I" model, oak case w/large round molding surrounding the white dial w/black Roman numerals & marked "Daniel Pratt's Son, Boston, Mass," drop case w/molding surrounding a red & black painted glass panel, signed eight-day weight movement, some flaking on dial, weight baffle w/crack, ca. 1895, 33" h. (ILLUS. on previous page) **1,792**

Frick Clock Co. Wall Regulator

Wall regulator clock, Frick (Fred.) Clock Co., Waynesboro, Pennsylvania, oak case, flat flaring stepped cornice above a long door w/arched glass panel opening to a round dial w/Roman numerals & seconds dial, stepped-out shelf support w/rounded & paneled front, late 19th - early 20th c. (ILLUS.) **185**

W.L. Gilbert Oak "Regulator No. 10"

Wall regulator clock, Gilbert (William L.), Winsted, Connecticut, "Regulator No. 10" model, long oak case w/molded pediment & cornice w/molding above a panel carved w/ribs & a scallop design above the round white dial w/metal bezel & black Roman numerals & subsidiary seconds dial, wood molding below the dial & over a long glass pane showing the pendulum & brass pendulum bob, the molded drop w/semicircular carved sides, time-only movement, missing seven oak balls at top, some nicks & scrapes to weight, ca. 1895, 52 1/2" h. (ILLUS.) **5,880**

Gilbert Wall "Regulator No. 16"

Wall regulator clock, Gilbert (Wm. L.) Mfg. Company, Winsted, Connecticut, "Regulator No. 16" model, walnut Renaissance Revival style long case, the high pediment top centered by an arched plaque w/bobbin-turned trim around a relief-carved mask & above a carved dentil band, a wide frieze band over the case w/a long narrow glazed door w/arched top flanked by incised & scroll-cut side pendants & opening to a dial w/Roman numerals suspending a long pendulum w/mercury weights, scroll-carved detail on lower sides of case & drop cornice at bottom w/detailing similar to the top, ca. 1875-85 (ILLUS.) **12,320**

Fine Gilbert "Regulator No. 11"

Wall regulator clock, Gilbert (Wm. L.) Clock Co., Winsted, Connecticut, "Regulator No. 11" model, Victorian Eastlake style walnut case, the high pediment w/a sawtooth-carved crestrail rail over a cornice above a frieze band of small knobs & a sawtooth band, the long case w/reeded panels above the round-topped glass front flanked by reeded pilasters, a molded base above a narrow sawtooth apron supported by angular cut support brackets flanked by lower back panel, eight-inch dial w/Roman numerals & small seconds dial, wooden pendulum w/large brass bob, eight-day movement, time & strike, ca. 1885, 7 1/2 x 17 14", 50" h. (ILLUS.) **2,000-2,200**

frame enclosing an arched-top glazed door opening to the white-painted sheet metal round dial w/Roman numerals above the long pendulum & large round brass bob, flat narrow molded base w/corner drops, ca. 1900, from a railroad dispatcher's office in Indiana, 19" w., 65" h. **1,760**

Massive Austrian Wall Clock

Wall regulator clock, grand sonnerie type, tall walnut case w/arched cove-molded cornice w/three urn-form finials, a carved floret & small triangular panels in the arch above a plain frieze band above the reeded case sides w/carved scroll brackets at the top corners, a tall inset arch-top keylock glass door w/molded frame over the brass bezel & white 9"-d. dial w/black Roman numerals & brass center ring, a three-foot long pendulum w/large brass bob, three small cylindrical weights, beveled base molding w/corner ball drop finials & ogee base drop ending in a small rectangular section w/ball drop finial, 66-beat time & strike movement, Austria, ca. 1895, 69" h. (ILLUS.) **5,600**

Wall regulator clock, Howard (E.), Boston, Massachusetts, railroad-type, quarter-sawn oak, a flat crest above a stepped cornice w/bracketed sides & small knob finials above the narrow reeded side

E. Howard "Regulator No. 10"

Wall regulator clock, Howard (E.) & Co., Boston, Massachusetts, "Regulator No. 10" model, figure 8-shaped walnut case w/molded round top & bottom panels, scroll crest w/bull's-eye center & conforming base drop, top molding over the white dial w/wood bezel & black Roman numerals, the waisted center section w/a glass pane reverse-painted w/black & gold border & center panel showing pendulum stick, the bottom panel glass reverse-painted in black & gold w/center circle showing pendulum bob, time-only movement, some dry splits to bezel, bottom repaired, replacement weight a proper Howard casting from 1976, ca. 1910, 33" h. (ILLUS.) **4,480**

E. Howard & Co. "Regulator No. 7"

E. Howard & Co. "Regulator No. 6"

Wall regulator clock, Howard (E.) & Co., Boston, Massachusetts, "Regulator No. 6" model, figure 8-shaped walnut case w/molded round top & bottom panels, scroll crest & base drop, top pane over the dial w/wood bezel, black Roman numerals & subsidiary seconds dial, the waisted center section w/glass pane reverse-painted in black, red & gold, the bottom glass panel reverse-painted in black, red & gold w/center circle showing pendulum bob, time-only movement complete w/Geneva stopwork, original hold-down tabs & proper signature, touch-ups to dial, tablets restored, pendulum stick renewed w/original hardware, replacement baffle, ca. 1874, 58" h. (ILLUS.)... **25,200**

Wall regulator clock, Howard (E.) & Co., Boston, Massachusetts, "Regulator No. 7" model, figure 8-shaped walnut case w/molded round top & bottom panels, scroll crest w/finial, upper section enclosing the white dial w/wood bezel & black Roman numerals, the center waisted section w/a glass pane reverse-painted w/black & gold border around a center panel showing pendulum stick, the bottom glass panel reverse-painted in black & gold w/a center circle showing pendulum bob, ogee base drop w/rounded drop finial, time-only movement, replaced top trim, finial a Victorian replacement, pendulum stick w/sprayed gilding, replacement baffle, flaking to bottom tablet, center repainted improperly, ca. 1880, 50" h. without replacement finial (ILLUS.) **10,640**

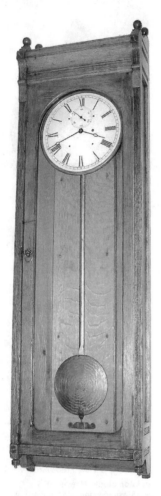

E. Howard "Regulator No. 89"

Wall regulator clock, Howard (E.) & Co., Boston, Massachusetts, "Regulator No. 89" model, simple rectangular oak case w/four corner knob finials on concave-front cornice, ribbing along corner panels on front & sides, arched glass panel over white dial w/black Roman numerals & subsidiary seconds dial, the door w/brass lion pull, corner drop finials at base, pendulum bob w/fancy engraved pattern, original No. 1 iron weight, time-only movement, old spliced & glued break on door, lion pull replacement for original lock, ca. 1889, 65" h. (ILLUS.)...................... **4,480**

E. Howard & Co. "Regulator No. 9"

Wall regulator clock, Howard (E.) & Co., Boston, Massachusetts, "Regulator No. 9" model, walnut figure 8-shaped case w/molded bull's-eye finial over molded round frame around the white signed dial w/black Roman numerals, the midsection w/glass panel w/beveled frame & reverse-painted border in black & gilt conforming to waist, the gilt pendulum stick showing through center, the lower circular glass panel w/reverse-painted concentric circles of black, gilt & deep red, w/pendulum bob showing through center, base drop finial, time-only movement, weight & baffle replaced, ca. 1910, 37" h. (ILLUS.).. **9,240**

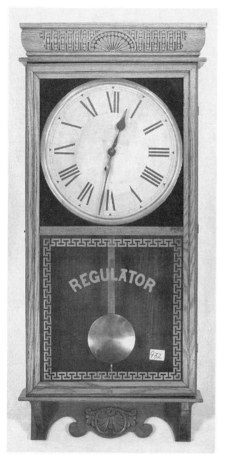

Ingraham Western Union Regulator

Wall regulator clock, Ingraham & Co., Bristol, Connecticut, "Western Union" model, long oak case w/a flat rectangular top w/a wide cornice lightly carved & centered by a fan device above the flat case molding enclosing the tall, wide two-pane glazed door, the upper pane w/black corners centered by the large brass bezel & dial w/Roman numerals, the lower pane w/a gilt Greek key border band & the word "Regulator" over the pendulum & large brass bob, short base brackets flank the scroll-cut & carved drop backboard, late 19th - early 20th c., 37" h. (ILLUS.) **338**

German Ebonized Wall Regulator

Wall regulator clock, long rectangular ebonized wood case w/a flaring stepped cornice supporting a high center crest w/a roundel over flaring molding & large ring-turned corner finials, two three-quarter round colonettes w/baluster-form tops & bottoms flank the tall arched glass front w/a brass bezel & white round porcelain dial w/Roman numerals, the multi-rod pendulum w/a brass ring bezel enclosing a white plaque printed w/"R-A," molded base over a ribbed band & long ogee base drop w/drop finial flanked by corner drop finials, eight-day spring time & strike movement, some restoration, Germany, ca. 1890, 37" h. (ILLUS.) **504**

Ornate Mini Black Forest Clock

Wall regulator clock, miniature Black Forest-type in an ornately carved walnut cuckoo clock-style case w/peaked top overhanging cut-out fruit & leaf decorations vining around sides & base, half-round columns flanking arch-topped glazed door w/more vine decoration over the white porcelain dial w/molded brass bezel & center ring & black Roman numerals, a brass three-bar pendulum w/a brass ring-form bob inset w/a porcelain plaque lettered "R - A," extensions of side columns form drop finials a fluted horizontal base rail also w/turned end finials & square blocks w/roundels, needs a 00 key but crank works, replacement hands, missing small carved rail of leaves on top, Germany, ca. 1890, 12" h. (ILLUS.) **1,792**

New Haven Clock Co. Wall Regulator

Wall regulator clock, New Haven Clock Co., New Haven, Connecticut, "No. 2 Office Regulator" model, long black walnut case w/octagonal molded top section enclosing the round white dial w/brass bezel, black Roman numerals & subsidiary seconds dial, the long rectangular molded drop case w/a glass panel showing the wood pendulum & large brass bob, the base drop replaced w/saw-cut pine stained to match (should have S-curve w/walnut veneer), front of edges & door all w/cross-cut walnut veneer, time-only weight movement, w/weight running down left side of case hidden from view, replacement hands, ca. 1880, 41" h. (ILLUS.)...................................... **1,400**

German One-weight Regulator

Wall regulator clock, one-weight regulator in the Viennese style, long walnut veneer case w/arched cornice & three turned finials, the base w/narrow reeded pilasters w/scroll-carved brackets at the top & base corners flanking the tall glass front over a brass bezel & white dial w/Roman numerals, single weight & long pendulum w/large brass bob, base tapering center drop & three drop finials, original time only movement, drop finial switched to top at some point, other five finials replaced, Germany, ca. 1880, 44" h. (ILLUS.) **840**

Austrian Wall Regulator

Wall regulator clock, rectangular walnut case w/molded pediment topped by molded cornice w/gallery w/finial at each corner, broken-arch crest w/finials, sides of case w/slender ring-turned baluster-form columns w/molded rectangular bases & capitals flanking the door panel w/arch-top molded inset for dial & pendulum, the round dial w/worn Roman numerals on silvered chapter ring, pendulum w/fancy grid overlay w/engraved cross pieces, the pulleys, dial center & weights all w/matched engraving, molded base w/band of short half-round columns & drop finials at corners, molded base drop w/ring-turned drop finial, two-weight movement, Austria, ca. 1880, 61" h. (ILLUS.) **2,240**

Wall regulator clock, Seikosha, Japan, dark stained wood case, eight-day movement, time & strike, ca. early 1900s, dial 14" d., 51" h. **350**

Nice Sessions Oak Wall Regulator

Wall regulator clock, Sessions Clock Co., Bristol, Connecticut, oak case w/wide flaring flat cornice above the large two-pane door, the top pane reverse-painted in black w/a gold ring over the paper dial w/Arabic numerals, the lower pane banded in gold & printed "Regulator," showing the pendulum w/brass bob, molded base above cut-out side scallops & a scroll-cut backboard w/stamped designs, eight-day movement, time-only, original finish, foxing on paper dial, ca. 1900, 5 1/8 x 17 3/4", 36" h. (ILLUS.)... **700-800**

Sessions "Regulator E" Wall Clock

Wall regulator clock, Sessions Clock Co., Bristol, Connecticut, "Regular E" model, pressed oak case, a large wide octagonal top w/molded bands around the brass bezel enclosing the original paper dial w/Roman numerals & outer calendar date band w/Arabic numerals, the pointed drop case w/stamped molding on the glazed door printed w/"Regulator," pendulum w/large brass bob, eight-day time & strike movement, ca. 1915, 16 1/2" w. top, 38" h. (ILLUS.) **850-950**

Sessions Clock Co. "Regulator E"

Wall regulator clock, Sessions Clock Co., Bristol, Connecticut, "Regulator E" store model, tall rectangular dark wood case w/molded pediment decorated w/bands of carved floral & beaded decoration, the body w/carved border decoration framing the two-pane glass door, the upper pane over the dial w/brass molded bezel, black Roman numerals for time & Arabic numerals for date, red subsidiary hand, the lower pane w/gilt scroll border & word "Regulator" over the brass pendulum & bob w/crisscross decoration, the base w/scallop-cut apron w/carved floral decoration, eight-day time-only movement, soil on dial, backboard separated & reglued, ca. 1908, 38 1/2" h. (ILLUS.)........... **504**

Wall regulator clock, Stand (Jos.), Zwittan, Switzerland, walnut case w/shell-carved pediment flanked by finials over stepped cornice, central glass door flanked by reeded engaged columns, tapered base flanked by drop finials & ending in a carved shell, three-train weight-driven chiming movement, enameled dial w/Roman numerals & signed by the maker, late 19th c., 52" h.. **1,265**

French Mahogany Wall Regulator

Wall regulator clock, tall rectangular mahogany case w/a long glazed door w/small carved scrolls flanking the arched top, a wide brass bezel enclosing the porcelain dial w/Roman numerals, a long gridiron brass pendulum w/harp design over the large brass disk bob, eight-day time-only pinwheel movement, France, late 19th - early 20th c., 61" h. (ILLUS.)... **2,138**

Wall regulator clock, Thomas (Seth) Clock Co., Plymouth, Connecticut, model #60, mahogany case, brass pendulum & weight-driven, 18 1/2 x 60"...................... **10,750**

Thomas "No. 2" Wall Regulator

Wall regulator clock, Thomas (Seth) Clock Co., Plymouth, Connecticut, "No. 2" model, tall oak case w/a large molded round top enclosing the brass bezel & painted dial w/Roman numerals & sweep seconds hand, the long rectangular drop base w/a tall rectangular molding enclosing a glass pane over the cylindrical brass weight & large brass pendulum bob, ca. 1890-1900, 17" w., 36" h. (ILLUS.) **1,800-2,000**

S. Thomas "Regulator No. 1 Extra"

Wall regulator clock, Thomas (Seth) Clock Co., Plymouth, Connecticut, "Regulator No. 1 Extra" model, rosewood-veneered case, the large twelve-sided top section centered by a round molding enclosing the brass bezel & painted dial w/Roman numerals & sweep seconds hand, the long rectangular drop case w/long glass door showing the pendulum w/a very large ornately scroll-pierced teardrop-form brass bob, eight-day single-weight movement w/original label on panel in front of weight, ca. 1875, 20" w., 40" h. (ILLUS. below left)............................ **3,000-3,800**

S. Thomas "Regulator No. 2"

Wall regulator clock, Thomas (Seth) Clock Co., Plymouth, Connecticut, "Regulator No. 2" model, long oak case w/wide round molding around the large replaced dial w/Roman numerals & sweep seconds hand, the long case w/a glass front showing the heavy cylindrical weight & pendulum, refinished, ca. 1884, 5 1/2 x 15 1/2", 36" h. (ILLUS.).................................... **1,000-1,200**

Seth Thomas "Regulator No. 6"

Wall regulator clock, Thomas (Seth) Clock Co., Plymouth, Connecticut, "Regulator No. 6" model, long oak case w/molded arched top w/center carved decoration & spike-topped spool corner finials on ogee molding, scroll-carved molding around the original dial w/black Roman numerals, subsidiary seconds dial & brass bezel, tall lower glass pane shows the pendulum & brass bob, short three-quarter round reeded columns w/drop finials at the top & bottom front corners, ogee base drop w/knob drop finial & corner drop finials, hands, weight & case hardware all original, recabled eight-day time-only movement, ca. 1884, 49" h. (ILLUS.) **4,592**

Thomas "Regulator No. 2"

Wall regulator clock, Thomas (Seth), Clock Co., Plymouth, Connecticut, "Regulator No. 2" model, long quarter-sawn oak case w/large round molding around the white dial w/black Arabic numerals & subsidiary seconds dial, a long rectangular drop case w/glass door w/spring/bullet latch showing the brass weight & pendulum bob, molded base, recabled time-only movement, original dated label on rear shows manufacture by ST division of General Time Corp., wooden bezel has warped & been reglued, ca. 1947, 35 1/2" h. (ILLUS.) **896**

S. Thomas "Regulator No. 2" Model

Wall regulator clock, Thomas (Seth), Plymouth, Connecticut, "Regulator No. 2" model, mellow caramel-colored hardwood case, a large top round molding enclosing the white dial w/black Arabic numerals & subsidiary seconds dial also marked "Seth Thomas," long molded rectangular drop case w/a glass door over the weight, pendulum & large brass bob, time-only movement, good inside label, ca. 1890, 36" h. (ILLUS.) **1,960**

S. Thomas Regulator "No. 2" Clock

Wall regulator clock, Thomas (Seth), Plymouth, Connecticut, "Regulator No. 2" model, oak case w/large round top molding enclosing the brass bezel, white painted zinc dial plate w/black Arabic numerals & subsidiary seconds dial, the long drop w/rectangular molding around the glass panel showing the original weight & pendulum w/large brass bob, time-only movement, paint flaking on dial, ca. 1900, 36" h. (ILLUS.) **1,568**

Seth Thomas "No. 2" Wall Regulator

Thomas "Regulator No. 2" Clock

Wall regulator clock, Thomas (Seth), Plymouth, Connecticut, "Regulator No. 2" model, oak case w/large circular top enclosing the white dial w/black Arabic numerals, subsidiary seconds dial & marked "Seth Thomas," bezel made of eight segments of solid oak, over a long drop case w/bevel-bordered glass panel showing pendulum, molded base, time-only movement, minor flakes on dial, ca. 1912, 35 1/2" h. (ILLUS.).............................. **1,764**

Wall regulator clock, Thomas (Seth), Plymouth, Connecticut, "Regulator No. 2" model, walnut case w/round top & long molded drop on shallow base, top glass panel over white signed dial w/brass bezel, black Roman numerals & subsidiary seconds dial, bottom panel w/glass-paned door over original weight & pendulum, original label in case & stenciled production date of March 1899 on rear, small veneer repair, some crazing, tension spring is weak, 1899, 36" h. (ILLUS.) **1,960**

Seth Thomas "Regulator No. 2"

Wall regulator clock, Thomas (Seth), Plymouth, Connecticut, "Regulator No. 2" model, walnut & mahogany veneer case w/a large round top molding enclosing the white dial w/black Roman numerals, long drop case w/molding at top & bottom, the tall glass door decorated w/a gilt stenciled design of a flying eagle & star within garlanded arch over an oval cartouche & "REGULATOR" all on a black ground, shallow ogee base drop, time-only movement, excellent label inside, ca. 1870, 34" h. (ILLUS.) **2,016**

Seth Thomas "Regulator No. 3"

Wall regulator clock, Thomas (Seth), Plymouth, Connecticut, "Regulator No. 3" model, tall oak case w/12-sided molded top frame w/two tiny baluster-form drop finials enclosing the round white dial w/black Roman numerals & subsidiary seconds dial, the long rectangular drop w/molded glass-paned door w/gilt-stenciled "Regulator" within a scroll design (should have a plain clear glass pane), molded base w/conforming corner drop finials & shallow drop, #62 time-only movement w/72 beats, cut pinions & maintaining power, original label inside case bottom, some veneer lifting & splits, ca. 1920, 44" h. (ILLUS.) **2,464**

Seth Thomas "Regulator No. 7"

Wall regulator clock, Thomas (Seth), Plymouth, Connecticut, "Regulator No. 7" model, walnut case w/molded outcurved cornice decorated w/shell carving, topped by crest of scrolls curving up at ends & a sunburst finial in center, dial frame w/molding at top & bottom & carved spandrels enclosing a white dial w/brass bezel, black Roman numerals & subsidiary seconds dial, connected to long drop by ribbed & molded band, the drop w/sides that scroll out at top & bottom, a contour frame around glass panel over weight & pendulum, flower-form decorations centered at top & bottom of frame, ribbed molded rectangular base drop suspended from molded base, time-only #62 movement w/cut pinions & maintaining power, some flaking on dial, ca. 1905, 48" h. (ILLUS.) **12,320**

Thomas "Regulator No. 30" Clock

Wall regulator clock, Thomas (Seth), Plymouth, Connecticut, "Regulator No. 30" model, tall golden oak case w/molded pediment topped w/a band of beading under the molded scroll-cornered tapering crestrail centered by a shell-form crest within a circle, reeded molding around the front w/an upper wood panel w/fan-carved upper corners & a scalloped lower border enclosing the large brass bezel & white dial w/black Roman numerals & subsidiary seconds dial, original weight & long pendulum w/damascene brass bob, w/a molded separate shelf w/tapering corner brackets & a scalloped baseboard centered by a floret, 80-beat time-only movement, ca. 1909, 49" h. (ILLUS.).. **6,160**

Seth Thomas "Regulator No. 8"

Wall regulator clock, Thomas (Seth), Plymouth, Connecticut, short "Regulator No. 8" model (3" shorter than long version), oak case w/molded pediment & crest w/sides that slant to small scroll ends from center molded arch, the dial frame w/carved sunburst spandrels around the white dial w/brass bezel, black Roman numerals & subsidiary seconds dial, original dial & hands, the bottom section w/contour glass panel showing pendulum, scroll-cut designs at tops of sides, molded base w/small apron & corner drop finials, weight, damascene pendulum, pulley & hardware, No. 62 time-only movement w/dead beat escapement & cut pinions, some wear to dial, pendulum stick may be old replacement, ca. 1905, 52" h. (ILLUS.).. **9,800**

Victorian Eastlake Wall Regulator

Wall regulator clock, Victorian Eastlake style case, walnut, molded flat top w/blocked ears above molded sides w/slender colonettes flanking a tall arched glazed door opening to the round dial w/Roman numerals above the brass pendulum, line-incised & stepped-back bottom apron w/a row of knobs & scallop-cut rim, time & strike movement, original finish, ca. 1880, 8 x 15", 40" h. (ILLUS.)........ **650**

Wall regulator clock, Waterbury Clock Co., Waterbury, Connecticut, jeweler's-type, walnut & walnut veneer case, a flat flaring & stepped cornice above a narrow vine-carved frieze band over a narrow carved band over reeded blocks above an upper panel enclosing the round dial w/Roman numerals & brass bezel above a long glazed window over the large brass pendulum & bob flanked by narrow burl side panels centered by a diamond design, a molded & reeded base over blocks flanking a bottom panel w/fan carving, late 19th - early 20th c., 10 x 25", 75" h. **6,720**

Wall regulator clock, Waterbury Clock Co., Waterbury, Connecticut, Model No. 66, oak, a large round molded top section w/conforming door opening to the large white dial w/black Roman numerals, time & strike movement, a tall rectangular lower case w/a narrow band of beads above & below the tall rectangular glass front over the wood & brass pendulum, late 19th - early 20th c., 7 x 26", 58" h. **1,064**

Waterbury Octagonal Regulator

Wall regulator clock, Waterbury Clock Co., Waterbury, Connecticut, octagonal long-drop oak case, large octagonal top w/beaded band decoration around the large dial w/Roman numerals & Arabic calendar numbers around the border, long pointed drop base w/beaded molding around the glass door printed in gold "Regulator," eight-day movement, time & calendar, ca. 1900, 4 1/2 x 16 3/4", 31 3/4" h. (ILLUS.) **500-600**

Waterbury Advertising Regulator

Wall regulator clock, Waterbury Clock Co., Waterbury, Connecticut, octagonal long-drop regulator, large octagonal top w/beaded molding around the dial w/Roman numerals, the long pointed drop case w/beaded molding, the glass door printed w/advertising reading "Fine Clothes - Made To Order - H.M. Marks & Co. - Chicago - Established 1872," eight-day movement, time-only, original case finish, stained dial, ca. 1900, 4 1/2 x 17", 32" h. (ILLUS.) **800-900**

Waterbury "Regulator No. 20" Clock

Wall regulator clock, Waterbury Clock Co., Waterbury, New York, "Regulator No. 20" model, oak case w/a wide round molded top frame around the brass bezel & white dial w/Roman numerals & subsidiary seconds dial, the long base w/a glass door decorated w/a modern "Regulator" decal, pendulum w/large brass bob, rectangular cast-iron weights, time & strike movement, original Waterbury label, beat scale in case bottom, ca. 1905, 38" h. (ILLUS.) **1,456**

Arts & Crafts Wall Regulator

Wall regulator clock, Waterbury Clock Co., Waterbury, New York, "Regulator No. 82" model, long Arts & Crafts-style mahogany case w/molded peaked cornice above the long door, upper door w/wood panel around the white porcelain dial w/brass bezel, black Roman numerals & subsidiary seconds dial, the lower door w/two flat slats enclosing three panes of glass, wood pendulum w/brass disk bob, simple rectangular base, time & strike movement, faded label in bottom of case, ca. 1914, 41" h. (ILLUS.) **1,120**

Waterbury "Regulator No. 9" Clock

Wall regulator clock, Waterbury Clock Co., Waterbury, New York, "Regulator No. 9" model, very tall oak case w/a high flaring cornice, three ball finials joined by slender twisted brass rods above a flaring gadrooned band over a fan-carved band above a narrow notch-carved band, all above the front frame w/reeded sides & small corner blocks, a tall arched glass panel over the round silvery grey metal dial w/black Roman numerals & subsidiary seconds dial, a single cylindrical brass weight & long pendulum w/large brass bob, the base w/ropetwist border over a scalloped front apron & quarter-round brackets flanking a back panel carved w/a large paterae, solid plate eight-day one-weight time-only movement w/Graham escapement, ca. 1891, 76 1/4" h. (ILLUS.) **15,680**

E.N. Welch Wall Regulator

Wall regulator clock, Welch (E.N.) Mfg. Co., Bristol, Connecticut, "Sembrich" model, tall black walnut case w/carved crown pediment w/carved decoration & scrolled sides, the tall arched top glass door w/scalloped wood molding around the white dial w/brass bezel, black Roman numerals for time surrounded by black Arabic numerals for dates, the lower glass printed in gold "REGULATOR," molded base w/ogee drop w/scallop-cut edges, original pendulum & large brass bob, original label on back, eight-day time & calendar movement, ca. 1890, 39" h. (ILLUS.) **1,680**

Welch, Spring & Co. Wall Regulator

Wall regulator clock, Welch, Spring & Co., Forestville, Connecticut, rosewood case w/round molded top & short drop w/reverse-painted glass panel, incurved stepped base, white painted dial w/Roman numerals, time & strike movement, finish on case partially stripped, some paint loss, ca. 1878, 24" h. (ILLUS.).............. **448**

"Sembrich" Model Wall Regulator

Wall regulator clock, Welch, Spring & Co., Forestville, Connecticut, "Sembrich" model, walnut Victorian Renaissance Revival style case, a large plume crest & scroll ears on the flaring flat cornice over a line-incised frieze above the long rounded glass front over the dial w/Roman numerals, pendulum w/large brass

Picture Frame Wall/Desk Clock

bob, molded base w/slender tapering side brackets above the pointed & scroll-cut, line-incised front apron, eight-day movement, time & strike, refinished case, ca. 1880, 5 1/2 x 14", 39" h. (ILLUS. top right on previous page) **700-800**

Wall/desk clock, Werner Clock Mfg. Co., Akron, Ohio, oak rectangular "picture frame" case w/panel in border of deep intricate pressed designs resembling carving, the rectangular dial panel lithographed on paper by Werner Litho of Akron, Ohio & decorated w/ornate spandrels & a lower medallion resembling the Waterbury Clock Co. trademark, the dial w/Arabic numerals, can be hung on wall or set on desk, minor stains on dial, ca. 1900, 9" h. (ILLUS. at bottom of previous page)... **448**

Reproduction of Water Clock

Water clock, Pearson, Page, Jewsbury & Co., Birmingham, England, reproduction of a water clock, an open disk brass dial at the top of tall iron uprights suspending a water-filled metal cylinder, boxed metal base, marked "Indigo Smyth - Oxon - 1742," complete w/float & water receptacle, ca. 1918, 28" h. (ILLUS.) **448**

Glossary

Anniversary clock (a.k.a. 400-day clock): clock that needs to be wound only once a year

Arc: path the pendulum takes when swinging

Balance: wheel that regulates the rate of movement in clock parts

Banjo clock: clock that roughly resembles a banjo in shape, with a round clock face over a long drop

Barrel: cylinder in a clock that contains the timepiece

Beat: the ticking sound made by the working mechanisms of a clock

Bezel: supporting ring that surrounds the dial and holds the glass that covers it in place

Blinking eye clock: clock in the form of a human or animal with eyes that blink in time with the beat

Bob: end of a pendulum, generally disc-form

Boulle: tortoiseshell, ivory and metal inlay on wood

Bracket clock: clock with a specific style of case widely used in 18th-century England that sits in a bracket that attaches to a wall

Calendar clock: clock that indicates both the time of day and the day and month of the year

Carriage clock: small portable clock with a handle on top, usually with a brass framework and glass front and side panels

Case: the framework of a clock that contains the working parts

Chapter ring: part of the dial that contains the numerals and the marks for minutes and seconds

Cottage clock: a category of inexpensive clocks widely produced in the United States in the late 19th century suitable for use in working class homes of the era

Crystal regulator: shelf or mantel clock with glass sides, similar to carriage clocks but with a high-quality "regulator" movement

Deadbeat escapement: escapement with no recoil

Escapement: mechanism that regulates the movement of the pendulum or balance wheel

Fusee: grooved cone that equalizes the tension in a spring-driven clock, regulating its speed

Gimbal: bracket device, usually seen in ships' clocks, that supports a timepiece and keeps it level

Grande sonnerie clock: French term for a clock that repeats the hour strike on the quarter hour

Grandfather clock: tall upright floor clock, also known as a "tall case" clock

Label: paper inside a clock case that often had not only the name of the manufacturer but also operating instructions and advertisements for the manufacturer

Lantern clock: early clock form with a case that resembles an early lantern

Long case clock (a.k.a. tall case clock): another name for a grandfather clock

Lyre clock: a variation of a banjo clock with a wood case somewhat resembling a lyre

Mantel clock: clock meant to sit on a shelf or fireplace mantel

Mercury pendulum: cylindrical pendulum with a silvery look made to resemble those in France that originally contained actual mercury

Movement: the mechanism of a clock that produces motion

Novelty clock: clock that performs some movement in addition to keeping time or that is in a form or shape not normally associated with clocks

Number cartouche (a.k.a. signet): separate decorative panel in a dial on which a numeral is painted or attached

Open escapement (a.k.a. visible escapement): the working parts of a timepiece that can be seen through an opening, generally located in the center of the dial

Perpetual clock: calendar clock that automatically adjusts to the variations in the length of months and doesn't need manual adjusting from month to month

Pillar & scroll clock: usually attributed to Eli Terry, the style of case popular in the early 19th century that features broken scroll pediment and slender round columns

Regulator: usually a large wall clock with a long case enclosing the dial above a long pendulum, noted for its time-keeping accuracy

Reverse-painting: decoration painted on the back of a glass panel or tablet

Spandrels: decorations that fill the space in the corners around the chapter ring of a dial

Steeple clock: clock with a Gothic-style case with a peaked top and finials that resembles a church steeple

Strike train: gears that regulate the striking on a time-and-strike clock

Subsidiary dial: small dial incorporated into the main dial that indicates something beyond hours and minutes (i.e. seconds, days of the week, etc.)

Sweep seconds hand: subsidiary hand that sweeps around the dial, indicating seconds

Swinging arm: timepiece with a standing figure with an upraised arm holding the clock works, with the dial and pendulum forming one long unit that oscillates as the clock beats

Tablet: decorative glass panel on the front of a clock case, frequently reverse-painted or stenciled

Time-and-strike: clock that both indicates time and strikes the hours or increments of hours with a bell or gong

Tower clock: clock situated in the tower of a public structure

Wag-on-wall: a wall clock, the dial, works, weights and pendulum of which are exposed and not contained in case

Weights: heavy objects, usually cylindrical, that drive the movement in non-spring-driven clocks

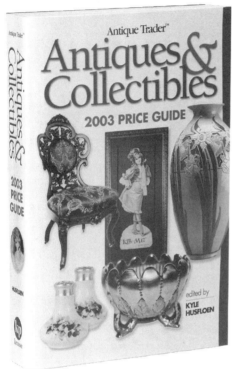

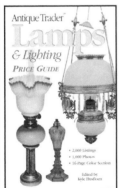

Keep Your Collection in Top Condition

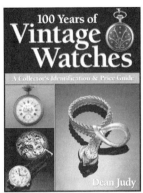

100 Years of Vintage Watches
A Collector's Identification & Price Guide
by Dean Judy

It's the perfect time to learn more about your collectible watches! In this brand new, full-color guide, you'll find detailed listings-including manufacturer, years of production, and invaluable pricing information-for more than 600 vintage wristwatches and pocket watches. More than 50 watchmakers, including Alpina, Cyma, Zodiak, Bulova, Elgin, Hamilton, are featured. Author Dean Judy also provides helpful hints for starting and maintaining a collection.

Softcover • 8¼x10⅞ • 224 pages
700+ color photos
Item # VWAT • $24.95

Making and Repairing Wooden Clock Cases
by V.J. Taylor and H.A. Babb

Re-create the beauty and elegance of traditional wooden clock cases using the historically authentic constructional plans, exploded drawings and expert tips provided in this fascinating book. Includes details for a wide variety of cases, styles and periods, from cuckoo and mantel clocks to magnificent long-cases.

Softcover • 8¾ x 11½ • 192 pages
30 b&w photos & 120 illustrations
Item #41464 • $19.99

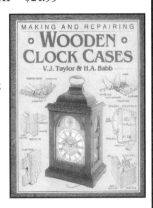

Repairing Antique Clocks
By Eric P. Smith

This practical guide, fully updated, teaches readers how to apply the tools, materials and techniques needed to repair and maintain all types of antique clocks without the expense of a professional.

Softcover • 6¾ x 9½ • 192 pages
50 b&w illustrations
Item #41365 • $18.99
